Nicole Fowler

SECOND EDITION

GROUP SKILLS
IN SOCIAL WORK
A Four-Dimensional Approach

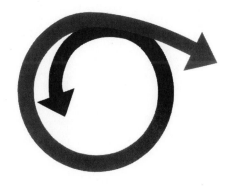

SECOND EDITION

GROUP SKILLS IN SOCIAL WORK

A Four-Dimensional Approach

Sue Henry

University of Denver

Brooks/Cole Publishing Company
Pacific Grove, California

Brooks/Cole Publishing Company
A Division of Wadsworth, Inc.

Printed in the United States of America
10   9   8   7   6   5   4   3   2   1

Library of Congress Cataloging-in-Publication Data

Henry, Sue.
   Group skills in social work : a four-dimensional approach / Sue Henry. — 2nd ed.
      p.   cm.
   Includes bibliographical references and index.
   ISBN 0-534-17106-0
   1. Social group work.   2. Social group work—United States.
I. Title.
HV45.H45   1992
361.4—dc20   91-24495
                                                                    CIP

Sponsoring Editor: *Claire Verduin*
Editorial Associate: *Gay C. Bond*
Production Coordinator: *Fiorella Ljunggren*
Production: *Greg Hubit Bookworks*
Manuscript Editor: *Tony Hicks*
Interior Design: *John Edeen*
Cover Design: *Lisa Berman*
Interior Illustration: *Susan Rogin*
Typesetting: *The Font Works*
Cover Printing: *Phoenix Color Corporation*
Printing and Binding: *Arcata Graphics/Fairfield*

PREFACE

Attention to groups in social work seems to have grown by leaps and bounds since the first edition of this book was published. Several textbooks have appeared; the journal *Social Work with Groups* has gained a solid footing in the professional literature; annual symposia on social work with groups are firmly in place as professional conferences not to be missed; the Association for the Advancement of Social Work with Groups (AASWG) has grown to an international professional organization, publishing its own newsletter; and there is growing accord between AASWG and the National Association of Social Workers and the Council on Social Work Education regarding standards and education for group work practice. The use of groups in agency and private practice seems to be riding the crest of a wave.

This second edition of *Group Skills in Social Work* is organized, as was the original edition, around the concept of skill as knowledge in action. Four dimensions of social work knowledge about people in groups interact to dictate the worker action to be taken. These four dimensions are (1) the stages of group development, (2) the contract form in effect, (3) the role and location of the worker vis-à-vis the group system, and (4) the program media utilized to enhance group social forces.

The book has been used by teachers and students in undergraduate and graduate programs in social work education, and also by practitioners. It has been used in this country and abroad. Even though it stands within a framework of knowledge, values, and skills that is specific to social work, it may be useful to group practitioners in other helping professions, as well.

Various assumptions set the boundaries of this book's approach to social group work practice. The assumptions about values are that groups are ubiquitous in society; that practice with people in groups is goal directed and goal oriented; that social work practice with groups is focused on the use of group social forces to help individuals, not on work with individuals in the presence of others; and that goals and means to goal achievement ought to be mutually determined between the worker and the group members. The assumptions about knowledge are that the concepts that define the group entity may be taken apart and studied separately without doing damage to the integrity of the whole; that practice is knowledge based; that groups go through stages of development; and that a worker's wisdom developed through practice is a valid source of knowledge. The assumptions about practice skills are that what a worker with a group will do is derived from her or his knowledge about the interaction of the four dimensions; that one worker with a group may suffice; that various roles may be taken by the worker in effective practice; and that the principles effective for work with direct service groups are equally applicable to groups for purposes other than direct service. These and other assumptions are identified as the book proceeds.

The focus of this book is not on self-help groups but on groups in which a professional social worker is present either to provide direct service to the individuals in the group or to provide staff service to an organization through the group.

This edition has revisions in five main areas. I have reconceptualized what was originally characterized as the conflict stage to include disequilibrium. I have added material about evaluation in groups and have described ways of utilizing goal achievement instruments in that evaluation. I have given more attention to cultural factors such as gender, race, ethnicity, and age. I have added several new tables and figures; and many of these are specific guides to worker activity at the various stages—for example, guides to analyzing and selecting program media. Finally, I have revised Chapter 10 to bring its conceptualization of worker skills into line with the general practice model of the other chapters.

The book is divided into ten chapters. Chapter 1 sets the context for understanding what groups can and cannot do and defines the various social forces constituting the group entity. Chapter 2 sets forth the model of practice used in this book. Chapters 3–8 present the six stages of group development, relate the four dimensions of the practice model to each stage, and discuss the worker skills appropriate to each stage. These chapters are illustrated with numerous practice examples. Chapter 9 addresses the issues raised by using coworkers with groups, by having groups with open membership and no time limits, and by recording group practice. Chapter 10 considers groups for purposes other than direct service.

Readers familiar with the original work will find that most of that content remains. Many new practice examples have been provided, and I have tried to tighten the connection between the examples and the principles they are intended to portray.

For the content of the book I have drawn upon many years of experience as a group worker, teacher, trainer, and consultant, and some of the practice examples come from that experience. Many people have provided examples from their practice: Diane Johnson, Gail Shattuck, Lee Oesterle, Walter Simon, Carla Posey, Kittie Arnold, Thana Christian, Barbara Bowen, Yolanda Chiu, Leslie Goetting, Eric Byrne, Tom Olbrich, Wilson Glover, Paul VonEssen, Leigh Abrahamson, John Anderson, Peggy Harrell, Janis James, Deborah Borman, Marilyn Moreno, Laura Vannoy, Cathy Miller,

Philip Hartmann, Sally Barrett-Page, Michelle Friedman, Ruth Parsons, and Katherine Vail. Thanks also to Big Sisters of Colorado, Inc. I express my deep appreciation to all of them for their willingness to share their work.

I am grateful for ongoing communication with Lois Miranda of the University of Wisconsin–Oshkosh faculty, for feedback on the book and for making available the work of her students as they acquired understanding of practice with people in groups. In particular, Kelly Muench and Pam Warren's charts of work with groups for other than direct service were helpful to me in clarifying the content of Chapter 10; Pam's chart of program media for those kinds of groups has been included in that chapter.

I also express my appreciation for what I have learned about social group work practice in agencies and from supervisors in those agencies. I am grateful to the schools where I studied—the School of Applied Social Sciences at Western Reserve University and the Graduate School of Social Work at the University of Denver—and the teachers I studied with. At two schools of social work where I have taught, the University of Pennsylvania and the University of Denver, I have been impressed with the students who willingly try group practice and share their experiences in a way that adds to what I know. I have found acceptance of the practice model at two schools of social work abroad where I have presented seminars: the Regional School for Higher Education in Social Services in Trento, Italy, and the School for Social Work Practice in Warsaw, Poland.

Members of groups I have worked with are thanked for what I have learned from them; most especially, I thank the women of the Women in Transition group and the Boulder County Safehouse Outreach Center group, not only for what they taught me about groups but also for letting me know their strength. I express deep appreciation and gratitude to two women who have been coworkers with me: Tory Pearlstein and Gale Stromberg. I learned so much from them.

Technical assistance was provided by Karen Kulp, of U.S. West Knowledge Engineering, Inc., who converted the printed text of the original edition to manuscript form so revisions could be made more easily. Joyce Ekanger, my secretary at the University of Denver, processed drafts of many of the figures in the book. Stacie Trexel undertook the burden of transforming citations and references to their present format. Linda Clark, assistant dean at the Graduate School of Social Work at the University of Denver, provided invaluable assistance in the computer aspects of producing the text. I thank them for this.

The late Dorothea Spellmann provided immeasurable assistance in the initial conception of the four-dimensional model, and I acknowledge her contribution. Margaret E. Hartford has always been a source of encouragement and support for my practice, teaching, research, and writing; I thank her for that. Miriam Turri's critical review of the original work was of inestimable value, and I thank her, again, for her continued encouragement to my work.

At Brooks/Cole, Sherene Miller was instrumental in managing the prospectus and contract process, and Claire Verduin has been a steady hand in seeing the project through to completion. I appreciate their respective roles in this undertaking.

Sue Henry

CONTENTS

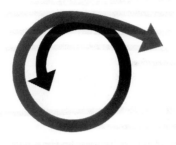

CHAPTER 1

CONTEXT

This chapter describes the uses of groups and defines the terms needed for understanding the concept of a group.

○

The Scope and Limitations of Group Uses

Anyone who considers using groups as a modality [method of treatment] for helping people should be familiar with the scope and limitations of the group form. Groups can be useful in helping people rehearse new behaviors or regain old ones, such as learning how to relate to other people, improving one's relationships with others, experiencing the giving and receiving of support, communicating with others, addressing intrapsychic dysfunctions, and expressing oneself more assertively.

Groups are helpful in creating a setting for persons to interact with people different from themselves, encounter their own values and attitudes, gain information about themselves and their behavior, and learn ways of changing it or handling situations more productively. Put simply, groups can be useful as a context for growth and change.

Groups can also provide a forum for persons to address issues, work collectively on issues, and participate in decision making. People may become aware that in collective decision making each person must give up something in order for others to have their needs met and goals achieved. Collective decision making can be more creative than individual decision

1

making because the options and resources are expanded and multiplied. People may discover that decisions reached collectively are more accurate because more information is generated, through feedback and interaction with others. They also may discover that group decision making is more time consuming and that a group tends to make fewer decisions in a given time than an individual does. However, the range of possibilities and options available to a group, and the greater accuracy of its decisions, may compensate for the greater time involved.

The group method of helping people has made a major contribution in its capacity to bring about change. To paraphrase Hartford's (1972, p. 31) formulation, change may be facilitated in and through the group medium, in an individual, in the whole group, or in the environment in which the group exists. This text discusses these three types of change and the dynamics that bring them about.

Within groups a certain amount of personal, sensitive information may be shared. The worker and the prospective group member should decide between themselves—and all the members should agree—about what kinds of material are to be shared. Personal matters outside the scope of the group's purpose, for example, should not become the material for group discussion. However, group members should not withhold relevant information that could be useful for the resolution of intrapsychic identity or interpersonal conflicts.   *existing within the self/psyche*

Groups cannot reduce time and cost factors. In a given time, a worker can serve more people in a group than individually. A worker can give 50 to 100% more face-to-face, worker-to-client time to group clients than to individuals—that is, one-and-a-half or two hours for a group as opposed to one hour for an individual client—and some time saving may be realized. However, groups require as much per person as individuals do, if the worker is conscientious about record keeping and about following up client information.

The increased income from offering a group may more than offset the cost of the time the worker spends for face-to-face contact, collateral activities, and recording. However, even under tight fiscal constraints, such cost-benefit considerations should not be the major determinant in the decision to provide group services. What should be critical is the assessment of the probable benefit to clients of being served in a group rather than individually.

Evidence suggests that the group form of treatment is contraindicated for people with certain diagnosed problems (Slavson, 1964). The worker should determine each person's capacity to receive therapeutic benefit from a group experience; indicators would be the type of problem and the degree of illness.

To sum up, groups help people rehearse behaviors, can assist growth and change, and can be an efficient way to make accurate decisions. On the other hand, groups cannot be the arena for handling irrelevant material, cannot be a time- and cost-saving instrument for serving people, and may not be helpful to people with certain kinds of diagnosed problems.

○
Definition of Terms

Throughout this book, certain social processes will be referred to, using terms from the social and behavioral sciences. The conceptual framework used here was originally developed by Grace Coyle (1930) and later modified (Coyle & Hartford, 1958; Goroff, 1972; Hartford, 1972).

Some writers on groups eschew a knowledge base in the social and behavioral sciences. They maintain that most of what is known in those fields has been developed on the basis of controlled laboratory experiments with paid subjects, isolated from the operation of real-life phenomena (Klein, 1970). They question whether those experimental findings can be utilized when social work is carried on in natural settings, with people enacting real-life situations spontaneously.

A similar argument is made by those who hold that the nature of a group "cannot be discerned by analyzing the separate characteristics of each component." In that view, a group can only be perceived as a gestalt, whole and organic (Schwartz, 1961, pp. 151–152, 158–159). This position is widespread in the profession. There is an ethos which holds that the phenomena with which social work concerns itself, precisely because they involve human beings, defy description. However, in this book the parts are broken down for purposes of description, explanation, and analysis. The totality cannot be addressed at once. Therefore, the social forces that define a group and those that cause it to function are presented as central dynamics in the life of the group. These changing social processes are portrayed at each stage of group development.

The discussion of what makes a group uses the following concepts (Coyle & Hartford, 1958; Hartford, 1972): membership selection and group composition; group goals; external structure (time, space, and size); internal structure (role differentiation); cohesion; communication and decision making; norms, values, and group culture; and group control and influence. These form the conceptual boundary of the entity group. The definitions presented here are brief, because this is a text on practice, although it rests firmly on a base of behavioral-science and social-science theory; and because this job has been done thoroughly elsewhere (Hartford, 1972).

Much of the discussion in the following pages comes from classics in the various fields of theory and research that social work draws upon. Readers will find many references to these first, enduring works. This is not because there has been nothing new in the succeeding years, but rather because the original sources were definitive.

Membership Selection and Group Composition

Membership selection is important because it is the people in the group, their behaviors and feelings, that will eventually create the other social processes.

There is much literature and research on the process of selecting persons to put together, in some configuration, in the expectation that the result will be a group that will work (Glick & Jackson, 1970; Hare, 1962; Hartford, 1972; McGrath & Altman, 1966; Richards & Polansky, 1959; Shalinsky, 1969; Shaw, 1971). Unfortunately, much of the literature is inconclusive and contradictory when it comes to guiding worker behavior. The enterprise of selecting the members of a group is guesswork at best. The factors taken into account are highly dependent upon what the worker chooses to believe from the literature, from research results, and from her or his own experience. Tools are available to guide workers in composing groups; the worker must choose whether to accept and act on them.

A study conducted by Shalinsky (1969), for example, shows that the FIRO-B technique may be used productively as a tool for composing groups. Shalinsky points out that thinking about group composition has usually focused either on the demographic characteristics of would-be members or on behavioral variables, which measure people's capacities to behave toward others and to receive behavior from others. Maloney and Mudgett (1959) suggest that the most compelling basis for choosing group members is homogeneity among the potential members with respect to the problem.

How alike should people be on any given characteristic when they are being considered for group membership? There is no simple answer. No formulas appear in the literature or research findings to say, "three of these and four of those." However, the law of optimum distance (Redl, 1951) is a useful concept. As soon as the first two or three potential members of a group have been selected, the normative range of their behaviors defines the range of tolerable behaviors for others recruited into the group. That is, whatever span of behaviors the early members tolerate in each other becomes the norm for the group. If behaviors exceed the tolerance level set by the initial members' behaviors, the group system may spin out of control and "explode." On the other hand, if the behavior of new members is more constrained than the initial span, the group may "implode" for want of variety and dynamic tension.

In practical terms, even though no magic formulas exist for concocting the perfect group, the question of heterogeneity versus homogeneity may be factored into the composition equation. This may be done by seeking members whose behaviors will be (a) sufficiently homogeneous in relation to group purpose to enable the group to be held together and (b) sufficiently heterogeneous in relation to the same important dimension to enable the group to move toward its goals. This strategy should result in a group process whereby members lend their strengths to others and receive back resources to match their needs.

These principles are only good for selecting the initial composition or for adding new members; they cannot reliably predict how persons will behave later in the life of the group. Future behavior depends on the interaction among members and the way people change under the influence of group pressure and worker intervention.

The purpose of the group aids resolution of the question of heterogeneity and homogeneity because it determines the criteria for choosing members. A group for therapeutic purposes needs to be composed of *class* people who are working on similar problems. A group for educational purposes needs to be made up of people with the same level of information in the relevant area. On the other hand, a task force needs to be composed of people with different skills, knowledge, and experience.

There is a growing body of literature that instructs social workers about ethnic, racial, socioeconomic, gender, age, and other cultural matters. *Social Work Practice and People of Color* (Lum, 1986) articles from the journal *Social Work with Groups* (Cassano, 1989; Davis, 1984; Kolodny & Garland, 1984; Lee, 1988; Morris, 1984; Reed & Garvin, 1983; Saul, 1982), and *Talking It Out: A Guide to Groups for Abused Women* (NiCarthy, Merriam & Coffman, 1984) all provide worthwhile information. The factors addressed in this literature are too numerous and specific to be discussed in blanket terms. To generalize across a population group or among population groups would be to ignore uniqueness and fail to take important differences into account. In the course of this book, as practice examples are presented and as worker actions are discussed, influencing factors such as ethnicity, race, age, gender, and socioeconomic status are brought out.

To summarize, group composition will be determined by the worker's predictions as to compatibility of needs and behaviors, similarity of problems, range of tolerance for deviance from behavioral norms, cultural and other characteristics, and skills related to the purpose of the group. The aim is to assemble a configuration *arrangement / gestalt* of persons with the potential to coalesce *come together and form one whole* and function as an entity.

Group Goals

Group goals could have been, just as logically as membership, a starting point for discussing group social processes, for it is in relation to a group's goals—which are the reason for its existence—that decisions are taken, interventions are made, and success is assessed. Group goals provide the momentum for what a group does. They become the star to steer by when monitoring progress. Schopler and Galinsky (1974) wrote:

> For a group to be effective, there must be sufficient consensus on which goals the group will pursue. Sufficient consensus means the group has enough support for particular goals to mobilize members.... Sufficient consensus exists when a majority of the members of the group system agree on goals and priorities. (pp. 201, 230)

Group goals are typically the product of three elements (Hartford, 1972). First, there are the individual members' understandings as to the purpose of the group, the members' expectations for the group, and their own expressed or unexpressed needs and objectives that they believe can be met within the group. Second, there are the worker's assumptions and expectations for the group as a whole, the assessment of each member's needs and level of functioning, and the worker's expectations as to how interventions will be directed. Finally, there is the agency's rationale for initiating a group, its purpose in choosing groups as a treatment method, and its general societal purpose. These various levels of goals become joined when a group of particular persons with a specific worker within a given agency setting comes into existence.

How does this convergence and synthesis occur? One explanation is that each person who decides to join a group comes with an unconscious or preconscious determination of what sector of the range of all possible agreements she or he is comfortably able to commit to. The group goal that emerges is the one that represents the best possible accommodation of all of these sets—the point where an equilibrium point of consensus can be found (Taylor, 1970).

A related question is how a group goal is to be understood: whether as the "sum of similar individual goals," as "individual goals for the same group," or as "a preferred location for the group" within its social environment (Cartwright & Zander, 1960, pp. 347, 349, 350); as a group level of aspiration, a "group performance goal" (Zander, 1971, p. 70); or as "an end state desired by a majority of group members" (Shaw, 1971, p. 294). This question has not been resolved in the literature. In this book the group goal is seen as a desirable end state for the group as a whole, which exists in the minds of the members of the group, and which can be identified by asking the members.

Group goal clarity is connected with clarity about the path to be followed in reaching the goal (Raven & Rietsema, 1960). This accords with Mills's (1967, p. 82) assertion that a group "whose members know what to do in order to reach their target ... [are] ... more likely to approach it than a group whose members do not have the 'know-how.'" Group goals are not always expressed in end-state terms, however; they are often stated in process terms (Henry, 1972). This finding leads to a consideration of the group goal as a starting point only, a relative statement rather than an absolute one. Goals become refined and reshaped as time elapses and members' experiences with each other and with the worker create a different entity from the one that made the initial agreement. This does not mean that an initial goal should be ignored; rather, it means that one should be aware of the group's changing goals as it zigs and zags through its life space. The first agreement sets the direction in which the group will go, and so the initial goal will always be there in one form or another; but its changing nature is an important dynamic.

The group goals and the selection of group members are two of the initial determinants of how a group will perform. Goals emerge from the interaction of member, worker, and agency purposes; they energize the members' and worker's behavior, provided they rest on sufficient consensus; they can be conceived as the desirable end state for the group as a whole; they are related to the path to be followed in reaching the end state; and they may be stated in terms of process as well as of end states. A group's initial goal should be considered as only indicating a direction because the process that unfolds in the course of the group's life will create changing goals.

External Structure

A third initial condition for a group is the external structure, whose elements are time, space, and size (Coyle, 1930). The decisions taken in respect to these elements set many of the initial boundaries within which members will interact in the service of their goals.

These elements are external because they originate from outside the group's own interaction. They help to shape and create these interactions; they are not created by them. They are structural because they give form to the group. The time element fixes the configuration in a particular frame and provides a base for conscious or unconscious investment in the experience. The space element locates the group in its environment and orients the group, emotionally and psychologically, to a home base—a place to identify with as the locus for giving and receiving help. The size element determines the network of available relationships and the communication patterns and role differentiation that will occur.

Time Decisions about the length of group meetings, the number of sessions, the frequency of meetings, and the timing of meetings all have an effect on the scope of goals that can be worked on (Hartford, 1972). In a short-term or time-limited format, the agreed goals need to be reasonably attainable within the predetermined time frame (Reid & Epstein, 1972). In a group designed to be more extended in time, the scope of the goals may be broader.

These time decisions will also affect the structure of the helping process. With a time-limited format, the work of the group needs to be focused, and attention to material not immediately relevant to the group's purpose will need to be curbed. With a long-term format, more exploration can occur.

Time decisions tend to affect members' levels of commitment to the group experience. In the same way that individuals tend to see themselves as working better under pressure, the "temporal goal gradient" (Reid & Epstein, 1972, pp. 92–93) may operate in a group of fixed duration: the energy expenditure and productiveness of persons may increase as the time allotted for goal attainment decreases. The degree of commitment that any member makes will be conditioned by the (probably unconscious) recognition of the amount of time available. In a long-term group, energy levels may seem to flow more placidly because of the awareness of the members that the ending point is somewhere off in the future. However, the energy can be expected to increase as the impending termination draws nearer.

Certain reasons for a group's existence may affect time decisions. For example, it has been suggested that groups oriented around crisis situations, and focused on anxiety reduction, may need to meet more frequently than groups addressing growth issues or deeper seated personality or character problems. Likewise, groups may need to meet more frequently in their initial stages than in the maintenance phases. In both instances, the frequency of association supports closeness and identification of the members with each other and helps to hold the group entity together (Hartford, 1972).

Space   A high priority should be given to providing a constant location for group meetings, so that members begin to form the awareness that this place is where they go to get and give help. The constant location reinforces a sense of being oriented in one's life space. It also enhances the group's identity, separating it in the minds of its members—and others—from all other groups (Coyle, 1930; Hartford, 1972).

How the area where the group meets is arranged is important. Churchill (1959) has demonstrated that the spatial arrangement of tables, chairs, and other equipment has the effect of prestructuring the content of group sessions. Whether the chairs are in a circle or around a table will affect communication patterns (Ward, 1968). Chairs in a circle may inhibit participation. However, in the case of persons experiencing difficulty in relating to others, a circle of chairs may stimulate participation, as the members feel more comfortable with each other.

If the group sits around a table, some people may not be able to keep all the others in visual range, and communication will tend to flow toward those who can be seen. A table may also represent a safety zone for members who are shy in relating to others; the table space directly in front of a member may symbolize that person's place of retreat. When feeling unable to communicate with others, members may remain focused on the area before them; when feeling able to risk communicating, members may see the territory in front of them as an island of safety to stand on while venturing forth and then to retreat to when danger seems imminent.

Physiological factors interact with the spatial arrangement of the place where groups meet. For example, in a room that is too warm, members will tend to sit farther apart; in a cool or chilly room, members will tend to draw their chairs closer together. In a very large area, members will tend to locate themselves in a pattern that allows for everyone to see everyone else at the limit of their peripheral vision. Research has found that the physical boundary of the group will be conditioned by the 20-foot range within which people are typically able to hear words spoken with a normal, well-modulated tone, pitch, and volume (Shaw, 1971).

All of these factors determine the manner in which members notice, speak to, interact with, and communicate with each other in verbal and nonverbal ways. From these interactions emerge leadership, interpersonal alliances, behavioral influence, conformity, and other patterns of behavior.

Size   The number of persons available for the distribution of labor will affect the efficiency and productiveness of the group (Bales & Borgatta, 1955; Hackman & Vidmar, 1970; Hare, 1962; McGrath & Altman, 1966; Thomas & Fink, 1963). There is no hard-and-fast rule about what the right size is for a group. The appropriate number of members is affected by the type or purpose of the group. For example, groups of four seem comfortable for people at their leisure when there is little pressure to produce a task result; groups of eight seem more productive for tasks; and groups of five seem best for discussion purposes (Jennings, 1953; Hartford, 1972).

A group of eight (as contrasted with a smaller group) is likely to include the pool of talents and resources needed to accomplish the group's task. As this group is task (or action) oriented, there needs to be less space for sharing or disclosing personal material, and thus, eight is a reasonable number for people to take into account and interact with. Part of the support for such a speculation comes from the wonderful notion of "the magical number seven plus or minus two" (Miller, 1956). The notion is that the human mind is able to contain, available for recognition at any moment, seven (plus or minus two) units of attention. If the units are familiar—for example, items on a grocery list—a person could reasonably expect to hold nine (seven plus two) items in mind. If the units are less familiar—perhaps the names of the planets of the solar system—a person possibly could retain only five (seven minus two) items. Thus, the size of a group might well be limited to nine people.

Research has tended to show that groups having an odd number of members (three, five, seven, etc.) tend to be characterized by an atmosphere of harmony and cooperation, whereas groups with an even number of members (four, six, eight, etc.) tend to be characterized by hostility and disagreement (Snyder, 1975). Perhaps people unconsciously want an odd number in case someone is needed to break the tie between opposing factions within the group. Under that expectation and given the presence of the odd-numbered person as "insurance" against disagreement, in a group of five perhaps the process is able to flow in a relatively harmonious mode.

However, Snyder (1975) found that all sizes of groups (from four through nine) had almost the same degree of satisfaction with their experiences; groups of four and five persons had slightly higher levels of satisfaction, and groups of eight and nine had slightly lower levels. Clearly, a group that becomes too large (e.g., 20 persons) cannot accomplish its task effectively because of the sheer burden of trying to keep all the other members in mind, and a group that is too small (fewer than four persons) may not have enough resources within it to be able to carry out its work. Between these two extremes, a group can be of any size appropriate to its purpose.

Time, space, and size, together with goals and membership, constitute the external structure in which a group will begin its life and proceed toward its goal, enacting and creating other social forces as it moves through the stages of its development. The internal structure is considered next.

Internal Structure

When the group begins to meet, role differentiation begins to evolve and to structure the group internally. The roles enacted by members determine the division of labor (Cartwright & Zander, 1960; Cunningham, 1951; Hare, Borgatta, & Bales, 1955; Hartley & Hartley, 1952; Shaw, 1971; Slater, 1955. The "labor" is of two types, and certain kinds of behaviors are needed for each. Homans (1950) postulated that each group is made up of an internal system and an external system. These systems evolve from clusters of behaviors that members utilize in relation to each other and on behalf of the group as a whole. The terms *internal* and *external* are used in this text to refer to systems as well as to structural elements. In both cases, *internal* refers to what goes on within the group as a result of processes and factors produced within the group by the members. *External* refers to what is outside the group—the result of forces imposed on the group or of factors in the environment outside the group—that nevertheless impinges on the group's functioning.

A cluster of behaviors is a *role* (Linton, 1936). For example, a person who tries to encourage the participation of other members, to help them feel good about their group experience or about the material they are reporting in the group, or about their participation might be called an "encourager." Another example: a member who reminds the others of the goal they are trying to reach or the task they are trying to accomplish, sorts out group discussion contributions in light of their relevance to the group's goal, and brings the group discussion back to focusing upon goal-related topics, could be called a "focuser." Other writers (Benne & Sheats, 1948) have described these roles and the behaviors associated with them.

Behaviors in both the internal system and the external system are needed for a group to be successful and productive. An encourager is needed to hold the group together; this and other roles having to do with the feelings among the members make up the group's internal system. Sometimes the internal system is called the expressive system, because it consists of what is expressed among the members. It is also called the social-emotional system, because it is concerned with the relations between members (the social aspect) and their emotional ties (Bales, 1950). When

Figure 1-1
Internal System

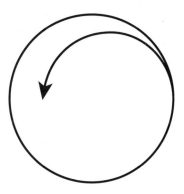

Figure 1-2
External System

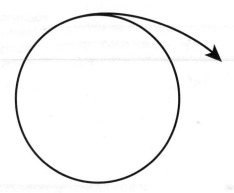

these behaviors are utilized, the group is able to stick together because of its members' feelings for each other. The group's internal system could be represented as in Figure 1-1.

Another system of behaviors that must be present in order for the group to be effective and successful, the external system, operates in the task arena. Behaviors such as those of the focuser keep the group oriented in the direction of its goal and moving toward goal attainment. Sometimes behaviors in this external system are called instrumental, because they enable the group to reach its goal (Bales, 1950). The group's external system could be represented as in Figure 1-2.

Figure 1-3
Integrated group system

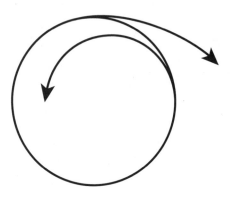

A successful and effective group will put the two systems together, as shown in Figure 1-3. Members will adopt certain roles which will both hold the group together and move it toward its goals. Different roles emerge and are emphasized at different points in the group's life. In fact, it is partly because of the process of role differentiation that a group may go through various stages of development (Dunphy, 1968). In the early stages of a group's life, more of the expressive, or internal system, behaviors are used, because the group needs to pull together before it can go anywhere. In later stages, the task-oriented roles need to be emphasized more in order for the group to get its work done (Hartford, 1972).

So, by the behaviors of members clustering into roles that enable the group to stay together and to reach its goals, the work of the group is thus divided among its members and the group entity is structured.

Cohesion

Some writers (Coyle, 1930) have called cohesion the "bond" that holds a group together. It can be recognized when people begin to refer to themselves as "we" or talk about "us" and "ours." Cohesion may also be recognized when members know and ask about other members, revealing that they have an awareness of the others and that those others have taken on some importance for them. Sometimes members indicate cohesion within the group by arriving early for meetings, as if to signal the importance the group has for them, or by attending regularly (Cartwright & Zander, 1960).

Cohesion is a bond that permits members to feel close enough to each other to allow their individuality to be expressed.

Festinger (1953, pp. 271–282) wrote of the "driving force acting upon the group member to remain a member of the group" and of "the restraining force which acts to prevent a person from leaving the group." In the seminal work in which he developed his ideas, Festinger (1953) put forward means of analyzing these forces, and he suggested applications of the processes he identified. He demonstrated that cohesion may emerge as a result of the group's response to some real or perceived threat to disband the group or to call upon it to produce something, or the threat represented by an "enemy" coming into the group's environment (Festinger, 1953).

Cohesion may be the attraction of members to each other, to the activities the group does together, or to the goals the group is working on; it may be the result of external pressures to remain together (Feldman, 1968; Hocking, 1941; Lott & Lott, 1965; Newcomb, 1960; Shaw, 1971; Stinson & Hellebrandt, 1972). Cohesion is produced internally, whatever its source. It arises out of the members' interactions with each other, their feelings for each other, their identification with each other, and the meaning of the shared experience. It is both a product and a determinant of the internal system. It is nearly irreplaceable in the business of group goal achievement and in the operation of the processes of social influence to bring about change in the group.

Communication and Decision Making

The energy on which groups run is communication, verbal and nonverbal. On the basis of what is communicated and how communication occurs, a set of people will interact and take on meaning for each other, consent together to attain some goal, and become a group.

A great deal of research has been done about communication patterns in groups (Bales, Strodtbeck, Mills, & Roseborough, 1951; Bavelas, 1960; Burgess, 1968; Hare, 1962). Much of it relates communication to the emergence of leadership; to persons who initiate communication, and those who receive communication, are perceived by others as leaders. Sometimes, where a person sits can affect the amount of communication received or initiated and thus can affect whether that person is viewed as a leader.

Where a person is located on the communication channels—her or his social position relative to other members—also helps determine that person's status within the group. For example, people who do not receive or initiate much communication may be viewed as isolates. Whether this position is self-imposed or imposed by others, an isolate in a group does not participate in the communication pattern of the group.

Communication is one of the processes in group decision making (Hall & Williams, 1970; Hartford, 1972; Kolaja, 1968; Taylor, 1970; Thibaut & Kelley, 1959; Vidmar, 1970; Zajonc, Wolosin, Loh, & Loh, 1970). Decision making is not restricted to groups formed for task or action purposes; it goes on also in groups for growth or corrective purposes. Such groups have to decide on group goals and determine the means for achieving them, and have to decide on membership policies. In the process of decision making, communications are exchanged among members in discussing ideas, beliefs, and points of view, in assessing them in the light of the group's common goal, and in arriving at a final point of agreement.

Seven methods of reaching agreement have been identified: (1) consensus among the whole group, (2) majority vote, (3) persuasion by a minority of group members, (4) averaging the individual opinions of group members, (5) persuasion by the member with the most expertise, (6) pronouncement by the member with the most authority after group discussion of ideas, and (7) pronouncement by the member with the most authority without group discussion (Johnson & Johnson, 1975). Some of these methods are more time-efficient than others but ignore the principle of participation; some observe the principle of participation but prove not to be time-efficient.

There may not be one best method for arriving at group decisions. The methods mentioned above may be used singly or in some combination depending on the kind of decision to be taken, how highly the group values widespread participation, the type of worker style or member-leadership style that emerges, or the stage of group development. What is important is that the group find a way to solve its problems and make its decisions. The members need to feel they are important to other members and to the life of the group, they need to recognize that they may have to give up some of what they want personally in order to achieve the greatest good for the greatest number, and they need to appreciate that people working in concert can be more productive than people working alone.

Norms, Values, and Group Culture

People's behavior may be influenced by others, producing a group system that holds together and gets its work done (Asch, 1955, 1956, 1960; Sherif, 1947; Siegel & Siegel, 1960). Norms emerge from the interactions of group members; and they may be overtly stated and enforced or conveyed subtly and covertly. A norm is a group's particular way of doing things, such as arriving on time, sitting in a particular pattern, speaking in a particular sequence, not interrupting other members, following the lead of certain prestigious members, or sharing or withholding certain information. A norm may have to do with not doing any of the above. The point is: norms communicate the group's own particular style, and they are expressed as "our way of doing things." A group norm may arise in various ways. The worker or an emergent member leader may enunciate that a particular behavior is the group's way of doing things; the members may then pick up the pronouncement and cause each other to behave in conformity to it. Or members may have some idealized expectation of how people ought to behave. This ideal may be embodied in a person within the group, one outside the group, or a person who does not exist at all but represents a kind of aspiration. Members will try to modify their behavior to emulate that person.

Norms represent what the group highly values; members will attempt to control each others' behavior in order for those values to be manifested in the group.

Norms are enforced by a range of rewards and sanctions. Members may praise each other, and shun or ignore an offender. They may elevate someone to an office, aspire to be seated near that person, or desire to be seen with her or him; or they may ostracize or exclude a member for failure to comply. They may badger, coerce, support, encourage, or emulate.

The group's culture is the distinctiveness that sets that group off from every other group (Hartford, 1972). Its culture emerges from the members' norm-conforming behavior. It says: "people who do things this way are people like us." This distinctiveness may be denoted by, for example, a particular style of dress or article of clothing, by the use of a particular vocabulary, or by a particular way of behaving. In whatever form this distinctiveness is expressed, it makes the members recognizable to themselves as "we" or "us" and to others as "they" or "them." Their style is the group culture that sets them apart.

Culture is linked to cohesion and may be taken as an indicator of it. Cohesion is conceptually defined as the sum of the forces attracting members to the other members, to the group itself and to what the group does (Cartwright & Zander, 1960); the group's culture may be one of those forces.

Group Control and Influence

Each member of a group is influenced by the other members and in turn influences them in the direction of her or his goals and the group goal. As Sherif (1947, p. 290), noted; "Once an individual identifies ... with a group and its collective actions, ... behavior is, in a major way, determined by the direction of the group action, whatever this direction may be."

A member's influence over other members is derived from the meaning that group membership holds for them. It depends on the group's goals, norms, cohesiveness, communication, and interpersonal interactions. In putting oneself in the position to influence and to be influenced, an individual aids, and is aided by, others in shaping behavior toward the attainment of individual and group goals. The emotional climate of the group may affect the degree of control or influence exerted. Group influence and control results in some loss or modification of self, as the individual identifies with the group and its direction of movement.

The use of group control and social influence in the service of change is discussed by Hartford (1972), who cites Newcomb and Sherif, and by Festinger (1953). People tend to alter their behavior to comply with the expectations expressed by others. This is particularly so when the individual has embodied, in part, in a group contract her or his goal of personal change.

According to Hartford (1972), change occurs through the group's influence not only because of people's need to be accepted and their fear of rejection but also because of their sense of responsibility and their desire to keep up with group standards and expectations. These standards and expectations are the norms of the group that will hold it together and enable it to do its work.

A thesis of the practice approach presented in this text is that the change sought by someone joining a group occurs at the confluence of goals, norms, cohesion, and group influence.

Summary

The social processes described in this chapter define the concept of a group, as that term is used throughout this book. No one of these processes or forces alone gives rise to a group; all of them must be present in some degree. As the text proceeds, these terms will be reappropriated and discussed in relation to the stage of development that the group has reached, the type of contract in effect, the role of the worker and her or his location with respect to the group, and the program media utilized.

This chapter surveyed what groups can and cannot do. It then focused on the theoretical base for social work practice with people in groups—the theory base that is drawn upon in this book.

In the following chapter, the elements of the specific model for social work practice with groups will be elaborated, paving the way for the remainder of the book.

References

Asch, S. (1955). Opinions and social pressure. *Scientific American, 193*(5), 31–35.

Asch, S. (1956). Studies of independence and conformity: Vol. 1. A minority of one against a unanimous majority. *Psychological Monographs, 70*(9), 1–70.

Asch, S. (1960). Effects of group pressures upon modification and distortion of judgements. In D. Cartwright & A. Zander (Eds.), *Group dynamics research and theory* (2nd ed.). Evanston, IL: Row, Peterson.

Bales, R. F. (1950). *Interaction process analysis.* Reading, MA: Addison-Wesley.

Bales, R. F., & Borgatta, E. (1955). Size of group as a factor in the interaction profile. In A. P. Hare, E. Borgatta, & R. F. Bales (Eds.), *Small groups: Studies in social interaction* (pp. 396–413). New York: Alfred A. Knopf.

Bales, R. F., Strodtbeck, F. L., Mills, T. M., & Roseborough, M. E. (1951). Channels of communication in small groups. *American Sociological Review, 16*(4), 461–468.

Bavelas, A. (1960). Communication patterns in task oriented groups. In D. Cartwright & A. Zander (Eds.), *Group dynamics research and theory* (2nd ed.). Evanston, IL: Row, Peterson.

Benne, K., & Sheats, P. (1948). Functional roles of group members. *Journal of Social Issues, 4*(2), 41–47.

Burgess, R. (1968). Communication networks: An experimental reevaluation. *Journal of Experimental Social Issues, 4*(3), 324–337.

Cartwright, D., & Zander, A. (Eds.). (1960). *Group dynamics research and theory* (2nd ed.). Evanston, IL: Row, Peterson.

Cassano, D. R. (Ed.). (1989). Social work with multi-family groups [Special issue]. *Social Work with Groups, 12*(1).

Churchill, S. (1959). Pre-structuring group content. *Social Work, 4*(3), 52–59.

Coyle, G. L. (1930). *Social process in organized groups.* New York: Richard R. Smith.

Coyle, G. L., & Hartford, M. E. (1958). *Social process in the community and the group.* New York: Council on Social Work Education.

Cunningham, R. (1951). *Understanding group behavior of boys and girls.* New York: Columbia University Press.

Davis, L. (Ed.). (1984). Ethnicity in social group work practice [Special issue]. *Social Work with Groups, 7*(3).

Dunphy, D. (1968). Phases, roles and myths in self-analytic groups. *Journal of Applied Behavioral Science, 4*(2), 195–225.

Feldman, R. (1968). Interrelationships among three bases of group integration. *Sociometry, 31*(1), 30–46.

Festinger, L. (1953). An analysis of compliant behavior. In M. Sherif (Ed.), *Group relations at the crossroads.* New York: Harper and Bros.

Glick, O., & Jackson, J. (1970). The effects of normative similarity on group formation of college freshmen. *Pacific Sociological Review, 13*(4), 263–269.

Goroff, N. (1972). Unique properties of groups: Resources to help people. *Child Welfare, 51*(8), 494–504.

Hackman, R., & Vidmar, N. (1970). Effects of size and task type on group performance and member reactions. *Sociometry, 33*(1), 37–54.

Hall, J., & Williams, M. S. (1970). Group dynamics training and improved decision making. *Journal of Applied Behavioral Science, 6*(1), 39–68.

Hare, A. P. (1962). *Handbook of small group research.* New York. Free Press.

Hare, A. P., Borgatta, E., & Bales, R. F. (Eds.). (1955). Small groups: Studies in social interaction. New York: Alfred A. Knopf.

Hartford, M. E. (1972). *Groups in social work.* New York: Columbia University Press.

Hartley, E., & Hartley, R. (1952). *Fundamentals of social psychology.* New York: Alfred A. Knopf.

Henry, S. (1972). *Contracted group goals and group goal achievement.* Unpublished doctoral dissertation, University of Denver.

Hocking, W. (1941). The nature of morale. *American Journal of Sociology, 47*(3), 302–320.

Homans, G. C. (1950). *The human group.* New York: Harcourt, Brace.

Jennings, H. H. (1953). Sociometric structure in personality and group formation. In M. Sherif (Ed.), *Group relations at the crossroads.* New York: Harper and Bros.

Johnson, D. W., & Johnson, F. P. (1975). *Joining together group theory and group skills.* Englewood Cliffs, NJ: Prentice-Hall.

Klein, A. (1970). *Social work through group process.* Albany, NY: State University of New York, School of Social Welfare.

Kolaja, J. (1968). Two processes: A new framework for the theory of participation in decision making. *Behavioral Science, 13*, 66–70.

Kolodny, R., & Garland, J. (Eds.). (1984). Group work with children and adolescents [Special issue]. *Social Work with Groups, 7*(4).

Lee, J. A. G. (Ed.). (1988). Group work with the poor and oppressed [Special issue]. *Social Work with Groups, 11*(4).

Linton, R. (1936). The study of man. New York: Appleton Century.

Lott, A., & Lott, B. (1965). Group cohesiveness as interpersonal attraction: A review of relationships with antecedent and consequent variables. *Psychological Bulletin, 64*(10), 259–309.

Lum, D. (1986). *Social work practice and people of color.* Pacific Grove, CA: Brooks/Cole.

Maloney, S., & Mudgett, M. (1959). Group work and group casework: Are they the same? *Social Work 4*(2), 29–36.

McGrath, J., & Altman, I. (1966). *Small group research: A synthesis and critique of the field.* New York: Holt, Rinehart & Winston.

Miller, G. A. (1956). The magical number seven plus or minus two: Some limits on our capacity for processing information. *Psychological Review, 63,* 92–95.

Mills, T. M. (1967). *The sociology of small groups.* Englewood Cliffs, NJ: Prentice-Hall.

Morris, S. (Ed.). (1984). Use of group services in permanency planning for children [Special issue]. *Social Work with Groups, 5*(4).

Newcomb, T. (1960). Varities of interpersonal attraction. In D. Cartwright & A. Zander (Eds.), *Group dynamics research and theory* (2nd ed.). Evanston, IL: Row, Peterson.

NiCarthy, G., Merriam, K., & Coffman, S. (1984). *Talking it out: A guide to groups for abused women.* Seattle: Seal Press.

Raven, B. H., & Rietsema, J. (1960). The effects of varied clarity of group goals and group path upon the individual and his relation to his group. In D. Cartwright & A. Zander (Eds.), *Group dynamics research and theory* (2nd ed.). Evanston, IL: Row, Peterson.

Redl, F. (1951). The art of group composition. In S. Schulze (Ed.), *Creative group living in a children's institution* (pp. 76–96). New York: Association Press.

Reed, B. G., & Garvin, C. (Eds.). (1983). Groupwork with woman/groupwork with men: An overview of gender issues in social groupwork practice [Special issue]. *Social Work with Groups, 6*(3/4).

Reid, W., & Epstein, L. (1972). *Task-centered casework.* New York: Columbia University Press.

Richards, C., & Polansky, N. (1959). Reaching working class youth leaders. *Social Work, 4*(4), 31–39.

Saul, S. (Ed.). (1982). Groupwork and the frail elderly [Special issue]. *Social Work with Groups, 5*(2).

Schopler, J., & Galinsky, M. (1974). Goals in social group work practice: Formulation, implementation, evaluation. In P. Glasser, R. Sarri, & R. Vinter (Eds.), *Individual change through small groups* (pp. 201–230). New York: Free Press.

Schwartz, W. (1961). The social worker in the group. *The Social Welfare Forum.* New York: Columbia University Press.

Shalinsky, W. (1969). Group composition as an element of social group work practice. *Social Service Review, 43*(1), 42–49.

Shaw, M. E. (1971). *Group dynamics: The psychology of small group behavior.* New York: McGraw-Hill.

Sherif, M. (1947). *The psychology of ego involvements.* New York: John Wiley.

Siegel, A. E., & Siegel, S. (1960). Reference groups, membership groups, and attitude change. In D. Cartwright & A. Zander (Eds.), *Group dynamics research and theory* (2nd ed.). Evanston, IL: Row, Peterson.

Slater, P. E. (1955). Role differentiation in small groups. *American Sociological Review, 20,* 300–310.

Slavson, S. R. (1964). A textbook in analytic group psychotherapy. New York: International Universities Press.

Snyder, N. (1975). An experimental study on optimum group size (Doctoral dissertation, University of Pittsburgh). *Abstracts for Social Workers, 12*(3), 34.

Stinson, J. E., & Hellebrandt, E. T. (1972). Group cohesiveness, productivity, and strength of formal leadership. *Journal of Social Psychology, 87*, 99–105.

Taylor, M. (1970). The problem of salience in the theory of collective decision-making. *Behavioral Science, 15*, 415–430.

Thibaut, J. W., & Kelley, H. H. (Eds.). (1959). *The social psychology of groups.* New York: John Wiley.

Thomas, E., & Fink, C. (1963). Effects of group size. *Psychological Bulletin, 60*(4), 371–384.

Vidmar, N. (1970). Group composition and risky shift. *Journal of Experimental Social Psychology, 6*(2), 153–166.

Ward, C. D. (1968). Seating arrangements and leadership emergence in small discussion groups. *Journal of Social Psychology, 74*(1), 83–90.

Zajonc, R. B., Wolosin, R., Loh, M. A., & Loh, W. B. (1970). Social facilitation and imitation in group risk taking. *Journal of Experimental Social Psychology, 6*(1), 26–46.

Zander, A. (1971). *Motives and goals in groups.* New York: Academic Press.

CHAPTER 2

A FOUR-DIMENSIONAL APPROACH TO GROUP SKILLS

In this chapter, the four dimensions of the practice approach of the book are presented, and the model of practice is built and discussed. These four conceptual dimensions interact so as to prescribe what the worker will do. This is the essential meaning of skill: it is "knowledge in action" (Phillips, 1957).

✕ Four-dimensional Model

1. Stages of group development
2. Contract form in effect
3. Worker location and role vis-à-vis the group
4. Program media used

The stages of group development are presented in somewhat more detail than the other three dimensions, because these stages provide the framework on which the book is organized.

○

1. Stages of Group Development

Schemas for describing the stages or phases of group development are as numerous as the writers who have written on the subject (Bennis & Shepard, 1970; Fried, 1970; Garland, Jones, & Kolodny, 1965; Hartford, 1972; Mills, 1970; Sarri & Galinsky, 1967; Shaw, 1971; Whittaker, 1970). Two models have most heavily influenced the practice approach of this book: "A Model for Stages of Group Development" by Garland, Jones, and Kolodny (1965) and "Stages and Phases of Group Development" in Hartford's *Groups in Social Work* (1972).

Whatever formulation is adopted, the movement from one stage of group development to the next is not linear. The stages are not discrete and finitely demarcated. Rather, the flow is spiral-like, with return to an earlier level of functioning for reinforcement and resolution of the issues of the previous phase before movement to the next level. This nonlinear progression seems to occur with both closed and open groups. A closed group is a fixed set of persons who begin their experience together and continue together for the term of the experience, without the addition of new members. An open group is a set of persons who begin and end their experience at different times, with new members entering and old members leaving the group. In this book, the closed group is presented as the general form. Differences between the two forms are discussed where appropriate, and the use of open groups is taken up in chapter 9.

The six stages of group development considered in this text are:

1. Initial
2. Convening
3. Formation
4. Conflict/Disequilibrium
5. Maintenance
6. Termination

The choice of terms to designate the stages, the definitions of these stages, and the descriptions of the specific dynamics of each stage are the responsibility of the author of this text.

The Garland, Jones, and Kolodny (1965) formulation helps the worker to recognize group development phases by the psychological connectedness of the persons who come together to form a group. That formulation defines five stages of group development: preaffiliation, power and control, intimacy, differentiation, and separation. In this book, their scheme was added to the contribution of Hartford's portrayal of phases of group development. Her design added understanding of stages of group development by the consideration of particular aspects of a pregroup stage.

Hartford (1972) contributed the notion of a convening stage. A worker *composes* a group; she or he *convenes* a set of people; and the people *form* the group. Hartford's term has been appropriated for use in this book. Hartford's pregroup phase has been drawn upon for understanding what occurs in the life of a group, and what a worker does, before the group forms. In this book, the first stage of life is called the initial phase; it is concerned with pregroup planning, assessment, interviewing, and membership selection—all done by the worker, or the worker in concert with others.

Initial Stage

As Hartford (1972) notes in her description of the pregroup phase, the idea for a group may originate in the mind of a worker who thinks it would be a good idea to have a group for a particular purpose, or in the minds of people who think it would be beneficial for them to be part of a group; or it may originate in an agency's administrative service decisions, which determine that group service is compatible with, or central to, the agency's function. Whatever the source of the idea, at some point a worker either takes or is given the responsibility to move the idea along. The worker then makes the idea known to other workers in the same agency or other agencies, to clients and potential clients, and to possible referral sources. The worker must clearly communicate the intended purpose of the group, what kinds of persons are most appropriate for inclusion, the projected time factors, and the intended treatment approaches or techniques. Many groups have never quite gotten off the ground because this vital step was not taken (Hartford, 1972; Schmidt, 1969).

The worker's vision of the group may be only vaguely formed, but it will determine the initial group composition and subsequent events. It cannot accurately be said that there are group dynamics at this point, but the embryonic group will be affected by the worker's actions in identifying the potential cast of characters and in projecting what the group will be like and how it can move toward attainment of its goals.

The worker needs to utilize her or his interviewing skills during this initial phase. Pregroup interviews figure prominently in the development of the various contracts which will be subsequently negotiated. These contracts are discussed in the second section of this chapter. The pregroup interview also provides the worker and the prospective member with a preview of the interactions and relationships that will exist when the group is convened and then formed.

In some instances, an intake interview is done by someone other than the person who will be the group worker. Moreover, the clients may be voluntary or nonvoluntary. Nevertheless, it is always important to conduct pregroup interviews.

b. Convening Stage

In the convening stage, the people whom the worker now convenes for the first time are entering a new situation, and the approach-avoidance dilemma described by Garland Jones and Kolodny (1965) occurs. The members of the new group size up the situation before deciding to commit themselves, and there is a general testing of the waters. The stages of group development can be seen as following a rhythm of separation and union; the initial and convening stages can be seen as moving from separation toward union (Schmitt, 1972). Inherent in that figure is ambivalence and struggle, resistance and choice. As one moves toward union with others, the desire to retain autonomy and identity is at war with the yearning toward identifying with and joining complementary figures. The worker takes a leading part in the events of this stage and acts as a surrogate for the group processes (Lang, 1972).

As the members struggle with the choice of belonging, the worker focuses on their resistances, helps clarify their aspirations and expectations, and aids their identification with each other and their common needs. The worker, while honoring their struggle, points out the possibilities that their choice to join, commit, and invest could bring to fruition. The worker models the behaviors that the persons themselves will use with each other once they choose to belong to the group.

c. Formation Stage

When the individuals who have been convened begin to interact with each other, establish interpersonal ties, take on group roles, create their own normative system, adopt a common goal, and act in relation to it, the group has formed. The key dynamic of this formation stage is choosing to unite with others. If the first two stages were a process of moving from separation toward union, in the phase of group formation the main feature is union. Cohesion indicators are evident, and communication and decision-making patterns are becoming established and functional. This is the first of two periods of strong attachment to other members, to the group, and to the worker (the second such period is the maintenance stage).

d. Conflict/Disequilibrium Stage

A dynamic of separation characterizes the fourth stage of group development. This stage has been variously characterized. One writer called it "storming" (Tuckman, 1965), another cast it as "disintegration" (Hartford, 1972), and others as "power and control" (Garland, Jones, & Kolodny, 1965). In the scheme being presented here, the dynamics of this state may be seen as conflict and/or disequilibrium.

ℯ. **Conflict**   Conflict is more than strong difference with another point of view, more than taking sides in a political sense. It is competition for the dominance of one's needs and desires over those of all the group members. Essentially, the conflict is over ownership of the group. Each member wants to separate herself or himself from all the others and fashion the group's experiences completely after her or his own design. This dynamic originates in a fear of losing autonomy and a resistance to surrendering too much of the self in favor of the greater good for the greatest number. It may be a reaction to the perceived implications of the attachment experienced in the formation stage. At any rate, the members pull back to reexamine what it means for them to be a member of this group and to rechoose commitment and investment (Brager, 1969).

ƒ. **Disequilibrium**   Alternatively, members' behavior may disturb the integrity of the group system tentatively achieved in the formation stage. The issue, in that case, may not be a conflict over ownership. It may be, as Hartford (1972) commented in citing Berne's work, that members of the group pause, in their evolution toward groupness, to deal with their functioning as a collectivity. Work on a task or on achieving integration continues, but from time to time the group may put it on hold to take stock of functioning, to evaluate the efficacy of its internal operations, or to observe its aims and processes closely. When this stage is seen as disequilibrium, the group operates in fits and starts, alternately working on the task and stopping to check its development. The watchful periods may reflect lack of clarity or agreement about the goal, uncertainty about the means to attain the goal, or questions about other choices of means or ends. "Issues which have been decided upon in previous deliberations may be reopened for further consideration" Hartford (1972, p. 82).

Maintenance Stage

When the members work through the conflict and put the disequilibrium right, they find themselves in a stronger attachment. This is the maintenance stage. In this stage, the sense of union or attachment is both qualitatively and quantitatively different from that of the formation stage. The initial choice to belong—the formation of the group—was done on faith. Until then, the events of the group had moved along smoothly; things looked good, and so it was safe and easy to commit oneself to the group experience. However, in the maintenance stage, the choice is deeper, firmer, and more informed with respect to what one has let oneself in for. The conflict stage has been passed, and equilibrium—albeit not of a static, flat-line kind—has been regained. Like the calm after the storm or making up after a fight, a deeper level of appreciation for what one has chosen is reached. Members are drawn more closely together. Decisions come more easily on the consensus pattern; norms operate smoothly and efficiently; the differentiated roles run the group's systems at an effective pace. All is well; it is a good time in the life of the group.

Some have characterized the maintenance stage as a quiet period, even as a "slump" having a "dead-level quality" (Smalley, 1971, p. 1287). On the contrary, this stage is more often a period of growth, of forward movement both for the individuals who comprise the group and for the group itself, in terms of the maturity and efficacy of the group's functioning. Many of the issues around joining, achieving what is sought, and obtaining what is needed have been resolved at this stage, so energy can be devoted to working on the help that the group exists to provide. Goals are typically in place by this time, and effort can be put into directing the group's internal structural processes—roles, norms, and communication patterns—toward the group's goals. Gains come fairly quickly and can be consolidated and extended to areas of functioning both within and outside the group.

The maintenance stage is a time when members begin to refer to themselves as "we" and to identify "our way of doing things." These indicators of cohesion express the meaning of the group experience for the members, the value of belonging, and the members' identification with each other. The uniqueness of this group, its difference from all other groups, becomes evident. Members take responsibility for the functioning of the group, attend to all of the internal and external forces that operate the social processes, and attend to the needs and growth of self and others.

Even though this level of stabilizing and consolidating gains maintains itself efficaciously, it has within it the seeds of its own termination. No experience can sustain itself at such a pitch; some kind of self-correcting mechanism operates to help members move on from this stage. If the members stayed in the maintenance stage endlessly, the usefulness of the group would be defeated; their purpose in joining the group was to improve social functioning, to acquire satisfying interpersonal relationships outside the group, or to attain insight into their internal, intrapsychic processes.

In the realization of these facts—whether unconscious, preconscious, or conscious—the members come to face the reality that this group experience, like all things, must come to an end. As the end approaches, even while the group is still in its maintenance stage, there begins a process of transition to the termination stage. It is a process that makes the final separation possible, and it rests on the security gained from the union that occurred during the maintenance stage.

Fried (1970), terming this transitional phase "individuation," has proposed that the attainment of individuation is, in one way or another, the end goal of all therapeutic endeavors. Without individuation, the union could become a stagnant and stifling state wherein persons would be unable to free themselves from the mass. Unless persons are able to move on from the cohesiveness and bonding of the earlier stages, being together could easily become an end in itself, a displaced goal, and individual goals and objectives could be lost sight of. Moving into and through this transitional stage of individuation is the best possible basis for a successful outcome of group membership.

Termination Stage

When the transition has occurred and members have discovered their capacity to function effectively on their own, the stage of termination is entered. At first glance, it might seem that an ending is simply an ending and that a group experience simply ceases once the ending point is reached. However, the actuality may be quite different. In order for the conclusion of any experience to be useful, time needs to be spent in preparation for it.

Members should be given an opportunity to become accustomed to the imminent ending, offered a chance for review and evaluation, and allowed time to stabilize the changes that have taken place in relation to the goals agreed to at the beginning. Moreover, people need to be able to express their feelings about the ending of an experience which has had meaning and significance for them. Many of these feelings are favorable, and people need the chance to express their appreciation for the growth that has occurred and for the context within which it happened. Sometimes, however, the realization of the impending loss of a supportive group will produce in people an expression of negative reactions, and the final stage may be marked by a chaotic regression to earlier stages of functioning. In either case, the central theme of this stage is that of mourning. Time needs to be made available to allow the handling of that emotional set.

For all of these reasons, the stage of termination needs to be prepared for, entered into, and moved through in the same fashion as all the prior steps. The focus of effort ceases to be on connection with the group as a whole; it turns to a deeper connection with the self, a deeper rootedness within one's own resources, and a greater reliance upon one's own capacities (Fried, 1970). This is possible, in most cases, when the psychological connectedness with others has been made and strengthened, has been supportive and productive of the security to be one's own person, and has promoted risk taking. Separating oneself from a group experience will be more successful when the prior stages have been fruitfully negotiated and the final stage skillfully facilitated.

The foregoing discussion sets forth the scheme of stages of group development used in this text. The next section examines the worker skills related to the contract that the members of the group agree to.

$$\bigcirc$$

2. ✳ Contract Forms

The second dimension of worker skill is the type of contract in effect at any given time (Croxton, 1974; Henry, 1974; Maluccio & Marlow, 1974; Seabury, 1976). The idea of a contract to express intention and responsibility in an

pects of each person's individuality in recognition of the greater good or larger ends to be served by collective effort. In that process, each person does not surrender her or his uniqueness or autonomy but rather commits energy to the therapeutic benefits to be derived from participation with others.

The worker contributes to the fashioning of the mutual contract by sharing her or his assessment of the clients' situations, her or his conception of the group's purpose and the potential benefits to be derived from belonging, and her or his own formulation of what could be possible for each client. When a group has formed and is ready to work, the mutual contract will reflect member, worker, and agency goals.

Beyond the mutual contract lies the interdependent contract, representing the best expression of the collective aim and intent of all parties concerned. In the interdependent contract, member, worker, and agency goals have given way to an agreement or understanding that

> contains reference to the group as a whole, to the intended outcome, to group content and to means of treatment. Member roles and worker roles are implied, if not explicit, thus suggesting something of group structure, as well.
>
> Clearly, the Interdependent contract is the common property of the group as a whole, since it contains the purposes, goals and objectives of the clients as individuals and as a collectivity. (Estes & Henry, 1976, p. 619)

Logically, when the group-oriented contracts have been fulfilled, the group will end. However, if the experience of group membership has been valuable, each member ought to be able to generalize her or his gains to life outside the group. For this, one final contract form exists: the independent form.

The goals reflected in an independent contract emerge from the group experience. Their content and mechanisms for implementation will have been shaped out of the interaction with other group members and the group worker. At the termination of the group experience, the independent contract will be a measure of the effectiveness of the group in helping the individual.

In making a contract, the worker should aim at clarity as to the group's goals, specificity in identifying those goals, and explicitness of the terms of the contract. The worker should begin addressing, with the group, the question of what they are doing together and what they will accomplish through the group experience. The worker should elicit oral statements from group members, write them down, and check them with the group for agreement. This will help to make a contract that is clear, specific, and explicit (Henry, 1974).

Veiga (1974) found that, of all the variables studied, the one that most consistently contributes to goal attainment is the simple act of putting goals in writing. Some may argue that writing is obtrusive, that it interferes with the therapeutic process. The counterargument is that human memory cannot be relied on, especially in the face of the intense self-interest of group members with respect to their own needs and goals. The position taken here is in favor of a written contract at each stage of contract negotiation or renegotiation and for each type of contract.

Taken together with a contract for group goals, a tool for measuring goal achievement has potential value. If goal achievement is measured at several points in time, adaptations can be made in the group's internal processes (program, structure, cohesion, and communication) and in the worker's intervention strategy, to keep the group oriented in the agreed direction or to renegotiate the contract. This measuring device might be a scale that the members complete, individually or collectively, each time the contract is reviewed for reaffirmation or renegotiation. It might be the contract itself, copied for each member, the members being asked to evaluate progress in narrative terms. A Goal Achievement Questionnaire has been developed for these purposes (see Chapter 7).

The contract should be used for evaluative purposes at each transition point. The discussion, initiated either by the worker or by group members, should address the question, "How are we doing in relation to what we said we wanted to do?" The question might be elaborated to specify such matters as the number of meetings, the use of time, or participation and communication patterns, as set forth in the group's mutual contract. Any term of any contract may be adjusted at any point. It should always be clear *what* is being agreed to as well as *who* the parties to the agreement are. The emphasis throughout should be on reciprocity and mutual agreement by all parties to all terms.

The individual contract exists prior to and long after the person's membership in a specific group. However, at a certain point, some of the individual's life goals and objectives might match the purpose for which a group exists. They are appropriated into a reciprocal contract between that person and a worker during the pregroup interview in the initial stage of group development. This reciprocal contract continues through the convening stage and up to the time of group formation.

At that point, members can mutually consent to a common goal and the means of achieving it. A mutual contract comes into existence between the members and the worker, and it continues through the formation stage and the conflict/disequilibrium stage, into the maintenance stage. The mutual contract helps hold the group together as it passes through its conflict/disequilibrium stage. It represents the members' initial aspirations and promises, and appeals to those aspirations are the best enforcement mechanisms for holding the group together.

When the group has regained its equilibrium in the maintenance stage, one of the forces aiding its reintegration is the formation of an interdependent contract. That contract, agreed between the group as a whole and the worker, expresses a group goal, one that is oriented to the group more than to the individual members. The interdependent contract continues through the termination phase to the point when the members leave each other and the group experience.

The group then ceases to exist, but the <u>members establish for themselves an independent contract that helps carry the meaning of the group experience with them</u>. This contract is what the members promise themselves they will do as a result of what they gained in and through membership in the group. The independent contract may become part of the person's individual contract, which is ongoing through life but is now reshaped by the impact of the person's having belonged to the group. The interrelation of the first two dimensions of the practice model presented in this book is shown in Table 2-1.

Table 2-1
Stages of Group Development and Contract Forms

Contract Form	Initial	Con-vening	Formation	Conflict/ Disequilibrium	Main-tenance	Termi-nation
			Stage of Group Development			
Individual	X———————————————————————————— X —					
Reciprocal	X—————————X					
Mutual			X ————————————— X			
Interdependent					X ——— X	
Independent						X—

3. Worker Role and Location

The third skill dimension is the role taken by the worker and the location of the worker vis-à-vis the group. The worker is not a member of the group but has a particular function with respect to it; therefore, the worker should occupy an appropriate location relative to the group.

The worker's role—and thus, her or his location vis-à-vis the group—is different from that of a member for several reasons. First, and most crucial, the worker has a different responsibility toward the group than any of the members have. The worker has to be the agent of the agency and to exercise professional judgment and skill in composing, convening, and serving the group. No member has these responsibilities. Second, the worker selects the members of the group; the members do not select the worker. Third, the members have been selected on the basis of some need or problem—identified by them or by someone else—for which the group is thought to be an appropriate setting for alleviation or resolution. The worker is not there to have her or his needs or problems addressed.

Certainly a worker may grow and change, professionally and even personally, as a result of association with a group; but that is not the worker's main purpose with the group. Of these factors, the crucial one is the enactment by the worker of a set of professional behaviors that are different from the behaviors of the others present.

The term *role* has been used to denote a cluster of specific behavioral patterns (Linton, 1936). Members enact help-seeking, problem-resolving, self-focused kinds of behaviors. The worker's behaviors are help-giving, resolution-facilitating, and other-focused. Since the perspective is different, the two sets of actors do different things and stand in different orientations to each other. The knowledge base or resources that each set of actors possesses is also different. In carrying out her or his function, the worker employs knowledge of individual and collective behavior, of planning, and of interventive techniques. The members employ self-knowledge to the extent that they can; they use their own definitions of their goals and aspirations; and they draw upon their own sense of what they are willing and able to do to achieve those goals. These knowledge bases are differentially utilized in the group experience.

The different roles necessarily imply different orientations to each other. Thus, the two sets of actors occupy different locations in the life space they jointly occupy. The worker remains apart from the group because she or he has composed the group—like a stage director choosing the actors, setting the stage, arranging the actors with respect to the setting, cueing their lines, but not becoming a player herself or himself. The analogy extends further; the worker, like a director, will also coach the members on how to portray mannerisms, gestures, inflections, and emotions, how to explore the motivation for behavior, and how to play to each other.

Several theoretical bases undergird the idea of the worker in a role and location separate from the group. Various approaches to social work with groups have been taught (Churchill, 1970; Council on Social Work Education, 1964; Hartford, 1972; Papell & Rothman, 1966; Schwartz, 1964). Each of these approaches stands on a different theory of psychology, social psychology, or sociology of small groups (Whittaker, 1970). It may be said that each approach implies a different worker orientation to the group and a different set of worker roles in relation to the group. The location and behavior of the worker will reflect the worker's view of what is going on among the set of people. This location and role may change according to the stage of group development.

Lang (1972) developed the idea that there are different orders of groups, reflecting the particular needs, capacities, and characteristics of the people who comprise the group.

The *role* of the worker may be cast along a continuum ranging from primary to variable to facilitative, depending on the worker's function and on the cluster of interventive behaviors utilized by the worker. Similarly, the *location* of the worker vis-à-vis the group may be cast along a continuum ranging from central to pivotal to peripheral, depending on the worker's position and on the degree of the worker's involvement in the group's processes. Thus, a worker may be central and primary within the group, or pivotal and variable, or peripheral and facilitative (Lang, 1972).

A worker enacts certain roles and occupies certain locations with respect to the group. The worker does this in order to maximize individual and collective contributions to group-as-a-whole functioning. Certainly, a set of persons does not begin its existence in a state of whole-group functioning. Necessarily, worker interventions need to be directed toward meeting a group in its embryonic form and moving it as far as it can go toward a mature and viable form, taking into account the capacities of the persons who comprise the group.

Table 2-2

Stages of Group Development, Contract Forms, and
Worker Roles and Locations

			Stage of Group Development			
Contract Form	**Initial**	**Con-vening**	**Formation**	**Conflict/ Disequilibrium**	**Main-tenance**	**Termi-nation**
Individual	X———————————————————— [Work Stage] —————————					X—
Reciprocal	X———————	X	Worker in pivotal location, variable role		Worker in peripheral location, facilitative role	
Mutual		Worker in central location, primary role		X ——————————— X		Worker in central location, primary role
Interdependent					X ——— X	
Independent						X—

There is a natural progression of worker function and position corresponding to the stages of group development and the existing contract form.

Primary Role and Central Location

At the outset of a group experience, the worker's role is to select candidates for the group. This is a primary role. The worker is in a central location as she or he gathers the persons who will comprise the group. The worker retains this primacy and centrality during the course of planning the external structural features of the group (matters of time, space, and size), prethinking the nature and function of the group, projecting an outline of the sequence of events, conducting the pregroup interviews, and negotiating the reciprocal contract between the worker and each prospective member.

The worker continues to be primary and central as the members are convened for their first session and the reciprocal contracts begin to be blended into a mutual contract. The worker retains this role and location by initiating and directing the group's discussion, by watching out for the participation of everyone (encouraging some to talk more and others, perhaps, to talk less), and by monitoring the feeling tone in the group's meeting atmosphere.

Variable Role and Pivotal Location

As the group forms and as it moves to a new level of connectedness, the worker intentionally takes a variable role and occupies a pivotal location with respect to the group. As the worker steps back from the central location and primary role, the members begin to supplant some of what the worker has been doing. In the vernacular of cinematography, the worker fades out as the group system comes up. However, because the group's (internal and external) systems are not yet stabilized at full functioning capacity, the worker needs to let the process run at its own speed and sometimes needs to move back in to help keep the system afloat. This is why the worker's role is referred to as variable, and the worker's location as pivotal. This role and location will be part of the mutual contract that is being negotiated at this time.

The worker's variable role and pivotal location continues during the conflict/disequilibrium period. When the group experiences upheavals, it may be stabilized and made able to weather the storm by the fact that there is a common agreement to refer to and the fact that the worker is standing ready to facilitate the process.

Facilitative Role and Peripheral Location

When the group enters its maintenance stage with a new level of integration and maturity, the worker assumes a facilitative role and occupies a peripheral location. The group has achieved full capacity to govern itself, and the worker now needs to be available in a resource role rather than a primary one. She or he will be at the boundary of the system because the group is maintaining itself, internal and external systems are "go," it conceives of itself as an entity, and it is functioning in a self-directed way.

Return to Primary Role and Central Location

When the group moves into its termination phase, the members are preparing to disengage from the system and to fashion their own independent contracts; they therefore give less energy to the group entity. The worker must be prepared to move back into a central location and a primary role in order to insure that the group experience may end well for its members. There is the appearance—and, sometimes, the reality—of a return to earlier stages of functioning, and the worker's taking the primary role and central location helps to sustain the group through this regression. Successful movement through this phase is aided by the worker's knowledge of the dynamics of ending and of the need for members to separate from the group and take up their own independent courses.

The interaction of the three dimensions considered so far—the stages of group development, the type of contract in effect, and the role and location of the worker—is shown in Table 2-2.

Program Media

The final dimension of worker skills is the program media that are utilized to enhance the group's process. A program medium is what the group is doing together, verbally or nonverbally. Whenever a worker chooses an exercise (such as fantasy trips), employs psychodrama, directs a client to converse with an empty chair as her or his alter ego, encourages the free-association monologue of one member in the presence of others, or engages the group in collective problem solving, that worker has elected a program activity.

The notion of program has been heavily relied on within social group work from the beginning. In fact, there was a time when program was thought to be the "tail that wagged the dog" (Wilson, 1976, pp. 25–26). The behavioral effects of activities upon individuals and upon the climate of the group and upon the emergence of the entity itself were first observed by Newstetter in 1935. At that time, schools of social work taught a whole array of interventive techniques that used such media as arts and crafts, dancing, games, rhythmics, music, and dramatics. The social work educators were clear regarding the purposive use of these media, as were their students who became practitioners and theoreticians of the art. Their colleagues, however, both within and outside social work, saw these techniques as fun and games, recreation for its own sake. Programming in group work was held in some disdain as being lightweight and lacking intellectual content.

Undaunted, and spurred by a recognition of the value of program media, social work educators went on teaching this content well into the 1970s. In the meantime, research was done on the effects of program as an interventive technique. A small but solid body of research and theoretical literature has been produced (Crawford, 1957; Gump, 1955; Gump & Sutton-Smith, 1955; Henry, 1964).

A basic assumption of the practice model described in this text is that the social worker should have a plan of action for the group she or he is serving. This plan of action is based on the worker's assessment of the needs of the group and the individuals who comprise it. The worker gathers facts about the needs that can be met within the group, particularizes those facts for the purpose of framing a plan of action to meet those needs, involves the individuals in helping frame that plan, and then intervenes in the group to help effect growth and change both in the group and in the individual members. In addition, the worker assesses the stage of development of the group in order to clarify the nature of the processes into which she or he intervenes.

An essential ingredient of the plan of action is the program media that will be used. Use of program media is an interventive tool of the social worker, and these media may be utilized for differential ends. When used for assessment purposes, program media reveal the needs and interests of group members according to the responses evidenced by them. When used for treatment purposes, program media are intended to meet the needs and interests of the group members.

A number of sources, both theoretical and empirical, have contributed to the understanding of the program dimension of group skills in social work (Middleman, 1968, 1983; Shulman, 1971; Vintner, 1967c; Wilson & Ryland, 1949). Program media serve a variety of functions; they can be used to modify the climate of a group interactional field, or to alter the activity itself in order to produce desired effects in clients. Program media can benefit individuals and groups, they can affect group content, and they are useful for facilitating a group's beginning, middle, and ending processes. A worker's knowledge and skills should include an understanding of individual and group interactional behavior in relation to program media. These media not only further certain values and enhance group processes but also affect the very nature of the interactional behavior and the group's emotional climate.

Research has shown that the emotional tone of a group session and the positive or negative quality of interactions among group members is altered from before to after the use of certain program activities (Henry, 1964). With a group of latency-age children, the game Spud (played with a ball) requires the members to unite against chance. The game Hangman was played on a chalkboard; it, too, requires members to unite against chance, and to forestall aggressive behaviors. These games evoked positive interactional behaviors. The activities of cooking and coloring, which constrain the control that members have over their own behavior, evoked negative interactional behavior.

The positive or negative behavioral effects of a program medium depend not only on the intrinsic nature of that activity but also on the stage of group development; the level of physical, emotional, social, and intellectual development of the members; the emotional atmosphere; and the purpose for which the activity is used. Workers with groups therefore need to carefully weigh and analyze any medium utilized to alter the behavioral pattern manifested by group members.

The framework for analysis of program media developed here is an amalgamation of the work of Vinter, Wilson and Ryland, and Middleman.

From Vinter (1967c) and the work of his associates comes the notion that a program medium may be analyzed on the basis of the behaviors elicited or provoked by the intrinsic requirements of the activity itself. Thus, in considering an activity for use with the group, the worker should scrutinize it with respect to guides to conduct, source of those guides, physical movement, skill level, interactiveness, the nature, form, and extensiveness of the activity, and the manner of distribution of rewards. If the activity is found to be appropriate for the group members' needs and capacities, the worker will proceed to initiate or allow its use. If some aspect of the activity is inappropriate, the worker may either alter the activity or select a different medium.

From Wilson and Ryland (1949) comes the notion that certain individual and group values are derived from program activities. The individual values are physical, social, emotional, psychological, and intellectual growth. The group values are cohesion, norms, and role differentiation. The worker's analysis, in this framework, consists of an assessment of what is needed by—or what is possible in—the group, individually and collectively. The worker then introduces an appropriate activity to meet those needs.

Middleman (1968) contributed the notion that the stage of the group's development is a factor in the choice of program activities. She used a process orientation (beginning-middle-ending) in thinking about groups, and she associated certain program media with each stage of the group's process. According to Middleman, the particular dynamics of each stage will cause the members of a group to behave in certain ways. The worker's intervention will modify members' behaviors toward the next stage of the process.

From these sources and from the empirical research done in this area, a framework for analyzing and selecting program media has been devised for this text. Program media are related to the processes of building, sustaining, and ending a group. The framework will help the worker to determine what the group should be doing at any given time. This is done by examining members' needs, their capacities to engage in a given activity, and the behavioral outcomes associated with that activity.

The description of the four-dimensional approach to social work practice with groups is now completed. The model is set forth in its entirety in Table 2-3.

From the matrix shown in Table 2-3, the worker can determine what they should or could do at any given time with respect to stage of group development, contract types, worker role and location, or program media. Once the worker knows what is occurring in any one of these four dimensions, what the worker will do will be prescribed by the way that dimension interacts with the other three. The decision points that eventuate in worker intervention may be derived from the matrix according to a "degrees of freedom" notion, and guides to worker behavior follow. For example, when the group is in its convening stage, the contract will be of the reciprocal type, the worker will be in a central location and will play a primary role, and the media to be utilized will be of the group-building type. Another example: when the worker is in a peripheral location and playing a facilitative role, it follows that the group will be in the maintenance stage, with the contract form shifting from mutual to interdependent, and the group engaging in sustaining kinds of program media.

Table 2-3
Four-dimensional Model of Group-work Practice

	Stage of Group Development					
Contract Form	Initial	Con-vening	Formation	Conflict/Disequilibrium	Main-tenance	Termi-nation
Individual	X———————————————————————— X —					
Reciprocal	X——————————X		Worker in pivotal location, variable role		Worker in peripheral location, facilitative role	Worker in central location, primary role
Mutual		Worker in central location, primary role	X ——————————————— X			
Interdependent					X ——————— X	
Independent						X—
	Group-building activities	Group-sustaining activities				Group-ending activities

Social work has tended to avoid a prescriptive stance with respect to teaching skills. This tendency has come from a wish to avoid giving a mechanistic or technical appearance to the practice of social work. However, the position taken in this text is that the knowledge base upon which social work practice rests—whether that base is derived from other disciplines or generated from within social work itself—has become sufficiently well developed to allow us to be prescriptive. That development has reduced the likelihood of turning out technicians able to execute only a limited number of highly specialized skills with only a limited degree of decision making. The analysis proposed in this book results in a range of possible interventions, from which one may be selected by the exercise of discretionary judgment.

Table 2-4 lists the stages of group development, the dynamics of each stage, its theme, and the worker skills required during that stage. This table comprises the practice model advanced in this text; Chapters 3–8 discuss these dynamics, themes, and skills in relation to the stages of group development.

Table 2-4
Stages, Dynamics, Themes, and Worker Skills

Stage	Dynamics	Themes	Worker Skills
Initial	Planning Membership selection Pregroup interviews leading to reciprocal contract	Preparation	Conceiving the idea Recruiting and selecting participants Conducting pregroup interviews and negotiating the recriprocal contract
Convening	Approach/avoidance Milling process Sizing up Parallel play	Entry	Observing and assessing Modeling entry into new situations Facilitating connection
Formation	Emergence of norms Role differentiation Coalescing Committing to group Coming to terms with goals	Joining	Supporting and encouraging participation Helping the synthesizing process Monitoring the consolidation of interactional patterns
Conflict/ Disequilibrium	Struggle for ownership Gaining own, collective power Dynamic tension Managing in conflict situations	Power and ownership	Turning issues back to the group Holding the system steady Creatively using the conflict
Maintenance	Consensus-like form of decision making Security and belonging Differentiated roles Norm conformance Beginning of differentiation	Work	Guiding and steering Supporting Encouraging expressions of difference
Termination	Bringing closure to the experience Finishing unfinished business Leaving as individuals Recapitulation and evaluation Stabilizing and generalizing change Projecting toward the future	Individuation	Preparation for separation Directing and focusing expressions of feelings about termination Facilitating the ending

[Handwritten annotations: "vital life of Group" (next to Dynamics); "assembling" (next to Convening); "coming together and form one whole" (next to Coalescing); "pos. + neg. behavior" "role models" "Getting Group going" (next to Worker Skills of Convening)]

Summary

This chapter has presented a discussion of the four dimensions that frame the practice approach of the book. The central thesis is that four dimensions interact so as to prescribe what a worker with a group will be doing at any given time; these are the stage of group development, contract form in effect, the role and location of the worker, and the program media.

The model presented here is prescriptive, in that it tells what the worker should be doing; it is processual, having a beginning, middle, and ending and elements that change over time; it is integrated, the elements being linked together and changing together and it is positive, being growth oriented and favoring possibilities and potentialities over pathology.

References

Bennis, W., & Shepard, H. (1970). A theory of group development. In T. Mills & S. Rosenberg (Eds.), *Readings on the sociology of small groups.* Englewood Cliffs, NJ: Prentice-Hall.

Brager, G. (1969). Commitment and conflict in a normative organization. *American Sociological Review, 34*(4), 482–491.

Churchill, S. (1970). *Worker behavior and rationale in troublesome management incidents in groups.* Unpublished doctoral dissertation, University of Chicago.

Council on Social Work Education. (1964). A conceptual framework for the teaching of the social group work method in the classroom. New York.

Crawford, J. (1957). *Impact of activities on participant behavior of children.* Unpublished master's thesis, University of Michigan, Ann Arbor.

Croxton, T. (1974). The therapeutic contract in social treatment. In P. Glasser, R. Sarri, & R. Vinter (Eds.), *Individual change through small groups.* New York: Free Press.

Estes, R. J., & Henry, S. (1976). The therapeutic contract in work with groups: A formal analysis. *Social Service Review, 50*(4), 611–622.

Fried, E. (1970). Individuation through group psychotherapy. *International Journal of Group Psychotherapy, 20*(4), 450–459.

Garland, J., Jones, H., & Kolodny, R. (1965). A model for stages of development in social work groups. In S. Bernstein (Ed.), *Explorations in group work.* Boston: Boston University School of Social Work.

Garvin, C. (1969). Complementarity in role expectations in groups: The member-worker contract. In *Social Work Practice, 1969.* New York: Columbia University Press.

Gump, P. (1955). The 'it' role in children's games. *The Group, 17,* 3–8.

Gump, P., & Sutton-Smith, B. (1955). Activity-setting and social interaction: A field study. *American Journal of Orthopsychiatry, 25,* 755–760.

Hartford, M. E. (Ed.). (1964). *Working papers toward a frame of reference for social group work.* New York: National Association of Social Workers.

Hartford, M. E. (1972). *Groups in social work.* New York: Columbia University Press.

Henry, S. (1964). *An exploration of the association between group interactional behaviors and four program activities.* Unpublished master's thesis, Western Reserve University, Cleveland, OH.

Henry, S. (1972). *Contracted group goals and group goal achievement.* Unpublished doctoral dissertation, University of Denver.

Henry, S. (1974, October). Use of contracts in social work with groups. Paper presented at the School of Applied Social Sciences Alumni Association Symposium, Cleveland, OH.

Lang, N. (1972). A broad range model of practice in the social work group. *Social Service Review, 46*(1), 76–89.

Linton, R. (1936). *The study of man.* New York: Appleton-Century.

Maluccio, A., & Marlow, W. (1974). The case for the contract. *Social Work, 19*(1), 28–36.

Middleman, R. (1968). *The non-verbal method in working with groups.* New York: Association Press.

Middleman, R. (Ed.). (1983). Activities and action in groupwork [Special issue]. *Social Work with Groups, 6*(1).

Mills, T. (1970). Toward a conception of the life cycle of groups. In T. Mills & S. Rosenberg (Eds.), *Readings on the sociology of small groups.* Englewood Cliffs, NJ: Prentice-Hall.

Newstetter, W. I. (1935). *What is social group work?* Proceedings of the National Conference of Social Work (pp. 291–299). Chicago: University of Chicago Press.

Papell, C., & Rothman, B. (1966). Social group work models: Possession and heritage. *Journal of Education for Social Work, 2,* 66–77.

Phillips, H. U. (1957). *Essentials of social group work skill.* New York: Association Press.

Prisoners sign contract for correction. (1971, December 13). *The Denver Post.*

Reid, C. (1969). *Groups alive—church alive.* New York: Harper & Row.

Rose, S. D., & Feldman, R. A. (Eds.). (1986). Research in social group work [Special issue]. *Social Work with Groups, 9*(3).

Sarri, R., & Galinsky, M. (1967). A conceptual framework for group development. In R. D. Vinter (Ed.), *Readings in group work practice.* Ann Arbor, MI: Campus Publishers.

Schmidt, J. T. (1969). The use of purpose in casework practice. *Social Work, 14*(1), 77–84.

Schmitt, A. (1972, November). The pattern of Rankian growth process. Paper presented at the annual meeting of the Otto Rank Association, Doylestown, PA.

Schwartz, W. (1961). The social worker in the group. In *The Social Welfare Forum* (pp. 146–177). New York: Columbia University Press.

Schwartz, W. (1962). Toward a strategy of group work practice. *Social Service Review, 36*(3), 268–279.

Schwartz, W. (1964). Analysis of papers. In M. E. Hartford (Ed.), *Working papers toward a frame of reference for social group work* (pp. 53–61). New York: National Association of Social Workers.

Schwartz, W. (1966). Neighborhood centers. In H. S. Maas (Ed.), *Five fields of social service: Reviews of research.* New York: National Association of Social Workers.

Schwartz, W. (1971). On the use of groups in social work practice. In W. Schwartz & S. R. Zalba (Eds.), *The practice of group work* (pp. 16–31). New York: Columbia University Press.

Seabury, B. (1976). The contract: Uses, abuses, and limitations. *Social Work, 21*(1), 16–21.

Shapiro, S. B. (1968). Some aspects of a theory of interpersonal contracts. *Psychological Reports, 12,* 171.

Shaw, M. E. (1971). *Group dynamics: The psychology of small group behavior.* New York: McGraw-Hill.

Shulman, L. (1971). 'Program' in group work: Another look. In W. Schwartz & S. R. Zalba (Eds.), *The practice of group work*. New York: Columbia University Press.

Smalley, R. (1971). Social casework: The functional approach. In J. B. Turner (Ed.), *Encyclopedia of social work* (p. 1287). New York: National Association of Social Workers.

Thomas, E. J. (1967). The socio-behavioral approach: Illustrations and analysis. In E. J. Thomas (Ed.), *The socio-behavioral approach and applications to social work*. New York: Council on Social Work Education.

Tuckman, B. W. (1965). Developmental sequence in small groups. *Psychological Bulletin, 63*, 384–399.

Veiga, J. F. (1974). Life goals inventory. Mimeographed.

Vinter, R. (1967c). Program activities: An analysis of their effects on participant behavior. In R. Vintner (Ed.), *Readings in group work practice*. Ann Arbor, MI: Campus Publishers.

Weathers, L., & Liberman, R. P. (1976). The family contracting exercise. *Journal of Behavioral Therapy and Experimental Psychiatry, 6*, 208–214.

Whittaker, J. (1970). Models of group development: Implications for social group work practice. *Social Service Review, 44*(3), 308–322.

Wilson, G. (1976). From practice to theory: A personalized history. In R. W. Roberts & H. Northen (Eds.). *Theories of social work with groups*. New York: Columbia University Press.

Wilson, G., & Ryland, G. (1949). *Social group work practice*. Boston: Houghton Mifflin.

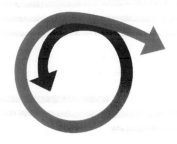

CHAPTER 3

THE INITIAL STAGE

In the initial stage of group development, an individual contract is being shaped into a reciprocal one, the worker is in a primary role and central location, and group-building program media are being used.

In this chapter, reference is frequently made to a "group purpose." The purpose of a group is the worker's conception of the group's possible function. This is distinct from the group's goal, which is the mutually agreed statement of a desirable end state. In the initial stage, therefore, there is only a group purpose; the goal emerges later.

The discussion also refers to "prospective members." These are persons who are interested in joining the group. Until the group is actually composed, convened, and formed, however, the selected persons are not actually members. In the initial stage and the convening stage, therefore, there are only prospective members.

Role and Location of the Worker

In the initial phase, the worker is in a primary role and a central location. There is work to be done before the group convenes for the first time, and

43

even before any specific person has been identified as a member of the group. Four main skills are required at this stage: conceiving the idea of a group, recruiting and selecting participants, conducting pregroup interviews and negotiating a reciprocal contract, and doing initial planning.

Conceiving the Idea

As Hartford (1972) has written, someone must conceive of the idea of having a group. This idea may come from the function of the agency itself, from the worker, or from the clients.

Agency as Origin   The decision may be taken at the administrative or managerial level that the agency will conduct groups for certain purposes and to serve specific needs.

In at least one community mental health center in which research was conducted, there was a standing policy that groups were to be the treatment method of choice (Henry, 1972). This policy was advocated by the chief administrator of the center, and groups of all kinds abounded there: parent education groups, multifamily groups for parents and "problem adolescents," young adult groups to correct dysfunctional patterns of social relationships, and educational groups for overweight adolescents. All manner of problems and many combinations of clients were treated through the group method.

However, not every client presenting herself or himself for service was automatically placed in a group. When people appear for treatment at an agency and their situations mitigate against group treatment, sound therapeutic planning would contraindicate their placement in a group. For example, the literature on psychiatric diagnostic categories appears to show that group treatment is contraindicated for people in certain categories (Anderson, 1977).

In many adolescent residential facilities (short- or long-term), daily groups are the order of the day. Sometimes groups are offered twice a day or more for those adolescents in residential settings who are not in school. Daily groups are functionally consistent with the agency's program, because the aim is to correct faulty means of establishing interpersonal relationships and to offer alternative modes of relating, and this is one of the aims of these residential facilities. Daily groups are also structurally consistent with the agency's program, because such services are designed to provide a treatment milieu. In one such type of setting, adolescents live in groups, eat together in a group, study together, play together, and spend their leisure time together. Adolescents generally tend to associate in groups whether they are in a residential treatment facility or not; but for therapeutic purposes the tendency may be maximized in the structure—and therefore in the treatment program—of such settings.

However, there is sometimes too much peer pressure, and behavioral contagion may reach epidemic proportions. Moreover, some residents may not be appropriate for group service.

In another example, the decision to allocate social work services or recreational resources to residents of a settlement-house neighborhood was made on the basis of Erikson's (1968) conception of the life cycle. Social work service was provided at the points of identity crises that occur as an individual makes the transition from one life-cycle stage to another. This decision resulted in social work groups being available, for example, at the time children entered latency and were leaving home for school, at the time that young people left latency to move through puberty into adolescence, and at the time of moving from adolescence into young adulthood. Recreation was the service method of choice, to meet the social needs of members who were solidly in any of the life-cycle stages.

A final example comes from a multipurpose, community-based agency serving the informal education needs of women and girls. The agency was engaged in a self-study, action-research project (YWCA of Metropolitan Denver, 1969). The aim was to assess the agency's standing in its community, its public image, and its fulfillment of its mandate to provide service to women and girls of all races and creeds and its success in meeting the social, education, and leisure-time needs in its community. In the course of the action-research, it was determined that a large unserved Hispanic population existed not far from the agency. Paying attention to the cultural factors that affect the social outlets which young and old Hispanics are allowed, the agency explored with the women of the area the desirability of having a mother-teenage daughter group. A two-generation group was proposed as a way of strengthening Hispanic cultural norms, thereby legitimating the experience for both the older and the younger women. The purposes of the group were, first, to provide opportunities for mothers and daughters to socialize and communicate more freely with one another, thereby helping to strengthen that subsystem of the family system; and second, to provide activities traditionally associated with female roles, such as sewing, crafts, decorating, and cooking. The group's meeting place was to be a neighborhood church with a strong positive community image. The offered group thus fully regarded the culture of its potential members.

The decision whether to offer group services will depend upon the worker's analysis of the requests for services, of whether certain types of problems repeat themselves among clients, and of the particular agency's function in society.

Worker as Origin The idea to have a group may begin in the mind of a worker, who then sponsors the idea within the agency and designs a group with a particular purpose in mind.

In a public welfare department, a caseworker became aware of great social isolation among the Hispanic women in her caseload. To help them break this isolation, she devised a plan for a group, proposing a cheerful, comfortable, and convenient meeting place. She secured a promise that the agency would provide transportation and child care and would assign a Spanish-speaking coworker, as some of the women spoke only Spanish. A program outline with budget estimates was developed, and the proposal was successfully carried through department channels.

Another example: a school social worker at an elementary school realized that a large number of the children came from families where the parents were either in the process of divorcing or were just recently divorced. This seemed to affect the children's school performance both academically and socially. The social worker approached classroom teachers and the principal with a proposal to establish a group for children of divorce. She was given clearance to proceed and received many referrals—enough to compose more than one group. She then set about designing a group that used exercises and discussions from affective education resources, tailored to address the problems of children going through the trauma of their parents' divorce.

Another worker conceived the idea for a group of chronically mentally ill clients in a community mental health center. She wrote:

●

The need for another group activity for the chronically mentally ill clients at the mental health center drop-in center seemed apparent from the extra unstructured client time I observed and the boredom exhibited by the clients. Drop-in center attendance was declining during time periods when there were no activities planned for the clients to participate in. I discussed my perception of the need for more activities with drop-in center clients and staff. I also determined what activities might be of interest to clients; this was done by talking to staff and clients and by conducting a brief survey. Next, the idea was presented to my supervisor. After receiving a go-ahead, the idea was presented at a weekly staff meeting and was met with support and enthusiasm.

●

Client as Origin   Sometimes a set of clients of an agency will ask it to provide a group service.

For example, a group of adolescent women who participated in the sports and recreation program of a neighborhood branch of a metropolitan YWCA approached the youth program director and asked if they could have a club (Ryland, 1967). A large number of youth clubs already existed in the agency, but none of these young women had joined any of them. The women were an informal "natural group," always together but not involved in any formal, organized group. What they sought was formal recognition for their self-identified group and the use of agency resources—principally in the person of the youth worker to whom they looked as an ego ideal—to work on improving their individual and collective self-image. Their request was granted, and the group ultimately became one of the strongest clubs in the agency.

When the first idea for a group has been formed, from whatever source, the group is conceived to exist for a specific purpose. From that point, the step to considering who should or could be a member is a small one.

Recruiting and Selecting Members

The worker begins to make known the potential existence of the group and seeks referrals of persons who have the need or the interest to align themselves with the stated purpose. From this pool of interested people, the worker selects the persons who will eventually form the group.

Recruitment   The worker may publicize the possibility of the group's being created by making announcements in the agency or in public media such as newsletters, bulletin boards, and meetings of allied organizations. By means of referrals, personal recruitment, or public media, the worker identifies potential members and begins to assess them for their potential fit within the group.

For example, a group for women in transition was designed by a second-year graduate student of social work. She created a brochure that was sent to community mental health centers and social workers in private practice, and was placed, with permission, in those offices. The cover of the brochure stated:

●

ARE YOU A WOMAN WHO IS:

- Changing careers?
- Beginning or ending a relationship?
- A new mother?
- Coming out of the closet?
- Adjusting to children leaving or returning home?
- Resolving retrospective incest issues?
- Going through any other major life changes?

...THEN YOU ARE IN TRANSITION
AND WE CAN HELP MAKE IT A POSITIVE
GROWTH EXPERIENCE.

WOMEN IN TRANSITION
a support group

●

The inside of the brochure further described the aims for the group, defined transition, and concluded: "Healthy growth requires an environment of support and nourishment. Group process with professional facilitation can provide such an environment."

Announcements of the beginning of this group were placed in newsletters of Lesbian organizations, periodicals aimed at women readers, and weekly "alternative" community newspapers. Contrary to the experience of many therapists in private practice and others who have employed these avenues of publicity, the response to these efforts was sizable. That provided the opportunity for selectivity in group composition—putting the right mix of persons together; but it also meant that a great deal of time was spent in pregroup interviews. The benefits of this approach made the effort worthwhile, in the long run.

Seven women were initially selected for membership; two of them subsequently withdrew. By the fourth meeting, therefore, the group consisted of five members, with the workers. It lasted for a total of 20 weeks. When this preset period ended, the members chose to continue meeting on their own as a self-help support system. They were still meeting a year later.

Another social worker designed a physical fitness group that had the secondary purpose of connecting teenage girls and career-oriented women in a kind of mentoring and (as the worker termed it) co-coach relationship. She described her plan like this:

●

The group design brings together girls aged 14–18 and career-oriented women. Both the girls and the women need to work on weight control and improving muscle tone, physical fitness, and self-image. The primary purpose of the group is to help participants develop positive attitudes toward proper diet and exercise that will lead to a lifelong health level of physical fitness. At the same time, the activities and group discussions are designed to foster in the participants a feeling of control over, and knowledge of, the capabilities of their own bodies.

The purpose in partnering the teenage women with the career-oriented women is to establish a co-coach relationship and also a mentoring relationship that will encourage career exploration by the teenagers. This more subtle goal of the program will be achieved by the exposure of the young women to the ideas and activities of the older women on an informal basis, rather than any formal career exploration activities.

Recruitment for the group would be done in two phases. Teen members would be recruited through the sponsoring agency, high-school nurses and counselors, therapists, pediatricians, weight-control doctors, and hospitals. Adult participants would be recruited through women's professional and social organizations, weight-loss clinics, local businesses, schools, and corporations. Word of mouth recruitment will also be effective in obtaining adult participation.

People not appropriate for membership in the group would be women who have already achieved a competent level of fitness, as they may be intimidating to the other members; women who are extremely overweight and would not be able to maintain the group determined activity level; and women with addictive eating disorders, unless participation in the group is recommended by a doctor or therapist under whose care the women would continue throughout the duration of the program.

•

Recruiting as widely as possible, through outlets and referral sources appropriate to the persons one hopes to attract into membership, will assure a broad set of potential members, from among whom the best group composition may be achieved.

Selection   In selecting group members, the worker needs to be clear about the purpose of the group in order to ensure a homogeneous group composition, as the following example shows.

A worker in a children's hospital and her supervisor decided that a group for mothers of children being treated at the hospital would be a good idea. They had observed the mothers in the waiting rooms and lounges, and they thought a group in which the mothers could talk over their concerns and questions would be valuable. Deciding that the group should be open to more mothers than just those in the division where they worked, they contacted nurses and therapists in other parts of the hospital, asking each of them for two or three referrals. A fairly large number of names came to them, and they proceeded to plan for the group sessions and convened the referred women. This group never quite got off the ground. Attendance was very sporadic even though the women continued to come to the hospital regularly on behalf of their children.

The group's purpose and the criteria for membership selection had not been specified exactly. The request for referrals had been very vague and open, and pregroup interviews were not held. The result was a group of too great diversity of needs and types. Some of the women were focused on their children's conditions and sought information and reassurance. Others, referred from the division dealing with abuse and neglect cases, were focused on their own deprivations and legal situations and demanded a great deal of attention and support from the coworkers and from other group members.

There was too much deviance from tolerable levels of normative behavior. The group never coalesced, and ultimately it fell apart because there was no common goal clarity to hold it together. This experience accords with a research finding by Hartford (1962), which shows that worker failure to make explicit the purpose of the group was associated with a tendency for the group not to form.

Conducting Pregroup Interviews

Pregroup interviews should be held with all potential members of all groups. The major purposes of these interviews are to assess potential members' desire and capacity for group membership, to clarify the purposes of the group, to discuss the potential members' objectives and goals with respect to the stated group purposes, and to represent in miniature the procedures and methods to be used in the group.

The pregroup interview is also the time when the prospective member is asked to consider whether, given the worker's approach to working with people and given the nature of the group, she or he is interested in making time, energy, and financial investments in the proposed group experience.

The following account illustrates the place of pregroup interviews in the process of starting a group, after recruitment activity has been undertaken.

●

The idea occurred to me that it might be useful to develop a sexuality group for adolescent girls. The main purpose of the group, as I perceived it, would be to enhance the girls' search for identity and striving for personal growth through helping them to understand new dimensions of themselves.

My first task during this stage involved the recruitment of members. I contacted the nurse at the school, spelled out the purpose I had in mind, and asked for her help in identifying potential members who could use such a group. She agreed to provide me with the names of ten girls between the ages of twelve and fourteen who she felt would benefit from the group experience.

The next step in the process involved my meeting individually with each of the girls. These individual sessions served a fourfold purpose: (1) to make known my intended purposes for the group in order to determine the girls' interest in becoming involved in the group experience; (2) to involve the girls in making decisions concerning the day and time for the group meeting; (3) to establish a verbal contract with each of the girls in order to reach an agreement about our goals and expectations; and (4) to make use of relationship to begin engaging each of the girls in the group experience. At the conclusion of the individual sessions all the girls had expressed an interest in taking part in the group and all appeared to be suitable for group membership.

●

The following list illustrates the kinds of questions a worker will ask of prospective group members in a pregroup interview. These questions were framed for a group for primary caregivers of Alzheimer's disease patients.

1. What kinds of caregiving tasks are you currently doing?

2. What can your spouse/partner do for herself or himself?

3. Do you have help? From whom?

4. Do you need more help? What type? Do you know where to find it?

5. Do you have time away from caregiving responsibilities? If so, how do you spend it?

6. Rate on a scale of 1–5 (1 = lowest, 5 = highest) feelings of fatigue, isolation, frustration.

7. What concerns you most about your current situation? Least?

8. Do you think others in a similar situation may have something of value to offer you that would help your situation? Do you think you have something of value to offer them?

There are a number of ways of determining potential compatibility and complementarity among prospective group members. One important consideration is problem homogeneity (Maloney & Mudgett, 1959). Social and ethnic factors also enter the picture. For example, a worker composing a group of frail elderly in an inpatient setting noted that, although the inpatient population was ethnically homogeneous, there were differences between rural and urban members, and between members who were lower middle or working class and those who were upper middle or professional class. Such differences need to be assessed in the pregroup interview and later made explicit to the group as a whole.

Another important consideration should be the resolution of the question of heterogeneity vis-à-vis homogeneity within the embryonic group system. The adolescent sexuality group just referred to illustrates the handling of that issue.

●

In my next meeting with the school nurse, she gave me a list of the names of ten girls whom she felt might benefit from the group. I had previously given her two criteria to guide her in the referral process: that the girls should fall within the age range of 12–14 years and that they should have needs that fitted the purpose of the group as I had explained it to her. The nurse reported that her choice of girls had been made on the basis of her perception that these girls were "looking for something" in the way of attention and emotional support. This perception was based on the frequency with which the girls found reason to come to her office.

I questioned the fact that the list included the name of one 10-year-old girl. The nurse asked that I give this girl special consideration because, despite the age difference, she is very mature and appeared to be having difficulty with the physical and emotional changes that go along with the maturation process. I agreed to see the girl to determine whether the age difference would be a negative factor to her involvement in the group.

Besides this girl, two others were 12, three were 13, and three were 14 years old. Nine of them were Black, and they all lived in one of the two nearby housing projects. All of the girls knew each other, at least superficially, because of their contact in school. Otherwise, the girls on the nurse's list all had in common the fact that they seemed to be grappling with identity and self-image struggles.

●

Table 3-1 summarizes the procedures, content, and worker skills of the pregroup interview. A checklist of what the worker needs to consider during the interview process is given in Figure 3-1.

Table 3-1
Pregroup Interview Procedures, Content, and Skills

Procedures	Content	Skills
Hold with all prospective members	Potential members' desire and capacity for group membership	Assessing
Determine the suitability of the prospective member relative to the stated purpose of the group	Purpose of group	Giving information
Determine the prospective member's interest in group membership	Potential member's goals with respect to stated group purpose	Asking for information
Obtain the prospective member's contract agreement to a reciprocal	Procedures and methods to be used in the group	Clarifying
	Worker style, member style	Giving information
	Potential member's needs	Asking for information
	Potential member's commitment of time and energy, financial commitment	Achieving agreement
	Appropriate references to gender, race, ethnicity, and age	Sensitivity to gender, racial, ethnic, and age considerations

Figure 3-1
Pregroup Interview Checklist

Have I:

_____ held a pregroup interview with all prospective members?

_____ given information before asking for information?

_____ made certain that the prospective member understands what has been discussed?

_____ determined the prospective member's suitability for the group?

_____ informed the prospective member regarding her or his suitability?

_____ made some arrangements for anyone not accepted into the group to be referred to individual counseling or to another, more appropriate group?

_____ ascertained the prospective member's understanding of time, energy, and financial commitments?

_____ obtained the prospective member's agreement to all contract items?

_____ concluded a reciprocal contract, and made it available in writing, if that is indicated?

_____ given all information necessary for the member to get to the first meeting?

Negotiating a Reciprocal Contract   When a prospective member has been identified or referred for consideration for membership in the prospective group, part of what the worker will do is to transform the individual's individual contract into a reciprocal contract. In the pregroup interview, individual life-objectives of the prospective member are explored and discussed with the worker. Those objectives can be formulated as "something I want to work on for the time being." If they match the initial purpose for the group, they become the basis for the agreements that constitute a reciprocal contract.

An excerpt from a worker's record provides an example of such a discussion.

•

The initial purpose for the group being composed at the mental health center was to help young adults take more conscious control of the way they develop a social support system for themselves—basically to enhance their ability to meet and relate to others more effectively. Persons seen as eligible for selection were those who see themselves as isolated from others and passive or inexperienced in initiating or sustaining relationships with others.

Bob, a prospective member, came in for his pregroup interview at the suggestion of his counselor at school. He was a premed student and was experiencing a lot of pressure as a result of being a full-time student and having to work half-time. He felt that he did not have anyone to confide in. He wants to be able to release some of his pressures and get an idea how he can deal better with his demanding life. He indicated being lonely and would like to enhance interpersonal skills in getting to meet and know people.

We discussed the purpose for the group, and Bob agreed that it matched his needs. I mentioned that we would meet on Tuesdays from 6 to 8 P.M. at the center, and he said that was good for him. I let him know that what he expressed as his needs had also been expressed by others I was interviewing. We discussed confidentiality, and he agreed to respect others' confidential disclosures and stated that he expected the same. I told him the group would be composed of individuals of both sexes, all roughly the same age, and with similar expectations and experiences.

At the end of the interview, Bob wrote: "I want to use the group because I have a need to expand my contacts with other people, especially with women. I have a hard time expressing my feelings and have some hesitation in attending the group. However, I am willing to give it a try and will come to each of the sessions." He left, agreeing to return on Tuesday evening at 6 P.M. for the first meeting.

●

A reciprocal contract is agreed between each prospective group member and the group worker. It states that what the person wants or needs to work on can be appropriated into the generalized initial group purpose. The worker agrees (or not) with the prospective member that the group can serve her or his stated needs. Further, the worker and the prospective member exchange their perspectives of what each expects of the other, in behavioral terms (Estes & Henry, 1976; Garvin, 1969).

The record of the worker with the young adult social skills group continues:

●

In the course of discussing with Bob what the purpose of the group is and how the group would operate, I let him know what he could expect from me and what I expected from him. I told him that I would be present at all the group sessions and that, at least in the beginning, I would be pretty active in getting conversations and discussions started, as I would be the one person whom everyone knew. I said I would try to keep things focused. I explained that people should feel free, especially at the start, to share things or not, depending on how comfortable they were; but that, gradually, they would probably feel safer in letting things out.

I said that I would be trying not to let people hurt themselves (by putting themselves down, for example), hurt others, or damage the meeting room and property. I said that I considered what we talked about to be the private business of the people in the group, not to be shared with people outside, and that I expected everyone to honor that. Bob agreed to this. I told him that I expected people to attend the group meetings, to come on time, to be willing to share according to their comfort level, and to allow space and time for others to share, too.

I asked Bob what he expected to do and what he expected from me. He agreed that, although he had some hesitation about coming because he has a hard time expressing his feelings, he was willing to give it a try. He is willing to attend the sessions; he will call in if he's not going to be able to get to a session.

He expects me to help steer the group toward the members' being able to realize their goals; he expects me to be able to clarify things for the group as we go along; and he expects me to give attention to people's needs for help. He sees it as part of my job with the group to provide a comfortable setting at a mutually convenient time and place and to facilitate a nonthreatening atmosphere.

●

The process of establishing this reciprocal contract can also aid the prospective member's understanding of how the group will function. The worker should outline the procedures and methods to be used in the group. This would include the exchange of information and expectations as to what sorts of people will be in the group (without giving specific names), what the prospective member will be expected to deal with, and what expectations the prospective member might hold for own or others' behaviors as the group progresses. The worker should spell out initial expectations regarding attendance, being on time or informing the agency of lateness or absence, participation, and self-disclosure. The worker should specify procedure for paying fees. The worker should be sufficiently in touch with her or his own style with a group to be able to let a prospective member know what to expect from her or him.

To illustrate further:

●

In the pregroup interview, I let Bob know that my style is a bit low-key and that I tend to use humor quite a bit in relating to people. I said that I try to keep tabs on what's going on and that I tend to notice body language and comment on it. I outlined some of the things that the group would be doing—exercises and role plays, as well as talking—and said that I would be like a discussion leader most of the time. I asked about his previous experience in groups. Except for having been in clubs in high school and having been a youth counselor at the Y, he hadn't been in a group like this. He had no preconceived notions of what this group would be like. I pointed out that the way our conversation had been going so far was pretty much how the group would go: questions asked or issues raised and then discussion about them. He said it seemed okay and not as scary as he had thought; nothing about it had been hard so far.

●

Table 3-2 summarizes the processes and content involved in establishing a reciprocal contract. A checklist for this negotiation is provided in Figure 3-2.

Table 3-2
Reciprocal Contract Processes and Content

Process	Content
Discussion	What the person wants and needs to work on at this time
Negotiation	Statements, in behavioral terms, of what the prospective member and the worker can expect of each other, initially
	Congruence between the group purpose and the prospective member's objectives
Orientation	Procedural expectations: • attendance • on time • informing agency of lateness or absence • procedures for paying • participation • self-disclosure
	Ethical considerations: • confidentiality • access to records • worker interventions to keep people from harm to self, others, or property • social relationships (if appropriate)

Ethical Considerations   The prospective member comes to a pregroup interview with the overriding questions, "How much can I trust this person? How much can I trust what is going to happen to me?" The worker's message is, "I imagine you're wondering what is going to happen to you and how the others and I will behave toward you. The best way to know that is to meet with the group and see if you can and want to trust yourself, the others, and me."

The worker does not ask for blind trust; that would be unrealistic. More honest and reassuring is a direct communication about how the group will proceed: "It will be part of my task to see that the people in the group don't hurt themselves, other members, or any of the equipment or facilities in the meeting place. Some of the growth and change you and the others

Figure 3-2
Reciprocal Contract Checklist

Have I:

_____ included the prospective member's statement of what she or he wants and needs to work on at this time?

_____ stated what my style of work is?

_____ stated what group members can expect from me?

_____ included what they expect of me?

_____ included what they are willing to do?

stated my expectations regarding

_____ attendance?

_____ being on time?

_____ notifying the agency of absences or agreeing to pay?

_____ procedures for paying?

_____ participation?

_____ self-disclosure?

stated the ethical considerations regarding

_____ confidentiality?

_____ access to records?

_____ worker interventions to prevent harm to the member, to others, or to property?

_____ social relationships?

_____ reached an agreement with the prospective member that the group purpose and that person's objectives are congruent?

_____ resolved whether to put the contract in writing? If I decided on a written contract, have I put it in writing, given one copy to the prospective member, and retained one?

---

go through may be painful, but we want to try to prevent what is destructive and self-defeating."

This approach lets the prospective member know what can be expected from the worker—what her or his role and attendant behaviors will be. By being direct, honest, and open about her or his way of working with a group, the worker tries to assure that there will be no surprises along the way. This approach also communicates an expectation of member behaviors. It says that the worker expects the member to behave within certain boundaries of respect for self, others, and property, and that if those boundaries are exceeded, the worker will intervene to hold people's behavior in check. The worker might say something like, "I wouldn't support your doing something inappropriate to your goals or those of the other members. I will support your choices to act in the direction of your getting what you want and need." The message may not have much concrete practical meaning at the time of the pregroup interview, but it is a tangible point of reference to return to, if the need arises, as the group progresses.

Another ethical issue that should be raised during the pregroup interview is that of confidentiality. People being considered for the group may not have had previous group experience; they need to know what will become of the personal information they share with the worker in this interview and with the worker and other members in the group meetings. Even if they have been members of groups in the past, they need to know how their information will be dealt with in this case.

The worker should tell prospective members: "In the course of our group's meetings, you and the others may tell quite a lot about yourselves. You may say some things you've never told anyone else before. I'd like to talk about how we can respect each other's privacy about these things. I will talk about it again with the whole group. What do you want me and the other members to do to keep our discussions confidential? What are you willing to do in return?"

The worker will try to stress that disclosures should not be discussed outside the group meetings or in social conversations. Some groups even ask that group discussions not be taken up with therapists the members might be seeing on an individual basis.

The worker also needs to let the interviewee know what records are kept and what use they are put to (for example, statistical, clinical, funding source reporting, or supervisory). The prospective member should be told the agency policies and practices regarding access to her or his own records and regarding the worker's sharing of confidential information, and should be advised of her or his right to change position about access to records or about information being shared.

The worker should outline the statute governing licensing of practice and explain the privileged-communication clause, if that applies. Where appropriate, the interviewee should be asked to sign a consent for treatment and release of information.

Another ethical matter sometimes raised in pregroup interviews is that of social relationships between members outside the group meeting time. The question might arise around whether the worker may appropriately impose such a limit on members' behavior. This step would be taken in the light of a worker's best professional judgment that the people have been brought together for a specific therapeutic purpose and that their energies need to be given only to the group, not to individuals within it.

In such cases, the potential for creating individual relationships with group members should be minimized. However, there might be times when contacts outside the group would be appropriate. Support networks might be set up between members, for example, or members might practice their social interaction skills while traveling to and from meetings together.

Chance meetings, of course, cannot be avoided but member preferences about how these are to be handled ought to be discussed. A group of battered women meeting in the community outreach center of a safe house had a discussion on this subject one evening. All of the women were living in their own homes and continuing their daily routine activities. One woman said she had seen another member and that member's husband (known to the group as her batterer) at a shopping mall and had debated with herself about approaching her comember. She decided not to and raised her questions in the group meeting. The members agreed that they preferred not to be greeted in public.

In another group, the decision might be entirely different. The important point is that the matter of member preferences about handling chance encounters ought to be discussed and resolved *at the group level.* Members ought not to have to remember that Dee and Jean and Rose don't want to be greeted but that Nancy and Julie and Marilyn are okay with it. The responsibility to raise and clarify this matter is the worker's, and it should be done early in the group's convening period.

Other points of view are possible; others may choose to promote contact outside the group, for a variety of reasons. The stance taken here, however, in order to maximize the group as the means and the context of helping, is to minimize outside associations unless the conditions for them are clearly negotiated.

The limit on social relationships outside the group applies most forcefully to the worker. Because of the power differential between worker and group member, the potential for exploitation, the worker's responsibility to give equal priority to the needs of all members, and the possible loss of professional perspective, workers should avoid social and sexual relationships with group members. (National Association of Social Workers, 1979).

These are overarching professional ethical concerns; they should be incorporated into the practice of a social worker whatever her or his method, and they should be part of standing operating procedures. They are highlighted here because it is at this initial stage of work that a worker and client interact directly for the first time. The ethical issues bear greatest weight when worker and client meet.

Initial Planning

At the same time that recruitment and selection of members is going on, the worker will also be giving thought to developing a generalized outline for the entire group experience.

The worker needs to mobilize the agency resources for the group. The worker with the group of frail elderly sets out the "environmental support issues and the agency budget."

•

The group does not operate on a fee-for-service arrangement; rather, it is part of the infrastructure of the rehabilitation department. Some costs and expenses would be low; however, the group needs the following resources from the agency:

1. The worker's time needs to be allocated. The worker spends two hours a week with the group itself and four hours a week analyzing and planning for the meetings.
2. The worker's supervisor should spend one hour a week supervising the worker's group work.
3. The meeting room needs to be reserved for two hours a week.
4. The members' rehabilitation schedules must include two hours a week for the group meetings.
5. The nursing staff will be needed to transport the members to and from the meeting room twice a week.
6. The secretarial staff may be used to type up the oral history vignettes (the group's principal program medium). This would be within the range of three to nine pages for the entire group.
7. The following equipment must be obtained for the group meetings: (1) a record or tape player with good acoustics, (2) records or tapes of old-time radio and music, (3) a large calendar, and (4) a flip chart. The calendar will be used to emphasize the termination date, and the flip chart will be used by the worker when a primary role and central location are required.

•

The worker will also be giving thought to the size of the group, time factors, the place for group sessions, and the arrangement of the space in which the sessions take place. These external structural factors will have an impact on what subsequently occurs in the group.

Size To decide the best size for a group, the worker needs to know about "deviant tolerance" and about the effects of group size on group goals, goal achievement, and members' satisfaction with group experience. The worker should also be aware of members' usual emotional repertoire and "acquaintance volume" (Moreno, 1960, p. 55; Jennings, 1952, p. 316, 1953, p. 333). People generally have a preferred number or volume of persons with whom they can interact comfortably, and a repertoire of emotional and psychological exchanges at their command in interacting with others.

The settlement house referred to earlier, which used social work groups to aid its members through life-cycle crises, used the notion of acquaintance volume in composing groups. Prospective group members were asked, in pregroup interviews, about the number of other people they usually went around with. The information was then used to determine a range of group size compatible with all the members' tolerable acquaintance volume.

The group purpose is also a determinent of size, as was shown in chapter 1; for example, task-focused groups tend to be larger than groups for growth purposes. Group size is a strong determinant of the communication patterns that emerge in a group, and thus of the relationship of leadership to followership and role differentiation that subsequently occurs. The worker's task is therefore to put into action what she or he knows.

Time   The planning for use of time will involve determining the means—the media—by which the group will begin its work toward its goals. This planning may be modified later, to the extent of the members' capacity to engage in decision making on their own behalf. As the people who come together probably will be unknown to each other and as their decision-making processes and their system of norms have not yet had a chance to develop, the worker will need to enact her or his primary role and central location by developing the initial format of activities in planning for the group's use of time.

Initially, the worker will determine the length of meetings, the number of sessions, and their frequency, drawing upon her or his knowledge of the effects of such factors on members' investment and commitment quotient.

An example from practice with a social skills group for chronic schizophrenic clients illustrates the relationship between group composition and time factors.

•

In order for the group to provide maximum benefits to members, I suggested it meet three times a week. This would give members a chance to practice, on a regular basis, the skills they learn. It would also give them the opportunity to bring everyday problems to be addressed in the group setting. If the meetings were held less frequently, I believed clients would tend to lose interest between meetings and that continuity would be difficult to achieve.

With unlimited staff time, I would like to see the group meet seven days a week, for 45 minutes each time, in order to provide the most consistent support for members. These clients typically have fairly short attention spans and impaired abilities to concentrate, track themes, and so on. Requiring more than 45 minutes would be anxiety provoking for most, and intolerable for some.

Because structure and consistency are important, the group must always begin on time. Patients should be reminded about the group a few minutes before the meeting is scheduled to begin. Those who are sleeping should be awakened in time to have 15 or 20 minutes to get ready.

•

Space   The space in which a group meets can affect much that occurs in the group (Churchill, 1959). Spatial considerations will influence communication patterns and leadership patterns as well as the emotional climate of the group. The worker will initially decide such matters as whether to seat people around a table or in an open circle, how far apart to place the seats, where the worker locates herself or himself, and whether to use blackboards and easels. Later, the members themselves may rearrange their space in accordance with their own preferences.

The worker needs to obtain a place where the group can meet. The worker with the adolescent sexuality group, referred to earlier, relates her experience in finding a suitable location for the group, which initially had ten members:

●

The duration of the group would be ten weeks (or ten sessions); this seemed adequate for the purpose of the group. The length of the sessions was set at one hour; this seemed adequate to insure participation by all members without interfering with other obligations the girls might have after school.

Because I realized the importance of the physical environment and its effect on group development, I attempted to find a setting that would be conducive to positive group development. My options were limited, however. I decided that my own agency (a community mental health center) would not be a good setting because of its association with mental illness. I was concerned that adolescent girls might feel uncomfortable about coming to such a setting or that the flavor of the group might change to fit the setting. I also decided that the school would not be a good environment in which to hold the group meetings, because I wanted to avoid having the girls think of me as a teacher or think of the group as school related.

I was fortunate to be able to make arrangements to hold the group in a meeting room at a branch of the public library across the street from the school. I was able to see the room prior to the first group meeting and to set it up in such a way as to maximize opportunities for interaction while still allowing for the privacy of the members. This wasn't an ideal setting, because the girls didn't usually use the library, and because it's a fairly formal institution; however, I felt it would be suitable in terms of privacy and physical proximity to the school and the girls' homes.

●

The following example illustrates the space considerations for a group of frail elderly in an inpatient rehabilitation unit of a general medical hospital.

●

All of the members may have movement impairments related to their orthopedic difficulties. The group meeting should therefore be held in an accessible place.

The effect of hearing impairments is minimized by the selection of a quiet place to meet and a seating arrangement that has all the members fairly close to each other and able to see clearly each others' lips and facial expressions. The effect of visual impairments is minimized by utilizing large-scale visual materials. The effect of memory impairments is minimized by the worker summarizing the results of previous meetings at the start of each meeting and summarizing the result of each meeting at its end.

Most of the members have low physical stamina because they are recovering from operations. The meetings should therefore be fairly short and should include some periods of passive listening. Also, the worker should be sensitive to the members' energy level and play the "Oldies But Goodies" radio station when they are tired. Since long-term memory is usually good, reminiscing is a suitable activity.

•

Planning the Program Media

Another aspect of the worker's planning, in this initial phase, is to develop a kind of map of where the group can go and how it can get there. This will involve thinking about the activities to be organized to enable the group to move through its cycle of building, sustaining, and ending. The worker's planning with regard to the convening and formation stages should include thinking of those media that will facilitate the group's getting off to a good start. People need to be helped through initial periods of uneasiness. The program media should allow space and time for them to enter the experience at their own individual pace, but also provide for their acting together so that patterns of relating to others may be established.

The following proposal for an adolescent group illustrates a worker's planning for the group's movement through the building stages.

•

The proposed group will be set in the outpatient unit of a community mental health center and will meet once a week for six months for a total of 25 sessions. Members of the group would be boys, ages 16–19, who are seen as "out of control" by their family or "in need of supervision." Youths who are severely emotionally disturbed or who have extensive records of serious criminal acts would be inappropriate for the group. Referrals would be made primarily from agencies such as juvenile probation, juvenile diversion, the department of social services, and the school.

In the convening stage, the worker would have each member introduce himself and tell the others why he is in the group. The specific rules for the group would then be explained.

The media for this stage are focused on group building—field trips, for example. One meeting would be taken up by visiting the county jail; the next meeting would have the group talk about the visit. A trip to an adolescent treatment facility would be handled in the same way. These trips and meetings would intersperse some fun activities that could be used to help the individual members understand themselves a little better by taking a look at themselves and their behaviors. In the discussions, the worker would use a reality-oriented approach.

In the formation stage, the members would be encouraged to take more responsibility for what is to go on for the duration of the life of the group. In this stage, the media used would begin to be group sustaining; for example, the worker can have members role-play with each other. The focus would begin to shift from having the members look at individual responsibility to having them look more at group responsibility. The worker would continue to use a reality-oriented approach.

●

In thinking through the dynamics of the conflict/disequilibrium stage and the maintenance stage, the worker needs to plan for the provision of an emotional, interactional field that supports the group's internal struggles and supports the members' development of cohesiveness and identification with each other. A dynamic tension needs to be maintained that is strong enough to hold the group together even while the members' behaviors push at the outer limits of the system. This dynamic tension is a "sociopetal" force, analogous to centripetal force in physics (Osmond, 1959). The sociopetal force represents the group's own "gravity," and the members' behavior that pushes at the outer limits of the system is an opposite, "sociofugal" force. Media may be selected and utilized to permit group members to move to some extreme behaviors (as during the conflict/disequilibrium stage) and to enable their return to a state of balance or integration (in the maintenance stage).

The worker with the group of adolescent males continued the proposal:

●

As the group moves into its conflict/disequilibrium stage, the group may be asking for more power and control. Even if the group is not asking for this, the worker still may begin to transfer the power and control from herself or himself to members and to the group. The worker can explain this to the group when it is happening. For example, the worker might talk with the group about the fact that she was told initially that these youth were not in control and could not take responsibility for themselves. But, the worker would go on, it seems that maybe they can be in control.

Of course, the group is not going to just take over and become a well-functioning, cohesive group solving each others' problems. The worker will still move in to help the group process when needed and move out when possible, to further the process.

Media can help sustain the group's emerging sense of responsibility for each other. For example, when member A and member B are in conflict, the worker can have A role-play that he is B and B role-play that he is A, to help the members see things through another's eyes. This should help members to get the idea that they are all in this situation together and that nothing will happen as long as they work at cross-purposes.

For the group to enter the maintenance stage, it will need to be in control and depending on each other rather than on the worker. The worker will need to become more a facilitator and less a leader. The media needed for this stage are group sustaining, with the members deciding what they will do and how things will be run. Because of the 25-session time frame, the maintenance stage may be short. It is even possible that with this time limitation, the group may not reach the maintenance stage. In either case, the worker must be prepared to shift the focus from group responsibility back to individual responsibility, to bring the group to the termination stage.

●

The following comments further illustrate the planning for the group-sustaining stages. The first is from the worker with a drop-in group of chronically mentally ill clients at a community mental health center.

●

The time was chosen for when the worker was available and when there was a weekly block of unstructured time on the drop-in center's schedule. Interesting activities needed to be planned to make this group appealing to the clients. I felt that the approaching holiday season might be a means of initially creating interest for the group. I decided to plan specific craft activities such as making center-pieces for the center's Thanksgiving dinner, having a decorating day at the center, making tree decorations, and making holiday greeting cards.

Other activities will be available for clients to choose from: leather-work kits, woodwork kits, oil or tempera painting, macramé, crocheting, candle making, making ojos ("eyes of God"), and simple bead work. I also would like to plan a client arts and crafts show in the spring. Other activities may address therapeutic goals more directly, such as having clients draw or paint emotions, activities they enjoy, things from childhood, feelings about their mental illness, or dreams for the future, and then have a group discussion about what was drawn or painted.

●

The second example is from the teenager–adult women's physical fitness/mentoring group.

•

The reward structure issue, I think, has particular significance to my group. I need to be cognizant of the reward structure of the activities and also the type of reward (such as praise, group recognition, or a new skill level) that each member responds to best. Because of the physical effort involved in this group and because physical effort has not been a natural part of their lives, immediate rewards are going to be very important in maintaining member participation.

•

The worker should also plan how much time to allot to various program activities. For a group of two hours' duration, for example, NiCarthy, Merriam, and Coffman (1984) suggest the following:

Assembling the group and completing forms	20 minutes
Introduction and formal beginning	5 minutes
Brags	10 minutes
Activity (topic, exercise)	35 minutes
Break	10 minutes
Activity	30 minutes
Ending (phone numbers, safety check)	10 minutes

In planning ahead for the final stage, the worker needs to be sure that a launching pad will be available from which the members can venture forth into their own future. A sense of closure to the group experience is necessary, even while the experience and its meaning should remain available to members as a firm grounding, a remembered safe learning place. A resolution of unfinished business also needs to be reached, so that people will be able to go and leave the experience in the past where it belongs even while the results of the experience remain.

A planning guide for workers to use in mapping program media for the stages of a group's life is provided in Table 3-3.

Various other considerations need to be taken into account in planning program media: the ages of the group members, their social and emotional characteristics, cultural and ethnic factors, and physical factors. Some guiding questions are included at the bottom of Table 3-3 to help the worker to think through what is going on with the group as well as to give attention to the individual members' needs and capacities, and to select or modify program media accordingly.

Table 3-3
Program Media Planning Guide

Stage	Dynamics	Themes	Media

Initial	Planning
	Membership selection
	Pregroup interviews
	   leading to reciprocal
	   contract
		Preparation	Interview

Convening	Approach-avoidance Milling process Sizing up Parallel play	Entry	Get-acquainted exercises

Formation	Emergence of norms
	Role differentiation
	Coalescing
	Committing to group
	Coming to terms with
	   goals
		Joining	Trust exercises,
			   cohesion exercises

Conflict/
Disequilibrium
	Struggle for ownership
	Gaining own, collective
	   power
	Dynamic tension
	Managing in conflict
	   situations
		Power and
		ownership
			Conflict resolution
			   exercises

Maintenance	Consensus-like form
	   of decision making
	Security and belonging
	Differentiated roles
	Norm conformance
	Beginning of differ-
	   entiation
		Work	Collective projects

Termination	Bringing closure to
	   experience
	Finishing unfinished
	   business
	Leaving as individuals
	Recapitulation and
	   evaluation
	Stabilizing and general-
	   izing change
	Projecting toward the
	   future
		Individuation	Ritualized endings

Guiding Questions

- How is the chosen medium congruent with the dynamics of the stage?
- What aspects of the dynamics are emphasized? How are they furthered?
- What benefits accrue to given individuals? To the group as a whole?
- What aspect of the medium may be changed to aid the benefits to individuals? to the group?

Summary

In this chapter the following profile of worker skill has emerged. An idea to offer or have a group is conceived. The worker undertakes a primary role in making the idea known and by contacting potential members and referral sources and in doing initial planning for the group. In the beginning, the worker assumes a central location in recruiting and selecting prospective members; conducting pregroup interviews and assessing the needs, desires, and capacities of prospective members; addressing the homogeneity of group membership in relation to the group purpose; assessing the necessary degree of problem commonality; and selecting those persons for membership who seem to hold the promise of being able successfully to create an entity.

In the pregroup interviews, the worker takes a central stance in clarifying the initial purpose of the group, negotiating between the potential member's individual objectives and the initial purpose of the group, in order to determine the suitability of the group for that person and of that person for the group, and representing the procedures and methods to be used in the group. From these pregroup interviews is fashioned the reciprocal contract, in which each selected member agrees with the worker that what is sought may be found in the proposed group and by the means to be employed in the group.

The worker projects an initial structure for the proposed group, making decisions about the size of the group, its time and location, and the kind of space in which it will meet. The worker also mobilizes the necessary agency resources for the group. The final task of the initial phase is to develop a general outline for the program media to be employed in the life cycle of the group.

References

Anderson, J. R. (1977). Clinical diagnosis as a factor relating to optimal group composition. Class assignment, Graduate School of Social Work, University of Denver.

Churchill, S. (1959). Pre-structuring group content. *Social Work* 4(3), 52–59.

Erikson, E. (1968). *Identity: Youth and crisis*. New York: W. W. Norton.

Estes, R. J., & Henry, S. (1976). The therapeutic contract in work with groups: A formal analysis. *Social Service Review, 50*(4), 611–622.

Garvin, C. (1969). Complementarity in role expectations in groups: The member-worker contract. In *Social Work Practice, 1969*. New York: Columbia University Press.

Hartford, M. E. (1962). The social group worker and group formation. Unpublished doctoral dissertation, University of Chicago.

Hartford, M. E. (1972). *Groups in social work*. New York: Columbia University Press.

Henry, S. (1972). *Contracted group goals and group goal achievement*. Unpublished doctoral dissertation, University of Denver.

Jennings, H. H. (1952). Leadership and sociometric choice. In L. Swanson (Ed.), *Readings in social psychology* (rev. ed.). New York: Henry Holt.

Jennings, H. H. (1953). Sociometric structure in personality and group formation. In M. Sherif (Ed.), *Group relations at the crossroads*. New York: Harper and Bros.

Maloney, S., & Mudgett, M. (1959). Group work and group casework: Are they the same? *Social Work, 4*(2), 29–36.

Moreno, J. L. (1960). Organization of the social atom. In J. L. Moreno (Ed.), *The sociometry reader*. Glencoe, IL: Free Press.

National Association of Social Workers (1979). *The Code of Ethics*. New York.

NiCarthy, G., Merriam, K., & Coffman, S. (1984). *Talking it out: A guide to groups for abused women*. Seattle: Seal Press.

Osmond, H. (1959). The relationship between architect and psychiatrist. In C. Goshen (Ed.), *Psychiatric architecture*. Washington, DC: American Psychiatric Association.

Ryland, G. (1967). *Exploring human space*. New York: Young Women's Christian Association of the U.S.A.

YWCA of Metropolitan Denver (1969). *YWCA Denver Dares*. New York: Research and Action.

CHAPTER 4

THE CONVENING STAGE

After the preliminary steps have been taken, the set of persons who will eventually become a group meets together for its first session. In this convening stage, as in all the other stages of group development, what the worker does is conditioned by four dimensions of group life: characteristics of group dynamics in this phase of the life cycle, the contract form in existence, the role and location of the worker vis-à-vis a configuration of persons convened, and the program media available to maximize group social forces.

The preformation of a group may be thought of as having a private phase and a public phase (Hartford, 1972). In the initial stage, the worker was principally concerned with the private phase of the group's life. Conceiving the idea to have a group and seeking legitimation for that idea, recruiting and selecting members, interviewing prospective members and fashioning a reciprocal contract, and planning—all of those activities are essentially private; they involve the worker with only one or two individuals from time to time, and the prospective members are not yet known to each other. In the convening stage, the group goes public. Its members meet face-to-face, and the work begins.

○

Notifying Prospective Members of Time and Place

Before the people ever meet, the worker makes certain that all prospective members have been notified of the time and place for meetings. For four reasons, this activity is a necessary one. First, the agreement to present oneself at a given time and place is one of the terms of the reciprocal contract negotiated in the pregroup interview; prospective members therefore need to know when and where the first meeting will be.

Second, time and space are two of the crucial external structural elements of group life. Prospective members will have a sense, from the outset, that this is where help will be offered and received. That sense will provide a point of orientation for the prospective members.

Third, the worker's action in notifying prospective members of the time and place of the first meeting will help establish the worker in the prospective members' minds as the central person in the group configuration (Vinter, 1967b). This is the appropriate location for the worker in the early sessions. Another benefit to be derived from this worker behavior is to reestablish and reinforce the connection made between worker and client during the pregroup interviews. When this connection is recalled to the minds of persons selected for group membership, they will know that, when they arrive for the first group session, they will encounter at least one other person whom they have met and with whom they have some initial rapport.

Fourth, in notifying persons of the time and place of the first meeting, the worker should acknowledge the approach-avoidance dilemma that may be operating (Garland, Jones, & Kolodny, 1964). Selective remembering could occur, that is, people may or may not remember that they are to participate in the group experience. The worker should make sure each person knows that she or he has been selected as a potential member of the group. Symbolically, the worker's communication says, "I know you may have some ambivalence about getting into the experience before you, but I also want you to remember that we talked and you seemed to want to try this."

From my own experience and that of many other group workers, this act of notifying people of the meeting time and place is better done by telephone, whenever possible, than by written communication. The direct, personal contact and hearing again the voice familiar from the pregroup interview will help to focus the sensibility of prospective members on what lies ahead.

A social worker in a community mental health center was recruiting members for a group, to be composed of clients who were in a drop-in center program. She used the following methods to notify clients of the place and time of the first group meeting. She posted signs around the center, announcing the focus of the group and the date and time the group would begin; she listed the group activity on the large activity-schedule board in the main area of the center; she asked the client board to include an announcement about the group in their weekly newsletter, which is sent out to all agency clients; and she verbally told clients about the group and asked that they tell other clients.

The prospective members having been notified of the meeting time and place, they assemble there and the convening stage of group development begins to unfold.

○

Group Characteristics in the Convening Stage

The convening stage of a group's life cycle is marked by the approach-avoidance dilemma and by suspended judgment, pending the decision by prospective members to commit their energies to the experience before them. People feel ambivalent, and they engage in a "milling process."

✳ Ambivalence

In the convening stage, the members move from separation toward union. There is a struggle between the desire to retain autonomy and the desire to join with others. In this first meeting—and for several of the next meetings—this struggle and ambivalence are clearly seen.

The tendency to approach the new experience is manifested in a variety of ways. People may enter the first sessions in an open way, greeting others, reaching out to include others, and asking for their own inclusion. They may exhibit a too hearty conviviality, or reveal too much about themselves in their search for affection and inclusion. The countervailing tendency is for people to manifest avoidance behavior in their first encounters with the new experience and other members. They may enter cautiously, even shyly, holding back; they may wait to be reached out to. These opposite tendencies are at work not only within the whole set of persons but within each person as well. Their behavioral manifestations may be understood as *atypical* of the behaviors that the members will eventually come to use in their interactions with each other. In most cases, they are manifested only when the person enters new situations. However, the people may not have enough self-awareness to know that their current behavior is atypical, and it may therefore be difficult for them to know how to orient themselves to the others and establish relationships. So it is a tentative interactional field at first.

It should be understood that everyone present is sizing up the situation and testing the atmosphere in her or his own way. A beginning presents the unknown, and people generally tend to face the unknown with uncertainty. Despite whatever impetus or motivation brought the prospective members to these first meetings, there may also be at work in them the awareness, at some level, that they know who they are, how they behave in certain situations, and what their coping and adaptation mechanisms are. Their life may not be perfect, but at least it is known. Ahead of each prospective member is a whole unknown world. How much will they change? Will they like the ways in which they will change? Will they have control over what the changes are? What will become of their relationships with significant others as they change and as a result of the changes? These and other unsettling questions may occupy the minds and emotions of the prospective group members, perhaps at an unconscious or preconscious level. They act these uncertainties out in myriad ways: with bravado, with reticence, with premature self-disclosure, with false conviviality, with approach, with avoidance, with ambivalence.

The prospective members will also manifest a number of group-oriented behaviors. Some of the people will be seeking, or even vying for, high-status positions within the group. They will be searching for ways to create the impression (and perhaps to assure themselves) that they possess the social, emotional, and psychological wherewithal to be a leader or a model to others. This behavior may be an expression of their own self-affirmation (or wish for affirmation) and a sign of their essential health.

All the potential members will be acting from one or a combination of three basic human needs (Schutz 1958, 1966): the need for *affection* (to express and/or receive affection from others), the need for *inclusion* (to be included by and/or to include others), and the need for *control* (to control others and/or to be controlled by others). As Schutz portrays these needs, and as Shalinsky (1969) used them in research into group composition factors, they result in ingrained patterns of relating. This framework of behavioral variables is useful for understanding what is occurring as a set of people begin to encounter each other. It is also useful for assessing the beginning dynamics of the group's social forces so that appropriate interventions can be made.

✱ Milling Process

The interactional pattern of what goes on in the early meetings resembles what Grace Coyle (1930, pp. 30–31) called a "milling process." In more than a figurative sense, people mill or circle around each other in the psychological and physical milieu of the first sessions, until they identify others who seem to be tuned to their same emotional channel and to whom they can begin to relate.

●

A social worker describes the first meeting of an adoptive parents' group at a family counseling center: the group was to begin meeting at 7 P.M. I had the hot water ready for tea, coffee, and hot chocolate and a plate of cookies out for people to help themselves. The first couple arrived between 6:50 and 6:55. They helped themselves to the refreshments when I invited them to do so, without saying anything to each other. Mrs. D mixed the instant coffee and powdered creamer in the cup for herself and her husband, poured the water, and handed him the cup. He took it without a word. He stood a bit away from the table, nervously sipping his coffee. Very shortly, the Js came in; the Ds smiled quickly at them and looked away. I introduced the two couples; the men shook hands and the women smiled. Mrs. D started toward the table as if to help the Js get their beverages and then pulled back, turning toward her husband. They didn't speak.

A silence ensued; I said that we were expecting three more couples and that when they arrived, we would move to the other section of the room for our meeting. I indicated the area where sofas and occasional tables were arranged in a conversational grouping. At that point the Ws and Ms came into the room. The conversation they apparently had been having as they walked down the hall died away.

Mrs. M recognized Mrs. D and greeted her in a warm and friendly manner. They had known each other through their church denomination's citywide women's group. The Ms and Ds introduced each other's spouses, and Mrs. M drew the Ws into the circle. The Js were hanging on the fringe until Mrs. D turned to them and, asking again for their first names, introduced them to the Ws and Ms.

The men began to shift their locations until they were standing together in an open-ended circle interfacing with the women's open-ended circle. The movement made me think of a football play pattern; the final configuration was like a figure eight. The men were considerably less talkative than the women, but I noticed that Mr. J asked Mr. W whether the Ws were adopting their first or second child. When Mr. W replied that it was their second, the other three men began asking about how these meetings go, how long they'd had the other child, how she was doing, and so on.

The women, in the meantime, were comparing notes about how long they had been waiting to adopt, what age child they wanted, the arrangements they had made for the child's room, how their families were accepting the adoption. Mrs. J, who had been very quiet, turned to Mrs. M and asked if she was the one who had been on a local television interview show last week talking about the women's environmental coalition. Mrs. M acknowledged that she was.

As people emptied their coffee cups, they moved back to the table to refill them, wives and husbands sometimes meeting there and sharing information about the people they had met. At 7:35, I moved around the circle, which was now becoming more like one large, closed circle than a figure eight, and I suggested that we move to the meeting area. As the group drifted toward the sofas, I noticed that all of the couple sets had realigned: Mrs. J, Mrs. M, and Mr. D walked together, talking; Mrs. W and Mr. M continued the conversation they'd been having on the way into the room; Mrs. D and Mr. J chatted and settled themselves next to each other on the sofa; Mr. W refilled his coffee cup and filled in the last space in the seating arrangement between Mrs. J and Mrs. D.

●

This milling process will result, eventually, in dyads and triads, alliances and subgroups, which will coalesce and form the units of intervention for the worker as the people move toward becoming a group. These early liaisons will not necessarily continue throughout the life of the group.

○

Worker Skills

The worker skills utilized in the convening stage are observation and assessment, modeling, and facilitating connection.

Observation and Assessment

Observation and assessment help the worker to become aware of people's patterns of behavior individually and collectively, to identify intervention points, and to form a base for future monitoring of progress and reformulation of goals.

In becoming aware of people's behavioral patterns, the worker will be gaining an understanding of the emotional atmosphere of this particular configuration of people. In identifying intervention points, the worker will be attending to the connections being made by the people present and helping them to determine which of these are productive and which are not. The worker will then act to support or alter those connections.

In forming a base for future monitoring of progress and reformulation of goals, the worker will develop some sense of the baseline behaviors utilized by the persons present. This information will be useful in helping members with their contract negotiation and with the monitoring function performed by the contract. It will also help the worker set her or his goals in line with the stated purpose for the group. The growth held out as a reason for joining the group depends on the members' and the worker's having an idea of where they want to go from where they are now.

The social worker describes the observations and assessments made at the first meeting of the adoptive parents' group.

●

As I watched the couples arrive, I noticed the awkward silences both within couples and among them; this was especially true with the Ds and Js.

Mr. D seemed the most reticent. I knew from my pregroup interview that he, of all the men in this group, verbalized his desire for children most; but he also seemed the one who held on most tightly to the hope that he and his wife would still be able to biologically produce children. He showed a trace of sadness and regret that they needed to go the adoption route if they were to have children at this point in their lives.

In the pregroup interview, we had explored as fully as possible whether he would be able to accept the adopted child as his own and not as a stopgap or temporary solution. I felt that the adopted child might not be fully taken into Mr. D's affection if he weren't committed to the idea. Viewing the coming adoption as temporary could lead him to view the child itself as temporary—especially if the Ds were able to produce biological children at some future point.

I made a mental note to keep track of Mr. D's questions and comments in the group, to see if he seemed to be testing out the idea of holding back forming a bond with the adopted child. Such questions as, "How long does it take until you feel this is really your own child?" or "What if you really warm up to the child but he doesn't return your feeling?" would be clues that we would need to zero in on a discussion of attachment and the various ways this occurs. It might even be advisable to have a separate session with the Ds, if these clues emerged too frequently or with too much intensity.

Mrs. D seemed much more comfortable and eager about the adoption. A quiet woman who tended to defer to her husband's needs, she must surely have a strong determination to proceed with adopting and must be able to convey her commitment to the adoption, supporting his expressed desire for children. I thought she could be a good resource for helping her husband express this desire in the group so that he could receive support from the others. Also, Mrs. D's previous acquaintance with Mrs. M would be available to foster a supportive dyad in the group.

Mrs. M is an outgoing, active, and involved person, and I mentally noted that she would be one who could be counted on to initiate discussion areas, to ask forthright questions, and probably to share information more freely than others at first.

Mr. W, the one who shared with the other men that this was the Ws' second adoption, seemed available to speak in the same forthright manner as Mrs. M. He seemed to enjoy a high status among the other men. He's a man who speaks very directly, neither minimizing nor overstating the adjustments and the pleasures of adoption. Certainly, Mr. W would be a strong resource in the group's interactions.

Mr. J approached others easily, after the initial ice was broken; I noticed that he initiated the conversation with Mr. W about first or second adoption. I thought he would be a good one, in the group, for looking after the social-emotional climate; he seems to want to hear from others and find his own comfort level with their information and let others know about that.

Mrs. J does equally well in approaching others, although she seems to take a bit longer than Mr. J; perhaps she sizes up situations differently. She was able to initiate a conversation with Mrs. W about the women's environmental coalition and share that she is an aware and action-oriented person. She may not be initially as expressive as Mrs. W, but her thoughtfulness indicates that she may be one who will help keep the group on track. Possibly, too, she may be one who can suggest alternatives about ways to conduct the group and suggest things for the couples to do while preparing for the child and once the child is in the home. Although not assertive and outspoken, Mrs. J seems one who could fulfill a leadership role in the group.

Mr. M and Mrs. W had not particularly caught my attention during the period when people were assembling. I was aware that the Ws and Ms had been conversing as they arrived, and I noticed that Mr. M and Mrs. W had talked between themselves as the group moved to the meeting area and had chosen to sit next to each other. I see that they may need to be drawn into the whole group a bit more, at a later time. For the time being, however, they seemed to have formed a supportive dyad of their own—at least, they had a comfortable conversation going.

●

Modeling

The worker models the kind of behaviors that will be needed to sustain the group's internal social-emotional system and to move the group through its external environment to reach its goal. These behaviors include helping people feel comfortable, welcome, and included, and helping them focus on what they want for themselves and for the group. When the worker models ways of meeting new people, helping people feel comfortable with each other, putting questions clearly and asking for information straightforwardly, giving answers evenly and simply, she or he is presenting a set of behavioral options to group members and expanding their possible repertoire of behaviors.

In the convening stage, the worker skill of modeling has a particular importance because of its contribution to the social and emotional tone of the group as it begins. The persons who will comprise the group observe in the worker a manner of relating to people that may not have been available to them before. This will offer a kind of stability and hope to the new participants in the group venture; stability in the sense that the worker's actions are consistent, and hope that the behaviors being modeled are ways of behaving that they themselves can learn.

A worker with a group for people learning to use interpersonal skills modeled such skills when she helped a shy member interact with her and then with another member.

●

In the pregroup interview, Addie and I had role-played her entering a new situation. She remarked, "It's easy with you here to practice with; this is safe. I wouldn't be able to start talking to people in a room full of strangers." I asked if she would be willing to give the group a try for a couple of times. I told her she might be surprised to find others in the same boat with her, and besides, I would be at the group meeting and she could talk to me or observe what I was doing as I met the people coming in. With much hesitation and reluctance, she agreed to attend the first meeting on the following Thursday.

That evening, she entered the room timidly, but on sighting me, she came over and spoke quietly. I talked to her by herself for a while and checked out how she was feeling. Although she said she was still nervous, I took her to Brad to introduce her. She followed my lead in speaking to him, waiting for me to introduce a topic to which both of them could reply. I stayed with the two of them because they were the two who had the most isolated existences. Brad is an accountant in the office of a large plant and led somewhat the same kind of noncommunicative life as Addie.

When it was time for the group session to start, I invited people to sit around the table and, although Addie stayed a bit in my shadow, as I moved toward my seat I was pleased to hear her say to Brad, "Shall we go and sit down? It's time for group to start." These had been my words, exactly. Although she was parroting me, Addie had initiated speaking to someone else.

●

Facilitating Connection

The worker's skill of facilitating connection is a way of intervening in the milling process. The worker will be assessing who is being connected with whom, both naturally and by worker intervention.

The skill of facilitating connection is vital because the existence of a group entity is the sine qua non for productive growth and change. A working group will be both means and context of help (Vinter, 1967a; Hartford, 1972). Unless people become connected and form a group, the result is likely to be no more than work with individuals in the presence of others, and the advantages of mobilizing group forces will be lost. In the convening stage, facilitating connection is one of the primary acts, as this will provide the critical mass out of which growth and change will come.

In the beginning, the worker meets with individuals who are not yet members of a group. The individuals are unconnected to each other; they each have the worker as their point of linkage to the incipient system (see Figure 4-1). In facilitating connection, the worker will intervene to produce alignments or alliances.

Figure 4-1
Individuals (I) Connected to the Worker (W)

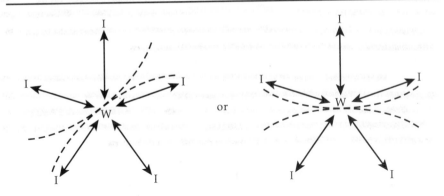

Converting the primary connections with the worker to primary connections between individuals will be a major task for the worker during the convening stage.

To summarize the characteristics of a group in its convening stage: members enter with varying degrees of approach and avoidance ambivalence, facing the unknown with uncertainty and manifesting a variety of behaviors to express their needs for affection, inclusion, and/or control. They encounter a worker who observes, assesses, and participates in their milling process as they seek compatible others to whom to relate. The worker models behaviors for them and facilitates their connections with each other. Facing directly both the tendency to approach and the tendency to avoid the experience, the worker can use what is being expressed to help the people clarify and state what it is they want from the experience and what they are willing to do to gain that.

Reciprocal Contract

The reciprocal contract exists between each individual client and the worker. It states that this group experience is the setting within which the prospective member seeks change-oriented goals that can reasonably be accomplished. The reciprocal contract form will continue for some time after the set of persons has begun to meet together, because it takes a while for the interpersonal relationships to produce a group. In the convening stage, therefore, the binding agreements will be between each client and the worker, and interactions, interventions, and communications will be structured and arranged on that basis.

At this convening stage, persons are testing the waters and determining whether to commit themselves; thus, the group forces are minimal. The situation will not remain in this state, but the prospective members need an initial opportunity to try out their relationship with the worker and to experience help offered and taken with respect to their own, independent objectives as stated in their contract with the worker. Only then can movement occur toward group formation and the mutual contract.

Nevertheless, at the first meeting the worker will engage all persons present in a discussion that establishes a group way of functioning yet allows each person's initial objectives to be addressed. The aim of that discussion will be to acknowledge collectively and individually that the persons present have something to work on, in and through the group. It will also stress that, even though what they have to work on is unique to each individual, they all have something in common.

A worker describes the reciprocal contracts of the members of a group:

●

This is a group of young adults, ages 24 to 31, who are nonassertive, who see themselves, somewhat, as the victims of others' interactions with them. They are not depressed persons in the clinical sense, but they are experiencing pain in their interpersonal relationships. The purpose of the group, at the family counseling agency, is to help people work on having, initiating, and maintaining satisfying interpersonal relationships. Reciprocal contracts had been negotiated with each person in pregroup interviews. There are three men and four women in the group. Their reciprocal contracts are as follows.

Lee (27-year-old male): I want to expand my contacts, especially with women. I have a hard time expressing my feelings and I'm a bit hesitant to come to the group, but I will agree to try it.

Laurie (28-year-old female): My biggest difficulty is initiating conversations with people; I just never know what to say. I'm very scared to join a group of strangers, since I have such trouble talking, but I'm agreeing to start the group.

Dana (24-year-old female): I want to meet people but I can't seem to make friends; people don't act like they're interested in getting to know me, so I don't spend much time where people are. I'm willing to come to the group to try out if I want to continue.

Yvonne (30-year-old female): I want to learn to make close friends, be more honest with people, and relate better with people my age. I do okay with older people; they're usually easier for me to talk to. I want to get along better with men. I guess I'm basically afraid of people; I don't trust very much and I want to learn to. I'm willing to come to three meetings of the group, and then I'd like to reasses whether I want to continue.

Dan (31-year-old male): I want to learn to express myself better interpersonally; I want feedback on how I come across in relating to people. If the opportunity comes along, I'd like to make some new relationships out of this group. I'm willing to commit myself to being part of this group.

Jennie (26-year-old female): I want to feel more comfortable talking to people; I'm most afraid talking with men. I'm basically a quiet and shy person and don't have friends to confide in. I'm willing to be in the group, but I don't want to have to start talking too much in the group.

Randy (28-year-old male): I'm under a lot of pressure as a full-time premed student with a part-time job on the side. I don't have anyone to confide in and have no place to release pressures. I feel lonely. I want to meet and get to know people and to improve my interpersonal skills.

•

When these people met for the first time, the worker reminded them of the pregroup interviews, reemphasizing that they would be asked to share what was going on with them but that they would be going at their own pace.

•

I asked them to introduce themselves, saying their name (only the first or both, depending on how they felt) and what their purpose is for being in the group. They all did that in turn; none of them spoke very long or very forcefully. They said basically what was summarized in their reciprocal contracts.

I asked if any of them had noticed what they had in common. Jennie said, "Well, it seems like we're all feeling isolated from other people and we want to get over that." I agreed with her observation and asked them if they could say what they want from the other people.

Dan repeated that he wanted feedback on how he comes across relating to people. Yvonne said she'd like to be able to talk or not talk and have that be okay. Jennie agreed with her and said that when she was feeling comfortable about talking, she'd also like to find some girlfriends and boyfriends in the group. Laurie said she'd just like to have the group wait for her when she tried to initiate something. Lee commented that he hoped they would be patient when he tried to say something about what he was feeling. Randy said he wanted to be able to let some of his pressure and tension out in the group.

The issue of confidentiality arose. Randy said he was in individual therapy and wanted to know if he could talk about the group with his therapist. I reminded the people about their agreement on confidentiality and invited them to respond to Randy.

Lee spoke up immediately and said, "I really meant it when I said I wanted things kept confidential. It's hard enough talking about my feelings with all of you; I don't want what I say to be told to anybody else." Laurie nodded vigorously. Jennie said that if she thought what she was talking about was going to be passed on, it would be harder than ever to talk. Yvonne said it was the same for her.

I turned to Randy and said, "It seems that the group is saying that we want to stick by our original agreement to keep things within the group. Can you live with that, or is it still an issue for you?" Randy asked whether that meant that he couldn't even tell his therapist that he was in the group. I said I didn't think it meant that but people were being pretty clear with him that they didn't want him talking about them, by name, or sharing their information with his therapist. He said he thought he was okay about that but would like to be able to bring it up again if it came up as an issue for him again. The others agreed, and Dana said, "Just like any of us should be able to bring stuff back here to check out."

I suggested a change of focus, from "What do you want from the others?" to "What do you think you have to give to the others?" They replied in rather specific and concrete terms.

Yvonne and Jennie felt they could give information to Dan on how he came across; Randy and Lee said they would be willing to help Laurie get in on the conversations in the group; they all agreed that they wanted to be able to be respectful of the others when they were struggling to say something or to participate. Randy asked, "But how can we do that?" I asked if any of them had any ideas about how people can learn from each other.

Jennie said she thought she had something to learn from Yvonne, who was at least able to talk to older people. Dana agreed, saying Yvonne seemed very self-assured and she would like to know how she could be that way. Lee said Dan didn't seem to have too much trouble talking with the women in the group and he'd like to know Dan's secret of success, since that was such a hard thing for him.

I said it sounded to me as if they were starting to map out the way the group would run; that maybe behind their suggestions were an outline or a format for the group sessions. Maybe they could do some role plays of situations and have someone else model for them; then they could try out doing something that seemed difficult for them, with the others giving them feedback and suggestions of ways to handle things. They seemed positive about that.

Dan asked if the group would be doing social things together like going out to plays or concerts or dinner. The rest of the people said, almost simultaneously, that they didn't want that; it wasn't what they bargained for and they weren't interested in that. I said it could be an outcome of their associating with each other, that they might find people they were interested in meeting outside the group when the group was over, but that we were all clear that socializing was not the goal of the group.

As it was nearing the time for the first meeting to be over, I returned to the matter of the reciprocal contract. I asked them if they had some ideas, now, about what the end product of their membership in the group would look like. Lee said he would be able to be more comfortable with women, would be able to talk with women, and would be able to say what he was feeling. Laurie said she would be able to start talking with people and would be able to keep a conversation going. Dana said she would be able to be comfortable talking with people her own age and would be able to trust.

Dan said he hoped to be able to make new relationships, whether in this group or not, and that he would have a better picture of how he comes across. Jennie said she'd be able to talk or not talk depending on how comfortable she felt, and not just be quiet because she was afraid of talking. Randy said he would be out from under some of his pressure and that he already felt a bit better just because he knew he'd found a place where he felt safe in talking and asking questions.

●

The discussion of means of group goal achievement should include attention to such factors as the number, frequency and duration of sessions, the times at which the session will begin and end, attendance requirements, fees (if applicable), the members' and the worker's behavioral expectations of each other, and possible program media to be utilized (Henry, 1972). Some of these contract terms may not be negotiable for one reason or another. For example, a group agreement on fees might be unnecessary.

At the first session the worker should take the lead. Reference should be made to the pregroup interview, in which the intended purpose for the group was presented and the individual objectives with respect to the projected group goal were discussed. The worker should acknowledge with everyone present that the initial agreement to join the group experience had to some extent conditioned the presence of all those attending. The reciprocal contract between each person and the worker should be referred to, in general terms.

These references set the framework within which the worker and the people present may begin to seek the common purpose for the group. The worker might start that process by saying something like this: "All of us have talked before about what this group is for and the potential benefits of the experience for each of you. You are here because what you want matches in some way what we have in mind in offering the group. Let's see now whether we can find some common way of expressing where the group is going and how we can go about reaching that point." The worker encourages the expectation that people's objectives can be realized and that their growth needs can be met through combined effort.

Finding a common expression of goals and means will be an unfolding process. The worker should make it clear that "We will start on it now but we won't finish the job now." At this stage, any conclusion will be tentative. Too early closure will result in unsatisfying—and ultimately nonproductive—behavior. The signs of premature closure are all too clear:

a compliant kind of assent is given to what appears to be a quick and easy solution. Because the assent is compliant and because the agreement is given for a quick and easy solution, it probably means that the mobilizing energy required to provide impetus to work has not been behind the agreement. In that situation, effort is expended only half-heartedly or not at all. The work devoted to achieving goals may flounder or meet outright resistance—nonwork. When that happens, the best recourse is to reexamine the decision—and perhaps the ingredients of the decision-making process—and get the agreement on target. A group will not move any faster than it is ready to move; it will move in its own direction and at its own speed.

The surest sign that the decision is off base is the failure of group members to commit time and energy to the task, as in the following example.

●

The adolescent group had moved smoothly through its first session, sharing individual members' reciprocal contracts and beginning to merge them into a statement of a common purpose for the group. At the beginning of the second meeting, I asked where their thinking had led them with respect to defining a common goal while still leaving space for their individual objectives.

Tim reacted to this question by saying, "Are we just gonna go on with more of that talkin' junk: 'Tim, what do you want?' 'John, what are your goals for being in this group?' 'Bob, what are you looking for?' Jeez, that's all we did last time. Why can't we just decide that we're gonna learn to control ourselves so we can stay outta trouble?" He glanced around at the others. "C'mon, Johnny, that's what you want, after all. Let's get it over with so we can start workin' on this group so we can get it over with. If we'd just decide on somethin', we could finish up on this jerky stuff."

John, not a very talkative boy, looked at the floor and then up at Tim and said, "Yeah, okay; I'll go along with you." Tim looked at the others, expectantly. None of them were glancing in my direction; mostly, they were staring at the floor or the wall.

"Okay," I said, "Is that what you all want? You want your goal to be to learn to control yourselves so you can stay out of trouble at school, at home, and with the police?" They shifted in their chairs, looked away from me and from each other, and a few of them mumbled agreement with the phrasing I had offered.

"Listen, you guys," Tim interjected again, "We only have to come to this jerk group ten times and here we are in the second meeting still beating around the same bush we ran around last week. Come on, get with it! Agree with the guy!" More of them spoke up in compliance with Tim's forcefulness.

"Well," I said, "if that's what you're going to go with, how do you see working on it? What do you think we should do for you to 'learn to control yourselves?' How are you going to learn that?"

Al suggested that they could each go to the school library and find a book on self-control or some other kind of discipline (weight lifting, athletics) and come back to next week's meeting and give a book report and tell the others what they got from the book. I asked if they were willing to go along with that. Unenthusiastically, they all said that sounded all right with them; they'd do it.

"Then," said Glen, "what're we gonna do with that? Take turns trying out each one of the ideas?" "Yeah, fine, that's okay," said Tim, impatiently. "At least we'd be doin' something instead of just sitting around shooting the bull about what we want to get outta this group."

Without much more discussion than that, they gave assent to the plan. As the group broke up, I reminded them of what they said they were going to do.

When the third session started, I picked up on Tim's wording of the group goal and Al and Glen's suggestions on how the media would be structured. "So," I asked, "who's going to start? What did you read that you want to tell the others about?" No one spoke. "Did anybody check out a book? Who found what?" I asked. More silence. Shifting in their chairs, they became even more uncomfortably silent and ignoring of each other and of me. "Did anybody do anything that you agreed to do last week?" I asked again. None of them had.

"Well, maybe we agreed on a goal too soon. It looks to me like everybody wasn't really committed to the way the goal was stated; maybe it sounded too 'groupy' and not enough of you in it. It makes sense to me that you wouldn't try to work on a goal you weren't committed to. Let's back up and start again where we were last week when Tim threw his idea out. What do you think?"

They visibly relaxed and picked up on a discussion of what they could say about their collective goal that left room for each of them to recognize his own objectives in it, too.

•

In the early stages of group life, the worker needs to keep a fairly close rein on the content of the discussion of where the group is going and how it is getting there. The worker should ensure that what is discussed is relevant to the goal; that members do not prematurely disclose irrelevant material; and that the initial working agreement is understood to be tentative. The worker needs to help the group agree to, and mobilize itself around, only what it can handle. Too early assent to ultimate goal statements or means of achieving goals can only lead to frustrated and frustrating behavior. The worker, using diagnostic and therapeutic skills, will help keep extravagant commitments in check.

•

With the group of retarded men and women who are candidates for community placement, we had structured a ten-week sexuality/human awareness group. In the pregroup interviews and in other group experiences with them (their cottage living groups, primarily), I had been trying to reinforce with them, "You are worthwhile and you are capable." After all, since they are candidates for community placement, it is important for them to hear that they are seen as being able and ready to live in the community rather than in the state home.

There was some initial embarrassment to handle. In the pregroup interviews, each member had said that she or he understood what the purpose of the group was and that she or he felt okay talking about sex in front of others. Nevertheless, there was some giggling and covering of faces or embarrassed stammering when we actually began to discuss their objectives in the context of a group goal.

One of the women, Lucy, who tried more than any of the others to play down her difference from persons in the community where she would soon go to live, impatiently said to the others, "All right now, you guys. Stop doing that. If you did that at the workshop, other people would think you were kids. If we are going to be on the outside with other people, we have to act like other people. I think we should see some movies and talk about our girlfriends and boyfriends, what we do with them and stuff like that."

This produced a horrified reaction in some of the others. "Oh, no! If we talk about what we do, the staff will find out and we won't be able to go live in the group home. Not me; uh-uh." Much as I tried to reassure them that talking about their sexual experiences and myths would not go outside our meeting room, they were well enough conditioned to the grapevine system of the state home not to trust that.

"Well, let's show some movies and get a doctor in here to talk about where babies come from, then," Lucy suggested. Extended silence followed. The members seemed to be recovering from the horrifying shock of Lucy's suggestion that they actually talk about what they do with their girlfriends and boyfriends.

"Look," I finally said, "It sounds to me like we need to get comfortable with just talking about girlfriends and boyfriends first. Lucy, let's hold on to your idea for a while and see how we do talking about girlfriends and boyfriends before we show movies or have a doctor come and talk to us. How do the rest of you feel about that?" Great relief showed on the faces of the other members. "Then, will you be okay if we start talking, next week, about what makes us like a boy or a girl and how we feel when they like us back?" They agreed to that proposal but checked out again that they wouldn't have to talk about "what they do."

•

With this first collective discussion of individual objectives and group goals, the worker should attempt to synthesize or summarize what has been said into a tentative new phrasing of each person's reciprocal contract. Although this contract remains an agreement between the worker and the individual, it will be influenced by the recognition that others are working on the same issues.

The worker should present this summary as something for each person to reflect upon in preparation for the next meeting. Away from the

intensity and immediacy of the exchange, they can reflect, recall, and repro-
cess what they want and what they are willing to do to get it. In this way,
people will come to their next sessions ready to take others into account
and ready to move, collectively, toward a mutual contract.

   The Goal Questionnaire shown in Figure 4-2 may be helpful for
ascertaining individual members' intentions in accepting group membership. At the conclusion of the first or second meeting of a new group, the
worker might hand each member a questionnaire form and ask each one
to think about the questions posed there and write her or his response.
The worker would then conduct a group discussion of the responses. In ·
that way, a start could be made toward the formulation of the group's mutual
contract. This process could be completed in one session, or it could constitute a homework task to be discussed at a subsequent meeting.

Figure 4-2
Goal Questionnaire

Write your answers to the questions alone, first. Then we will have a discussion to make a group statement of goals.

1. Why do you think all of you are here together?

2. What are you all going to try to accomplish together?

This is how the worker summarized the discussion in the first meeting of the young adult group working on interpersonal relationships:

•

I pointed out to them that they were already starting to define the common goal, even though they were putting it principally in their own terms right now. They were saying that they wanted to be more in command of their own ways of relating, rather than letting others define that for them; that they wanted to be able to have satisfying relationships with other people; and that they were beginning to have the idea that this was in their control.

I pointed out that some of their suggestions about the kind of support they felt they could give to the others outlined some of the ways the group would operate. I said we would be picking up on those suggestions right away. I reiterated that they had recommitted themselves to an agreement on confidentiality and that it sounded like they were willing to trust each other, although with some reservations until they knew each other better. They agreed with that summary.

I said that we were out of time, but that for next week's meeting, I wanted to ask each of them to think of ways of getting what they needed from the others. I said we would talk this over again, and next week we could start on some of the ideas they had suggested tonight. With that restatement of the common purpose each held for herself or himself in the group, the summary of their ideas for group media, and the reiteration of the confidentiality agreement, I had led into their "homework" assignment for the next meeting. The meeting then ended.

•

In stating who the parties to the contract are, it would be premature to refer to the group as a whole. The collection of individuals is not yet a group, and persons are still tentative with respect to their individual levels of commitment to the experience. References to the group as a whole will best be held in abeyance until people's behavior demonstrates that they are taking others into account and that they recognize that their individual purposes can be well served by joining and claiming a common purpose. Until cohesion is manifested in member behavior, until norms are operative, and until roles of leadership and followership have been differentiated, the group has not formed and a mutual or interdependent contract cannot be in effect.

Within the parameters of the reciprocal contract as discussed above, the set of people has a beginning point, "an initial working agreement," as Schwartz characterized the contract, from which to proceed.

Contract Review and Renegotiation

The reciprocal contract should include a reference to future times for reviewing and possibly renegotiating the contract. As the group changes, what the people agree to do will change, too. The worker should therefore help the people keep an open and flexible stance with respect to where they are going and what will occur on the way; one way to do this is to provide the structure for reviewing, reexamining, and, if necessary, renegotiating their agreement. Periodic rest stops in the life of the group will provide that structural opportunity.

No hard-and-fast rules exist to indicate when these periodic "check points" should occur. In some cases they might be at the point that the group moves into its next stage of development, particuarly the formation stage and the maintenance stage. In other cases, an existing contract supports and stabilizes the group system during a particular stage of group development, notably during the conflict/disequilibrium stage (discussed in detail in Chapter 6). The contract might also be reviewed and renegotiated at least once while the group is solidly functioning within each phase of its life cycle.

The young adult group initially agreed on four specific check points:

•

The group's reciprocal contract was for them to meet for 15 weeks to work on their issues of becoming more assertive and less victimlike in their dealings with other people, at home, at work, and with clerks in stores and offices. They would work on this by using role plays, simulations, and homework exercises.

They agreed, at the end of the second meeting, that we would start following the media structure we had developed together and that we would stop at the end of the 4th, 7th, 10th, and 12th meetings to check out with ourselves how we were doing and where we were going. We could stop at other points, depending on the members' needs and interests, but for sure we would stop to monitor at the end of those meetings.

•

The characteristics of a group in its convening stage and the contract issues at this stage having been presented, the two dimensions that remain to be discussed are the role and location of the worker and the program media utilized.

Role and Location of the Worker

In the convening stage, the worker occupies a central location and takes a primary role vis-à-vis the group system just as she or he did in the initial stages. Now, however, the worker is actually meeting face-to-face with the whole set of people assembled at once; the worker's orientation is now one-to-many rather than one-to-one. Nevertheless, this set of people is not yet a group; in front of the worker, in these first sessions, is a *collection of individuals*. The worker has established some initial connections through the pregroup interviews. She or he is, at this point, the central, special figure for each individual.

The worker may find that a person who had been talkative during the pregroup interview has gone suddenly silent; or an individual who was reticent in the pregroup interview may become voluble when confronted with all the other new persons. The behaviors manifested by prospective members during these first sessions is less important in determining what the worker does than is the necessity for the worker to pick up the tenuous strands of interpersonal ties that began to emerge during the pregroup interviews. As it is separate individuals who come to the first sessions, as the worker has made some earlier connection with each of them, and as the individuals are enacting their own best fashion of entering a new and unknown situation, the worker's attention will be most productively given to relating to each person as a separate individual.

Figure 4-3
Location of the Worker (W) vis-à-vis Individuals (I)
at the Convening Stage

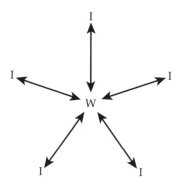

Figure 4-3 portrays the location of a worker vis-à-vis the individuals in the convening stage. It is not suggested that the worker literally put herself or himself in the middle of a circle. The diagram is figurative only; it is intended to reflect the worker's central, active, and directing relationship to the prospective group members.

The worker's central location serves several purposes. First, it gives each individual a channel of relationship with the worker. It reassures the individual that the worker is there for her or him. It is partly to symbolize the importance of each person that the worker will direct communication in the wheel fashion depicted in Figure 4-3 (Bavelas, 1960). Second, this location makes the worker the "central person" (Vinter, 1967b, pp. 20–23), common to all and at the same time unique to each. This location allows the worker to maintain and direct the communication process between the individuals.

Third, the central location allows the worker to observe and assess interpersonal patterns and capacities of the persons present and to intervene to support, facilitate, or modify them.

The responsibility to facilitate communication, to get people talking, and to have people begin to know each other is clearly the worker's. The worker's role at this stage is to help people connect with each other, to represent the communication channels between persons, and to help people feel at ease with each other.

Different positions may be taken with respect to the worker's role in these early stages, advocating that the worker let the group process take care of itself. However, the worker holds the information necessary to insure the success of the experience. The worker has interviewed and selected each person in the group. No other person in the group has met everyone else, has so much information about all the other people, or has formed an assessment of the other people's needs and capacities. In fact, no other person in the group has the responsibility to form such judgments.

Moreover, the worker has made a plan for a purpose-directed group experience. The worker's plan is never cast in concrete, but it does provide the road map for where the group will go and what route it will follow.

The worker possesses considerable power by virtue of the information she or he has. However much the worker may try to present herself or himself in an egalitarian posture, the members of the group are aware of what the worker knows about them, about other members, and about what the group is to do. No matter how much a worker may try to lower her or his profile and be just one of the group, the members will be conscious of this power differential and will expect a different role performance. Because of the power inherent in the worker role, it is the worker's responsiblity to be "communication central" and to facilitate the connections between people in the first meeting.

The worker should arrange the room spatially in accordance with what she or he knows about the people who will come and in accordance with what the worker has decided to do to get the group off to a good start. Chairs, tables, and other equipment will be in place; the worker will—if at all possible—make the room temperature and lighting levels comfortable; and the worker will be ready to greet people by name as they come into the room.

The first meeting—and subsequent meetings as well—may be conducted in a three-step sequence. First, the worker states the general plan or recapitulates what has occurred in the life of the group up to this point. Second, the worker draws attention to this session's business at hand. For the first meeting this will involve each person presenting herself or himself to the others and sharing initial goals for herself or himself and for the group as a whole. In subsequent meetings, this second phase will involve direct work on the matters for which the group exists. Third, the worker focuses on what will happen next for the group and for each individual. Regular use of this sequence gives continuity from one session to the next, and it gives each session a jumping-off point.

In the practice approach described in this book, the worker takes the initiative to set the tone for the meeting. She or he states the purpose of the group, describes how the sequence will go, and recapitulates the main items touched on in the pregroup interviews. This step is important in that it makes public and makes common property the conversation each person present has had with the worker in the pregroup interview. Symbolically, it also makes the worker the common property of all persons present. Whatever fantasies or expectations each person has had about the worker's being there for her or him alone are challenged by this act of the worker revealing that all have had prior communication with the worker.

This is how the worker opened the first session with the young adult group:

•

When they had all arrived and were seated around in a circle, I began by saying I was glad to see that they had all made it to the meeting. I started the session by stating what they each individually knew but which I wanted now to state for them all, together.

"Each one of you has had a session with me by yourselves where we talked about who the other people attending the group would be and what each one of you wanted out of being in the group. I talked to others who are not here tonight, too, but I decided that what each of you was looking for lined up to make a kind of common starting place. You are all near the same age and have similar issues, so it seemed like you would be the ones, of all those I interviewed, who would work best together. When we talked, I stressed that I would be giving attention to each of you and also to others. I know what each of you said to me in our interview, but it doesn't seem that I should say it for you here."

I said that I wanted to make clear what my task was, as I saw it. I repeated that I would be present at each meeting, and that I would help keep the discussions and their work on course. I would be listening to them separately and collectively, to help them keep moving in the direction they were saying they wanted to go. Sometimes I would make direct suggestions and sometimes I would raise questions for them to work through.

I reminded them that I would insure that they were not destructive to themselves, to others, or to the property of the center. I would also give them some cues for relating to people, if the way I went about that was useful to them. I asked whether that was clear and made sense.

I reiterated that I'd wanted to say these things with all of them present so they knew we were all starting from the same place and the same information. No other questions were raised, and I proceeded on the assumption that they were clear—for the time being, anyway.

•

At each step in the sequence of the first meeting, the worker should stop to ask for questions, to ask whether what has just transpired is clear, and to ask what people have understood of what has just occurred.

The worker then invites those present to make themselves known to each other (that phase of the session was described earlier in this chapter). Various means may be used for this; the important point is to be sure that each person has the chance to say her or his name and to say something about herself or himself. For some people this may be difficult; in those cases, the worker may decide the person's just saying her or his name is enough. Pressure to reveal more than the person is ready to say should be off at this point, just as the inclination of some to reveal everything should be guarded against. On the other hand, people should be there with some expectation (however minimal) to say something. It is important for people to understand, by direct encouragement and by example from the worker and the others present, that verbal participation is necessary and valued.

What happens in these early sessions will lay down a pattern for succeeding sessions, and the worker should make sure there is some verbal participation by everyone. This is one of the group norms that should be established from the beginning. The worker should state it as a ground rule of the group, to be reinforced both by the worker and by the others present.

The worker asked the members of the young adult group to introduce themselves, asked them what they wanted to say to Randy about confidentiality, asked them to talk about what they thought they had to give to the others, solicited ideas about how they thought people could learn from each other, and asked them to give their idea of the end product of their membership in the group.

•

In each case, I was either going for a specific reply from everyone or asking for those who felt most comfortable to say something. In that fashion, I was trying to insure that they all said at least three things and had the opportunity to say something a couple of other times.

In summarizing what they had said after each discussion point, I was trying to encourage their verbalization. I wanted to give the quieter ones space to talk, even if only a little, to give the more talkative ones space to contribute more. I believed that if the quiet ones heard others talking and knew that talking was difficult for some of them, they might take a chance and risk speaking, too.

•

Some workers encourage verbal participation by the use of check-ins at the outset of each meeting. A worker with a group of women in life transitions proposed metaphorical weather reports. The members were asked to give a summary of the preceding week in the form of a weather report and then to elaborate with specific details. For example: "The week was mostly sunny with a few periods of cloudiness," referring to periodic moments of doubt or uncertainty; or "I had mainly periods of turbulence and rapidly changing conditions," referring to a time of conflict or tensions.

Various metaphors might be used: summarizing one's week in song titles, describing one's mood in terms of colors, giving the preceding week a grade, or writing a letter of reference for the week. Some form of craft medium, such as a collage or a free-form color design, facilitate deeper expression of the members' assessments of their days since the last meeting.

A group of women at the outreach center of a safe house for battered women employed an oral report of the week, reporting highs and lows and their own sense of triumph of setbacks. Weight Watcher group leaders often structure these check-ins according to "celebrations" and "challenges." Whatever the device, the purpose is to elicit topics that may serve as a common theme for the work of the session.

In summary, in the early sessions the worker occupies a central location within the group system and, from that vantage point, takes a primary role in negotiating the group contract and in setting the tone and modeling appropriate behaviors.

The final dimension to be discussed is the program media utilized to maximize the group social forces in the convening stage.

◯

Program Media Analysis

A great wealth of information exists to aid a worker in selecting the media to begin a group (see, e.g., Cassano, 1989; Davis, 1984; Kolodny & Garland, 1984; Lee, 1988; Lum, 1986; Middleman, 1968; Morris, 1984; Reed & Garvin, 1983; Saul, 1982; Shulman, 1971; Vinter, 1967c; Wilson & Ryland, 1949). In this stage of planning, the worker will need to analyze the clients' capacities and characteristics and to analyze what program media will contribute to the desired behavioral outcomes.

Clients' Capacities and Characteristics

In deciding what the people will do when they are together, the worker needs to be aware of the persons' physical capacity to speak and to move, their emotional or psychological capacity to interact and to communicate, and their intellectual capacity to reason, to think abstractly, and to generalize from experience. In the following example, the program was modified to accommodate the members' capacities.

●

This group consisted of four women who were residents of a transitional living group located on the campus of the state training school for the retarded. This was the first such home for women. All four women had behavioral difficulties that limited their ability to cope with community living. These problems arose from a lack of interpersonal relationship skills. All had extremely poor self-concept. These difficulties usually presented themselves in acting-out episodes of verbal or physical abuse. The key in planning programming with this group has to do with the developmental capabilities of the members; however, this does not mean that the group is unwilling or unable to handle some material beyond their experience. It may be that experimentation will redefine some activities previously conceived as beyond the capabilities of the clients.

As a means of boosting self-esteem, the members were to record daily, with the help of staff, one thing that made them feel good about themselves. This activity did not work, because the staff were not committed to helping the clients think it through or to record. We adjusted the activity to a weekly procedure to be reported at the conclusion of the meeting. We recorded each item on a chart for everyone to see. This procedure worked beautifully and had meaning for the members—they never let the procedure be overlooked.

In utilizing specific media to enhance the purposes of the group, activity-oriented exercises were most helpful. Due to the conceptual limitations of the members, specific activities were designed to lead into discussions. Materials were used according to the members' functioning level. Magazine pictures were used for identifying feelings, for identifying likenesses and differences, and for making self-collages. Resources from elementary education material in the area of human awareness and development were found to be the most adaptable.

●

The worker also needs to be aware of the cultural background and experience of prospective members. This will affect how they feel about the mixing of the sexes or about sharing personal information with persons outside the family or culture. It will affect their perception of the amount of personal or social distance allowed between people, the appropriate way to speak (e.g., tersely or verbosely), the proper treatment of persons in authority or persons in various age groups, and the correct forms of address to persons of other cultural or age groups.

These considerations, along with the objectives of each person in joining the group, will be important determinants of the kinds of program media selected, as in the following example.

●

An International Wives' Club was established by a social worker from Hong Kong who was in the United States as a participant in the local affiliate of the Council of International Programs for Youth Leaders and Social Workers. The club was open to wives from abroad, with or without children. There were altogether fifteen members between the ages of 21 and 42 years. They came from a wide range of backgrounds and countries: Saudi Arabia, Nepal, Japan, Colombia, Chile, Brazil, Korea, and Indonesia. Most of them came to the United States as immigrants; some came with their husbands, who were students at universities in the area.

The worker organized the effort and recruited members. She also recruited volunteers, some from other countries—Turkey, Brazil, Japan, and England—who helped with transportation, crafts, recruitment of members, and the like. They, too, had valuable experiences and suggestions to contribute and share with the members of the club. Program for every meeting was planned with the volunteers and the members, to insure that they would meet the variety of needs of the members. Program content ranged from indoor to outdoor and active to sedentary activities.

The purpose of the group evolved, through the planning process, as being to help women from other countries, who were kept at home because of small children to make friends and have an opportunity to enjoy life more in this community; to help the women solve their language and cultural problems and adjust better; to provide them with some basic coping and survival skills; to organize a limited number of classes or activities that might meet their interests; and to provide child-care services and make the nursery a real school experience for children who were toddler age and up.

For most of the time, the members were engaged in craft making, sharing their different ways of life, learning simple expressions of one another's language, and practicing English. Field trips to areas of interest were also organized, to encourage the members to take their own families out on the weekends.

•

Behavioral Outcomes

Media are amenable to analysis on the basis of behavioral outcomes (Vinter, 1967c). It is possible to determine whether the behaviors utilized in any given activity will establish a pattern or result in an outcome that is productive for the group and for the individuals who comprise it. In planning for the early sessions of a group's existence, the worker should put together what she or he knows about the persons with what she or he knows about a contemplated activity to see if it will be appropriate. This is illustrated in the following example.

•

The school Parent Advisory Council for Title I (ESEA) schools was convening its first meeting of the school year. The officers had been elected in the Spring, and all eligible members had been contacted by telephone to inform them of this first meeting.

In planning for the first meeting, the officers decided that the most important thing was to create a positive and accepting climate, so that the people who hadn't attended a council meeting before would feel a beginning relatedness to each other and would feel comfortable. Because the council would be mainly concerned with decision making, the officers felt that it was important for people to feel at ease and able to talk. In order to do that, they would have to reduce the stranger feeling as soon as possible. So they decided to begin the meeting by using a get-acquainted game that would get people talking to each other.

The activity they selected used sheets of paper with six statements on them. Each person was asked to find, for each question, at least two other people at the meeting whose answers were the same as her or his own answer. When they found someone with the same answer, that person was to write her or his name on the blank following the question (see Figure 4-4).

Figure 4-4
Get-acquainted Questionnaire

Find two people who have these things in common with you. Ask them to write their names in the spaces provided.

Participate in exercise as much as you do

1. _____

2. _____

Feel as you do about the local professional football team

1. _____

2. _____

Have the same number of children as you

1. _____

2. _____

Had the same breakfast as you

1. _____

2. _____

Have the same favorite television show as you

1. _____

2. _____

Grew up in the same state as you

1. _____

2. _____

At first, people remained seated and talked only to the people on either side; then they began to talk across others; finally, they began to get up and move around. In the beginning, they were talking only to one person at a time, but soon small clusters gathered, and they began to visit with each other about other things than just the items that were on the paper. Dora and Annie, for example, discovered that they were from the same small town in South Dakota. By the time the chairperson called the activity to a halt and asked for the meeting to start, everyone was talking, seating patterns had changed, and the ice had been broken.

●

The analysis of behavioral outcomes must be related to the stage of group development. In the convening stage, the worker should be looking for media that will facilitate connection between people and provide space for persons to risk and share to the limits of their ability at this time. The media should help people become acquainted with each other and should help them focus on a desired end state for themselves and for the group collectively. The program media used at this stage need to take into account people's ways of entering new situations and their needs for affection, inclusion, or control.

The following record illustrates worker skill in this area.

●

At the first meeting of the adolescent sexuality group, only five of the ten girls who had agreed to take part in the group were present. Initially, there appeared to be a polite acceptance of the worker. The members participated enthusiastically in a group-building exercise in which they were asked to share information about themselves in a fairly nonthreatening way. Very personal information about some of the members' sexual activities was revealed during this time, in an apparent attempt to test the worker.

The issue of confidentiality was introduced by one of the members saying, "I'm not going to want to talk if I think you're going to spread it around the school." This was supported by other members. Tina and Irina wondered if this group was going to be boring. When the purpose and goals of the group were restated, the girls responded positively and offered suggestions of topics they would like to discuss in the group. The suggestion was made that members be allowed to bring food to the group. Another suggestion involved starting the group earlier and ending it later. Before the meeting was over, Tina began wondering when the time would be up so they could leave.

The members were not ready at this point to initiate activity or to operate on a personal level (aside from the sharing of very personal information, which seemed to be aimed at testing the worker). I therefore did much planning of activities and topics of discussion that would enable the members to become involved at a safe and comfortable pace and would not require a great amount of investment.

One of the activities I planned was the use of self-portraits at the beginning and again at the end of the ten weeks; at the beginning, they would be part of a self-awareness exercise and at the end, an evaluation procedure. I realize that the use of self-portraits is not a totally accurate method to determine the changes that took place during the group experience; however, I felt it would provide an interesting perspective. In the first meeting, the drawing afforded an opportunity for the girls to look up and talk to each other and to look down and pay attention to their drawing. This created a safety zone around themselves. They could stay within themselves, if they wanted; or they could reach out and talk and interact with the others if they wished. Drawing self-portraits seemed to offer exactly the island of safety they needed.

•

Summary

In the convening stage, groups are characterized by an approach-avoidance dilemma and by a milling process out of which interpersonal alliances emerge. A worker responds to these phenomena by using the skills of observing and assessing, modeling, and facilitating connection. The contract is of the reciprocal type, in which the agreement is between each individual and the worker. It states what is potentially available in the group experience and what the person is initially willing to do to achieve what she or he says is desired. The worker initiates a discussion about the reciprocal contract and makes a beginning reference to the contract forms that will come into being later on. The worker also mentions the future periodic points of contract review and renegotiation. The stage is set for adoption of the next form of contract, the mutual one.

Throughout, the worker occupies a central location vis-à-vis the system of people and takes a primary role in the interactions and social forces. The worker channels communication, observes and assesses individual and collective behavior, and generally acts as a surrogate.

The worker analyzes the characteristics and capacities of the persons present and the behavioral outcomes associated with specific activity media. The worker then selects the most appropriate program for the set of persons at the convening stage, to maximize the social forces that will facilitate the building of a group entity.

These worker actions and the interactions of the persons convened in the early sessions prepare the way for the formation of the set of persons into a group.

References

Bavelas, A. (1960). Communication patterns in task oriented groups. In D. Cartwright & A. Zander (Eds.), *Group dynamics research and theory* (2nd ed.). Evanston, IL: Row, Peterson.

Cassano, D. R. (Ed.). (1989). Social work with multi-family groups [Special issue]. *Social Work with Groups, 12*(1).

Coyle, G. L. (1930). *Social process in organized groups.* New York: Richard R. Smith.

Davis, L. (Ed.). (1984). Ethnicity in social group work practice [Special issue]. *Social Work with Groups, 7*(3).

Garland, J., Jones, H., & Kolodny, R. (1965). A model for stages of development in social work groups. In S. Bernstein (Ed.), *Explorations in group work.* Boston: Boston University School of Social Work.

Hartford, M. E. (1972). *Groups in social work.* New York: Columbia University Press.

Henry, S. (1972). *Contracted group goals and group goal achievement.* Unpublished doctoral dissertation, University of Denver.

Kolodny, R., & Garland, J. (Eds.). (1984). Groupwork with children and adolescents [Special issue]. *Social Work with Groups, 7*(4).

Lee, J. A. G. (Ed.). (1988). Group work with the poor and oppressed [Special issue]. *Social Work with Groups, 11*(4).

Lum, D. (1986). *Social work practice and people of color.* Pacific Grove, CA: Brooks/Cole.

Middleman, R. (1968). *The non-verbal method in working with groups.* New York: Association Press.

Morris, S. (Ed.). (1984). Use of group services in permanency planning for children [Special issue]. *Social Work with Groups, 5*(4).

Reed, B. G., & Garvin, C. (Eds.). (1983). Groupwork with women/groupwork with men: An overview of gender issues in social groupwork practice [Special issue]. *Social Work with Groups, 6*(3/4).

Saul, S. (Ed.). (1982). Groupwork and the frail elderly [Special issue]. *Social Work with Groups, 5*(2).

Schutz, W. (1958). FIRO: A three-dimensional theory of interpersonal orientation. New York: Holt, Rinehart & Winston.

Schutz, W. (1966). Interpersonal underworld. Palo Alto, CA: Science and Behavior Books.

Shalinsky, W. (1969). Group composition as an element of social group work practice. Social Service Review, 43(1), 42–49.

Shulman, L. (1971). 'Program' in group work: Another look. In W. Schwartz & S. R. Zalba (Eds.), *The practice of group work.* New York: Columbia University Press.

Vinter, R. (1967a). An approach to group work practice. In R. Vinter (Ed.), *Readings in group work practice.* Ann Arbor, MI: Campus Publishers.

Vinter, R. (1967b). The essential components of social group work practice. In R. Vinter (Ed.), *Readings in group work practice.* Ann Arbor, MI: Campus Publishers.

Vinter, R. (1967c). Program activities: An analysis of their effects on participant behavior. In R. Vinter (Ed.), *Readings in group work practice.* Ann Arbor, MI: Campus Publishers.

Wilson, G., & Ryland, G. (1949). *Social group work practice.* Boston: Houghton Mifflin.

CHAPTER 5

THE FORMATION STAGE

The formation of a group occurs throughout the interaction of the persons who comprise it. A worker composes a group by selecting the persons who will belong, and the worker convenes the group in its first meeting; but only the persons themselves can form a group (Hartford, 1972). However, the formation of a group will be affected by what the worker does with respect to each of the four dimensions; that is the subject of this chapter.

○

Characteristics of Groups in the Formation Stage

A group in its formation stage is characterized by the emergence of group norms, by the differentiation of member behaviors into roles that help hold the group together and move it toward its goals, and by the emergence of decision-making processes. Group norms are those verbal or nonverbal communications by which the group influences the behavior of its members. Norms control the group's way of doing things. They arise from what the members need in order to maintain themselves in some state of dynamically balanced, creative tension. Someone might say, "I always make better progress when I get positive strokes than when I get putdowns" (expressing a need for affection). Someone else might rearrange the seats or adjust the light or temperature level in the room without consulting the other people or the worker (expressing a need to control). In such verbal and nonverbal ways, people will try to affect the behavior of others. Each member attempts to fashion the group toward what she or he wants the group to be. However, a want from one member does not get the group anywhere unless it is also wanted by the other members.

Emergence of Norms

An example will illustrate this phenomenon. Johnson and Johnson (1975) designed an exercise to aid persons' understanding of joint effort in a group. The people stand in a circle in the center of a room with hands up and fingertips touching the fingertips of two other people. Wordlessly, using only pressure applied to the fingertips of the other people, each person must try to maneuver the group toward an area in the room where she or he wants to go. Of course, each one will have a different destination in mind, and each will resist the others' efforts. The group does not move.

Then the group is instructed to agree on a specific direction in which to move. Off they go! Some members apply pressure; other members yield to the pressure. Dramatically and kinesthetically, through this exercise, the group experiences that no one person is able to take the group where it collectively has not chosen to go. Only cooperation can move the group in a particular direction but cooperative resistance can prove a powerful obstacle, and moving a group off dead center will require accommodation to the wants of all members.

Norms give people cues to ways of behaving, a pattern for the way a session will proceed, and determine the way the whole group experience will go. A norm may be, for example, that one specific person is always the one who responds to the worker's question first, or it may be a fixed seating pattern or that lateness of no more than ten minutes is allowed. These are fairly superficial norms that pattern the time and space and interactions of the group. On a deeper level, a group may develop the norm that when a person has shared deeply emotional material the rest of the group will give positive verbal strokes, or will stay silent for a time, or will embrace the speaker. The norm may emerge that one particular member is always asked by the others what she or he is thinking or feeling on every subject.

Worker Behavior in Relation to Norms   The worker monitors and evaluates norms. If a norm tends to establish a pattern for the group's life that, in the best judgment of the worker, is productive for the individual affected and for the group as a whole, the norm should be encouraged.

A norm may, however, be counterproductive. For example, members may begin to sanction disruptive behaviors on the part of some other members. This disruption may be in the form of members getting up and walking around the room to get coffee while a low-status member is speaking or falling asleep or carrying on side conversations among themselves.

Members might be sarcastic or put down other members, threaten to leave the group or to put another member out of the group, respond by pointed silence when someone shares something important to them, or even threaten physical harm to another member. If any of these behaviors become the norm, one or more members may be left outside the interactional system.

The worker should discourage or modify such negative behaviors before they become ingrained. This is done by the worker intervening to call attention to the behavior.

The worker might directly confront a member's behavior, in this way: "Ray, we need to have just one conversation going on here. Would you and Jean please get in on the one that's going on here with the rest of us?" or, "Paul, your threat to have Carl put out of the group is something that isn't going to be carried out. Maybe you need to take a look at what it is about him that sets something off in you."

Alternatively, the worker might direct the group's attention to the dysfunctional behavior and ask the group to handle the issue. (Shulman, 1967). The worker might say something like, "It seems to me that there's an awful lot of traffic in the direction of the coffee pot whenever Peter starts to talk. Why don't we take a look at what's going on? Frank, what's your thought about that?" or, "You're indicating to me that Louise is talking too long. Shall we see what you all want to do about each other having time and space in meetings? Louise, would you be willing to let us know how you feel about the others' reaction to you?"

Direct threats of physical harm can be handled by referring to the contract terms agreed to during the pregroup interviews. At that time, the worker would have said, "I won't let you hurt yourself, another person, or any of the property in the room." As much as possible, situations should be handled within the group itself; however, there may be times when the worker needs to meet with a member individually to discuss that member's behavior in the group.

The norms that operate in a group are the patterns of influence that emerge from the accommodation of the members to each other. The group will accept a certain range of behaviors; any behaviors that fall outside that range may diminish the capacity of the group to stay together. When behaviors deviate from the group's normative range, the worker should assess the potential effect of this deviance on the future functioning of the group and should address, or engage the group in addressing, the deviation.

The worker may reinforce desirable norms by calling attention to their operation when they have become established. The worker may help enforce such norms by calling attention to members' actions that depart from the patterns of behaviors accepted by the group. This act on the part of the worker should not be arbitrary or unilateral but should align with what the group has laid down as its scope of tolerance (which will vary from group to group). Rarely do norms operate effectively by the worker's announcing, "These will be our norms."

In encouraging a behavior pattern, the worker may say something like: "We seem to be following a pattern in which Rita usually speaks immediately after I've said something to the whole group. You seem to be comfortable with this; you seem to trust Rita's understanding of what's going on. I'm okay with that if all of you are." This intervention makes public the observed behavior and then validates it, giving expression to what the others may have noticed and been comfortable with but been hesitant to confirm openly. The worker's observation that all others are comfortable is deduced from their tacit cooperation with the pattern. If this observation is not consensually validated when the issue is surfaced, then a rearrangement of the pattern will probably ensue. If the worker has accurately observed and commented in a way that encourages the behavior, the pattern will stand.

Sometimes a norm will emerge from a member's statement about what she or he would like to have happen. For example, after a few sessions, someone might say, "I don't know about anyone else, but I would feel that we are more open with each other if we turned and looked at someone when we have something to say about them." The worker might reply: "Anna is proposing a way for us to talk to each other in a more open way. How does that sound to all of you? Are you feeling that you want to do that?" The worker's intervention would be directed toward gaining the assent of the other members and then encouraging the suggested procedure by commenting on the consensus.

If Anna has high status—that is, if she is one to whom others look for ideas and ways of behaving—what she proposes is likely to be followed. If her status is low—that is, if others treat her as being marginal to the system and "not as good as the rest of us"—then her ideas, whatever their merit, are not likely to be regarded. In that case, the worker may choose to sponsor the meritorious proposal. The worker might say, "Anna has suggested something that sounds like a good idea. What do you think of improving the openness of our way of talking to each other by looking directly at the person you're speaking to? Do you feel you want to do that?" This intervention still puts the question to the group, but loads it with the worker's approval because the worker has assessed it as "good" for the group. (The acceptance of Anna's suggestion will also be good for Anna's integration into the group system.)

However, the group may not assent. In that case, the worker needs to be ready to support Anna even while communicating the rejection of her proposal.

A worker's recording of practice with a group of adult women with chronic mental illness, participants in a mental health center's partial care program, illustrates worker skill in helping the group to establish norms.

●

During today's check-in, the theme that emerges is a need for involvement in the larger community rather than isolating from it. I am somewhat surprised by this theme because of the isolating I note even among the members of the group when they are in the Chipeta House setting. Before the meeting begins, I have observed that the individuals singly and silently make their way downstairs to the music room. No discussion or interaction accompanies the members as they make their way to their respective seats.

As usual, Marla takes the seat "supported" by the wall behind her and the bookcase to her left. Once I take my seat, she will be to my right. Leann sits to Marla's right in a sinky chair which seems to swallow her frail, pale frame. Vicki— whose on-going self-conversations seem to place her on the edges of the group—sits alone on a long couch opposite me. She sits to Leann's immediate right, scrunched tightly against the arm of the couch nearest Leann. They share an end table which rests between them. Talkative Maria takes her seat to the right of the couch. Her chair touches no walls and she rests her feet on the coffee table in the center of the group's circle. Ginny sits to Maria's right and to my left, with her eyes downcast and hands stuck firmly in her jacket pockets. I pull my chair back slightly to include Ginny in the circle.

As we begin the check-in, I note that Vicki writes busily on a yellow pad. Later, as Maria begins to share her recent experience of shopping with a friend, Vicki interrupts with interview-style questions, while continuing to write on the pad. Marla responds tersely to the questions and attempts to continue her story. As I look around the circle, I note that only Maria and Marla seem aware of Vicki's note taking, and both women watch her closely as Marla speaks. When Marla finishes speaking, I take the opportunity to address Vicki's busyness today and request that she tell the group what she is writing. She explains that she's "taking notes," and I observe that each of the other members registers a look of surprise. As I ask her to explain more about why she is taking notes, Maria interjects, "Yeah, 'cause I don't like that." Vicki responds by explaining that her therapist has requested that she keep a journal.

After a pause, I ask Maria to say more about why she doesn't approve of the note taking. "Well, I don't like for someone to be writing down what I say . . ." (I note that Leann and Marla nod their heads in agreement, while Ginny again settles back into her former position with head down and eyes downcast.) ". . . I mean, this is supposed to be confidential," Maria says. I acknowledge her response with a nodded affirmation, then ask how others feel about what Maria has said.

Marla speaks up next. She agrees with Maria and specifically wonders whether Vicki is using names in her notes. Vicki says, "Yeah," and Marla requests that she erase the names. Marla also expresses concern that perhaps Vicki has misunderstood the concept of journaling. Leann—who sits on the edge of her seat now, looking straight ahead—interrupts Marla to interject, "Yeah, and you're not supposed to be writing while we're talking." She states that what others are saying is important. I reflect what I think I hear her saying, and as she turns to look at me, Leann affirms that I have heard her correctly. She continues, "Yeah; I mean, how else are we going to help each other?"

After a brief pause, I inquire of Ginny regarding her feelings about what we have been discussing. At first she says nothing, but after I reflect her earlier response—the look of surprise at discovering Vicki's taking notes—she agrees with Leann that "we're supposed to listen." I wonder about her own listening but do not verbalize this thought.

I offer a summary of what the group members seem to be expressing regarding confidentiality, listening, and paying attention. As I check out what I believe I have heard, all heads nod affirmatively, including Vicki's. I ask, "Do you agree, Vicki?" She answers yes, tears out the page in her note book and puts the pad away. After a brief moment of silence, Marla again picks up the previous theme and the group settles back into its former mode of listening while each member takes her turn at relating her individual experience.

●

Differentiation of Roles

Roles are sets of behaviors (Benne & Sheats, 1948; Biddle & Thomas, 1966; Linton, 1936). People come into any group experience with fairly well-established patterns of orienting themselves to the world around them and to the significant others in their various social environments. One person may notice the participation level of other people in a group and ask quiet ones to offer their thoughts and feelings. Another person may charge or recharge the energy of others when the pace tends to lag. Someone else may be the type who can come up with good ideas when the group seems stuck, or one who can suggest just where the group can go to obtain more information about something. People bring these behaviors, typical of them, into their formal group experiences.

A group may be thought of in terms of two subsystems: the behaviors that hold the group together and the behaviors that move the group toward achieving its goals. The sets of behaviors that help hold the group together are classified as social-emotional roles; those that help move the group toward its goal are classified as task roles.

The emergence of roles in a group is a natural one. Some people will adopt roles that help pull the group together and look after people's feelings about each other, themselves, and the group itself. Others will adopt roles that help the group clarify its goals and identify the means and resources needed for achieving these goals. In the formation stage, the worker will be doing a constant analysis of the behaviors being manifested by the members of the group.

Worker Behavior in Relation to Roles   The worker will assess the functionality of each role for the person adopting it. If a role is productive and satisfying for the person, the worker should encourage that set of behaviors. If the role does not attain for the person what is wanted, if it does not aid the person in her or his relationships with others, then the worker should try to move the person into a different set of behaviors.

That movement could be brought about in several possible ways. The worker could point out to the person that the behavior seems to be of the type that the person has identified as unproductive and a target for change, and the worker might suggest some other behavior to replace it. The worker could ask other members to give this kind of feedback, and might suggest that other members act as models or as monitors of change efforts. The worker could engage the person in an impromptu role play, leading the member into a rehearsal or improvisation of more productive ways of handling the situation. In each case, the aim will be to help the member learn goal-specific, functional sets of behaviors. As the individual member is experiencing this learning, the other members are also learning through the insight they gain into their own situations; if necessary, the worker may explicitly extend the learning.

The worker will also assess the functionality of each role for the group as a whole. This is the point at which the material discussed earlier with respect to a group's internal and external subsystems will have the most bearing. Behaviors in the two subsystems may be differentially emphasized, depending on the stage of group development (Hartford, 1972); nonetheless, role behaviors in both subsystems need to be present to some extent in all stages.

As the group matures, the member roles will become more differentiated. The worker should be ready to encourage roles that help to give shape and direction to the group's statement of goals, and roles that give rise to positive feelings about belonging to the group or about other members or the worker.

●

The adolescent girls' socialization group in the settlement house was organized in September. They were aged 11 to 14 years and, although all the girls knew each other from living in the same neighborhood and going to the parochial school there, they had not all been members of the same organized group before. They were working on a variety of socialization goals and on acquiring internal controls and limits. The roles that were emerging were both formal and informal. The formal roles were appropriate, as the group was organized in a club format.

Early in the year, the club developed a structure to be used in transacting business. At that point the worker was assigned the "president" role and only one other officer was designated: the secretary. Gradually the girl in the secretary's role began to assume more of the presiding function. This was less the result of the members' assigning that function to her than the result of her need for internal controls, which she projected onto the club as a whole and assumed for herself. She asked if the club could elect "regular officers." When they did, they elected nearly everyone in the club to an office.

The worker's task then became to assist the members in occupying the formal roles to which they had been assigned. Sometimes this meant meeting with the officer just prior to the club meeting; sometimes it meant interrupting the flow of business transactions to suggest what a particular officer needed to be doing at that point and to ask the agreement of the others as to the necessity of that officer's tasks being done. Essentially, the job of the worker was to mediate the group's functioning by clarifying the group maintenance behaviors that were necessary and by soliciting group assent to the worker's intervention.

With regard to informal roles, the girls' behavior in the group was like the interactional behaviors they experienced from each other in all the other parts of their lives. Theresa needed others to depend on her; she brought three other members into the group and remained related to her three "satellites." (The membership policy allowed for new members.) Her interactions in the group have been primarily focused on trying to be liked by everyone. She exhibited this need by trying to smooth any troubled waters; she did this by offering all sorts of suggestions and proposals or compromises to the group's way of behaving— even to the point of bribing the other members into settling their disputes by offering special treats from the grocery store operated by her grandmother, if they would just "try to get along with each other." The worker's role in relation to this was to help Theresa experience controls from the members with respect to sharing the group with others rather than exploiting it for her own ends.

The group assigned Janie the formal leadership position. This accorded with her informal status, in the group, of being the member with whom the others have the most reciprocated affectional ties and the member whom the others recognize as best representing their aspirations toward age- and gender-appropriate role enactment. The worker's role in relation to this was to support Janie's attempts to express the group's ideal image of her as one who could tend to business and also communicate to the other members her liking of them and caring about them. For each of the members, the help received both from worker interventions and from group relationships was, in one way or another, to be incorporated into the group interactions. The members could learn to share the center of attention and test out appropriate behavior, acquiring internal controls and limits.

•

In the beginning of the formation stage, members may be cautious in their use of the full range of behaviors they typically use in relationships. They will still be in the process of resolving their approach-avoidance dilemma and will therefore refrain from fully revealing themselves or utilizing with the others the repertoire of communication and emotional expression available to them. Moreover, members will not be rehearsing new behaviors, for two reasons. First, until they resolve the approach-avoidance dilemma, their behavioral repertoire will not yet be accessible for shaping and reshaping. Second, the group's normative system will not yet have taken hold sufficiently to cause members to acquire new, group-oriented behaviors. The worker's role at this stage is to be "the absent role taker." This means that the worker must be prepared to supply the behaviors that are not being taken by group members.

Workers, like everyone, have sets of roles and the attendant behaviors that are typical of them as persons. For example, a worker may be, by nature or by habit, more product-oriented or more process-oriented. A product-oriented worker will tend to pay more attention to the group's task system, whereas a process-oriented worker may be more aware of the needs of the social-emotional system. A worker with a group must do more than just perform a familiar role. The worker needs to be ready to enact any of the roles necessary to the full functioning of both of the group's subsystems.

Group Decision-making Processes

As the group of people begins to put its house in order—to create itself as a system—and get it moving toward its goals, the group will begin to operate a decision-making process. Prior to the formation stage, the group has been making decisions; now, however, the group will begin to have an identifiable pattern in the way it arrives at its decisions.

Seven methods of decision making have been identified, each with its own efficiency and effectiveness (Johnson & Johnson, 1975). However, such a classification describes ideal types; few situations in reality fit exactly into an ideal type. Each group will evolve its own most effective method, perhaps at times resembling one of the ideal types and at other times simply representing that group's own best way of making decisions. The way a group initiates an idea, deliberates over it, and makes a decision on it will be norm determined and role related.

●

Two decision-making patterns began to emerge for the girls' socialization group at the settlement house. In one, because the girls were together and in close contact with each other throughout the week between meetings, decisions were often made outside the group and brought into club sessions for ratification. This reflected the fact that in the minds of the members it was a friendship group, and had not yet become a formal, organized group. Naturally, the informal, consensual method of arriving at agreement appeared to suffice.

The second pattern went to the opposite extreme: the members used their highly structured pattern of formal offices to deliberate and arrive at a formal, majority-vote mode of taking decisions. Their manner of deliberation, however, reflected their transitional state in learning to acquire internal controls (which were often projected onto the group in attempts to control rigidly the behavior of all the others). It also reflected their transitional state in transferring their friendship group to a formal, organized group. In this second pattern, the methods employed by the girls were rather primitive: an individual who was attempting to control the group usually demanded attention by shouting or by pounding on the table. This provoked in the others a stunned silence, followed by cries that the shouter or pounder should "control herself." When things had quieted down, the girl who wanted to speak would very formally ask permission of the president and then put her proposal forward. This was followed by a very patterned sequence of debate. Members would put their hands up, be recognized by the presiding officer, say, "Excuse me, I'd like to say something," and only then proceed to address the group. Whoever spoke out of turn or disregarded the method was fined 1 cent.

When everyone had spoken, the presiding officer would solemnly call for the vote and the sergeant-at-arms would count the votes, write down the tally, and hand it to the president, who would announce the result. The outcome, of course, would already have been clearly obvious to everyone present, but this formal and patterned method of taking decisions reflected the needs of the members both to acquire internal controls and to translate their friendship group into a formal club.

●

The worker assesses the efficacy of the decision-making procedures and modifies those which are not productive for individuals or for the group. The report of the girls' socialization group continues:

●

It has been interesting to note that the girls will accept attempts at control from certain girls and not from others. In fact, the girls who demand the most order from the others are the girls who have the most difficulty themselves. Their control methods, when exerted on the rest of the group, are the most severe, most harshly applied, and most unrealistic in terms of what controls the other girls need. This results in either rebellion or appeals to the worker to mediate the severity of the method.

Mostly, I have functioned as a limit setter and clarifier. When the efforts at control have seemed to come from an individual member's own feelings of being out of control, I have tried to mediate for her between her own needs and the needs of the group: "Lois, I know you want the group to accept your idea and I know you think you have the solution worked out, but this group belongs to all the members and you'll need to wait and see whether everybody wants to go along with you. The group has a procedure and everybody agreed to stick to it, so ask to be recognized and get your idea in front of the group the way you all have agreed."

●

○

Mutual Contract

In the formation stage, the reciprocal contract is transformed into a mutual contract. This mutual contract represents a fledgling acknowledgment of the likeness of the individuals' goals and an acknowledgment of the potential benefits to each of them of joining a common enterprise. It is an agreement made by all the members with each other that they will commit to a specific goal, to be achieved by certain explicit means. The worker is part of this agreement as well, and so the parties to the contract may be thought of as being all the members and the worker.

The process by which the reciprocal contract becomes a mutual contract is one of abstraction from separate particular statements to a general one. In the convening stage, attention was given to raising the awareness of each individual that what she or he seeks in the group experience is like what the other individuals present seek. In the formation stage, the worker directs her or his efforts toward the discovery of a general statement of what the group wants and how that will be obtained. This "higher order" statement expresses the wants and needs of all the members without being the specific statement of any one of them.

The following example illustrates the flow of the contract transformation process.

●

This was a group of nine undergraduate students volunteering to serve as tutors and big sisters/big brothers to elementary-school children. The group was set up to deal with their experiences in their volunteer work, to help them explore their interest and ability in future careers involving work with children, to develop peer relationships that can augment their classroom learning, and to provide training in communication skills.

Each student was asked to write a statement outlining her or his reasons for participating in this group and agreeing to attend the group and to carry through on working with the children. In presenting their reciprocal contract statements at the group session, the students seemed quite definite that they were committed to those goals and were not simply parroting the stated purpose for the group.

After an initial orientation session, we spent a full group meeting discussing the mutual contract. Each member presented her or his reciprocal contract, and I presented my goals and expectations. My goals were to develop an atmosphere of honesty and trust in which each member could share her or his experiences with the child she or he was working with and could discuss the growing relationship between them. I wanted the group to help the members examine their skills and understanding of working with children and to further their understanding of effective relationships. Further, I wanted the group to provide an arena for the safe discussion and resolution of problems in their volunteer work. Finally, I wanted to have the group become a support system for the students in their formal educational program.

The students' goals varied; the following is a composite list: To develop a relationship between all the members to discuss successes, failures, and problems of the volunteer work; a place to share experiences and get feedback; a place to learn skills for dealing with people, such as communications skills; a place to learn about working with children; sharing of advice on how to deal with situations; a place to relate class material to the real-world situation; a place where we can help each other work out problems and share the fun and good things that go on; to provide an open discussion of relationships so we can learn from others' experiences and realize that we're not alone in the problems and that some things are normal experiences; a safe place for self-exploration.

The students accepted all these goals as they were presented. There was discussion and prioritizing of the goals, but no disagreement. This was the basis of our mutual contract.

•

The concept of an equilibrium point, originally used to account for decision-making in groups (Taylor, 1970), applies very well to the emergence of a mutual contract from a reciprocal one. The idea is that every person goes into a decision-making situation with a predetermined range of possible decisions she or he could agree to. The predetermination may be conscious, preconscious, or unconscious. Group decisions are made when the potential agreement ranges of all the individuals overlap. That point of overlap represents the best possible accommodation of all conflicting views; it is the equilibrium point for the group decision.

The process of forging a mutual contract parallels this pattern. The members have defined their individual ranges of acceptable objectives in their reciprocal contracts during the convening stage. The worker then helps them enlarge their awareness of the needs and objectives of the other persons present. In the formation stage, the worker directs her or his efforts at bringing the separate ranges into alignment at a point of common accord. This is done by focusing on phrasing a comprehensive—yet group-specific—statement that includes all the members' goals and their ideas about how to attain them.

The worker will adopt a "we" perspective rather than an "I" perspective. The members will begin to express what they seek as goals for the group as a whole; this is one of the features that distinguishes a mutual contract from a reciprocal one. The use of such phrases as "all of us," "each other," "we," and "us," indicates the emergence of cohesion in the group.

In the formation stage, not only do the parties to the contract change but the terms of the contract expand as well. The mutual contract will refer to the group as a whole; it will outline the direction the group is moving, member behaviors, worker behaviors, what the group will be doing together (the program media for achieving its goals), the meeting times, the number of meetings, the membership policy (whether open or closed to new members), the meeting place, and the fees; and it will provide for periodic review and renegotiation (Garvin, 1969; Hartford, 1966; Henry, 1972).

This is how the undergraduate group of tutors and big sisters/big brothers agreed on their mutual contract:

•

I then asked how the goals could be operationalized. We discussed the specific task and behaviors that would be needed to carry out the goals. The first priority was to develop a trusting atmosphere that would be conducive to sharing experiences, problems, and feelings. To operationalize that, everyone agreed to share their experiences. We agreed to take all sharing seriously and not to discount anyone's feelings or experiences, to listen attentively, and to structure sharing time in each meeting. We also agreed that regular attendance would enhance the trusting atmosphere.

The second priority was to learn skills for relating to the children. We agreed that sharing experiences and having each student try to help the others from their experience would help in the learning of skills. We agreed that we would set aside time for communication training and would attempt some role playing. Also, we would invite a teacher to give us some insight into working with elementary age children and would consider the possibility of inviting other experts if we wished, at a later date.

We agreed that, in order to foster a sharing atmosphere, we would maintain confidentiality unless the individual involved wished to have the situation discussed with school personnel. In order to foster an atmosphere of voluntary sharing, we would not ask each person whether they had something to share but would let all share as they felt like it. Each member would try not to dominate the group. Finally, we agreed that we would discuss the contract again at the beginning of the next semester to evaluate whether the goals were being met.

I explained that the foregoing would be our contract. One member asked if I was going to write up the contract for them to sign. We discussed this question and decided that we did not want a written contract.

●

Provision for renegotiation is an essential ingredient of a contract. Not to review and renegotiate the contract would imply that the group never changes. It does change, however, and what is sought and the means of reaching what is sought will also necessarily change. A statement of goals and means that is agreed to early in the life of a group will not be viable in its later stages; those who agreed together to do something, by certain means, will not remain the same, choosing to do the same thing by the same means. Time and events external to the group members' lives bring change. Within the group itself, the power of norm conformance and the cognitive and affectional accommodation of each member to other members and to the possibilities for individual goal achievement within the group will require members to act with reference to others in the service of their own goals.

Worker interventions that call attention to the dynamics of influence and control operating among the members should occur regularly, with the focus upon monitoring behavior and calibrating the means-goals equation. Through this effort, the groups' contract and members' engagement with it reflect the ongoing value of contract review and renegotiation. In this way, the contract maintains its viability as a change-inducing instrument and as a touchstone for members to chart their own individual and collective movement.

Members' awareness of their future need to reexamine their early decision was probably not very well developed in the convening stage. There was probably a sense of relief when the group was able to express its statement of its initial agreement on goals and means. The thought of restating what it will do and how it will do it was, in all likelihood, not present in people's minds.

In the formation stage, members will begin to be aware of the need to stop and take stock. They will be more cognizant of just how things are to go and how they are going, and of how the system operates. That cognizance will lead them to form ideas of alternative strategies for achieving goals. It may even lead them to reformulate their own view of the end state. More than that, the members will be gaining a deeper sense of connectedness with each other, the other members will have more meaning for them, and there will be more investment in each other's meeting their goals. The time will be ripe for group members to think about fine tuning their agreement on goals and means by providing for periodic review—and renegotiations, if necessary—of the contract.

The worker may need to initiate the discussions of the contract as a way of assessing the group's readiness to move into a mutual contract. Once that contract exists, the members will take more responsibility for contract monitoring and correction, when needed. That is inherent in the terms of the mutual contract: members agree to their own, the worker's, and others' expectations of behavior. The nature of the norms that have emerged and of the differentiated roles assumed is such that people will behave with reference to others' expectations. As the group matures in its level of functioning, members will come to expect of each other, rather than of the worker, that the group can sustain itself on the basis of what they do.

•

The contracting meeting initiated a different atmosphere in the group. At that meeting and in the two subsequent meetings, there has been a great deal of sharing and a very close feeling. Members said they appreciated the opportunity to express what they wanted to do and felt more a part of the group because of the contract meeting. They said they looked forward to the meetings and to meeting their goals. The new structure, allowing time for communication training and discussion, has introduced a more organized, comfortable flow to the meetings.

•

○

Role and Location of the Worker

Beginning with the formation stage, the worker moves out of a central location and a primary role within the group and into a pivotal location and variable role. The location is called pivotal because the worker alternately moves out to a peripheral place and moves back into a central place, as the group's processes require. The worker's role is variable because the worker will sometimes be merely facilitative and sometimes more active if the group's functioning makes that necessary. To be active is to enact the "absent role taker" role with respect to both the internal and the external system. To be facilitative is to enact a consultant role, furnishing resources to the group on a demand basis.

When the group has begun to operate its own internal and external systems, the worker needs to be the absent role taker within a smaller and smaller sphere of action. That is, as the members begin to take on and utilize a range of social-emotional (or expressive) roles, the worker will be able to move out of actively taking those roles, but will remain ready to move into an active role as needed, even in later stages of group life. The worker should neither hold on to the central location and primary role any longer than she or he needs to nor become peripheral and facilitative sooner than the group is ready for. To hold on too long is to rob the members of their opportunity to become self-sufficient and self-determining; to let go too soon is to abdicate the responsibility of serving the group with the best skill possible.

In the example described earlier, in which Anna suggested that each person face a group member when she has something to say about that member, the worker had three options for intervening; each option illustrates one of the roles a worker may assume.

Taking a primary role, the worker would pick up Anna's suggestion, weight the idea with her or his approval, and put the proposal to the group. The worker inserts herself or himself decisively and intentionally into the group's interaction network and acts on behalf of one member.

Taking a facilitative role, the worker would do nothing at the time Anna made her suggestion, leaving it to the group to manage Anna's contributions. The phrasing of Anna's comment, "I don't know about anyone else but I would feel...," invites other members to respond. When acting in a facilitative role, the worker waits for the others to respond and to use their initiative.

The worker in a pivotal role would act but would not weight Anna's contribution with the worker's support of the idea. The worker would simply put the question to the group, converting it to group property. The worker would then be ready to move into a primary role if the group's processing of the suggestion warrants that; otherwise she or he would let the group address the proposal unaided, and unimpeded, by worker behavior.

Worker Skills

The worker skills employed in the formation stage are those that encourage participation, help the synthesizing process, and reinforce interactional patterns.

Encouraging Participation

The worker will encourage participation by actively intervening as norms emerge and as role differentiation occurs. The worker will support norms and roles that are functional both for individual members and for the group as a whole and will modify or redirect norms and roles that are not functional.

An example of such intervention occurred in the adult group in the psychiatric hospital.

●

Bill was upset because, as he saw it, other people in the group weren't investing as much in "getting well" as he was. "Maybe you've all got the time and money to sit around and explore your navels but, dammit, I'm in here to get well and there hasn't been much going on that shows me that any of the rest of you want to do anything but be taken care of the rest of your lives!"

The others reacted in their typical fashions: some turned away or shrank into their seats; others got up and paced around the room; a couple strongly denied his words. The patterns of behavior being used by the members were regressive; that is, under Bill's attack they were reverting to the levels of functioning that they had at the time they entered the group.

I took a fairly confrontive stance with Bill: "Suppose you let up on people for a minute, Bill. You seem to be feeling that there are problems here, but I haven't heard anyone else support what you're saying. Let's check it out." I said, "Bill, I'm going to ask you to sit there and be quiet. If what you are saying is how everybody else feels, let's let them say it for themselves. But in the meantime, you are not to say anything to what anyone says. If you do, I'm sending you back to your room and the rest of us will iron out our problems."

I then began to address the others directly, one by one, asking them how they felt about what Bill was saying. They did have some issues and, with my drawing them out, they could articulate them. From there, we began to discuss ways to get them more involved in saying for themselves what they wanted by way of support from the others in the group. By the end of the session, we were more back on keel as far as the communication and support network of the group was concerned.

●

Helping the Synthesizing Process

The worker will help the synthesizing process by fostering the modification of members' behaviors into group-oriented behaviors. For example, in guiding the transformation of the members' reciprocal contracts into a mutual contract, the worker will aid the group in ways that will vary according to the group's needs and abilities. If the members initiate the discussion of a mutual contract, the worker will hold back from leadership; if they do not, the worker will initiate the discussion and suggest forms of expression to define the emerging mutual contract.

The worker will help bring into coherence the disparate behaviors of the group members. Operating in a pivotal location, the worker stands ready to intervene actively when that is indicated, and to abstain from action when the group gives evidence of its ability to sustain its own emergent system.

The example that follows concerns a divorce adjustment group. The worker helped the members sort out their conflict over individual members' styles and helped them blend their separate needs into a group-oriented focus. The worker enacted a variable role and occupied a pivotal location, alternately intervening to focus the discussion and letting it flow, according to the group's need and capacity for either behavior.

●

There had been some evidence, at the previous meeting, that the members were moving into the conflict/disequilibrium stage. Edie had tried too hard to take care of Anita, who had not been participating much. She had received a strong "leave me alone" response from Anita. Other members had tried to rescue both Edie and Anita, but neither had wanted the help. Appeals had been made to me to do something. Because all of this had come up near the end of the session, I had only commented briefly. I said it seemed to me that the different spaces occupied by each member were beginning to be more evident and that people were trying to see how they could keep their individuality while, at the same time, belonging to the group and getting something out of it for themselves. I suggested that we discuss this question more at the next session.

At this evening's session Edie brought up the subject. She said she was sorry if she had come on too strong last week but that she noticed that Anita hadn't been participating and she thought Anita wasn't getting what she needed from the group. Anita reacted again: "Let me decide that, will you? I didn't ask you to decide what I need and I sure don't need you to decide whether I'm getting what I want from this group."

I did not respond directly to the exchange between Edie and Anita but tried to elevate the issue to a group level. I asked whether anyone else had any ideas about what was going on in the group. Lisa said she was confused. She said she was feeling okay about herself and the group and assumed that everyone else was, too. She didn't know what to make of what happened at the end of last session. She did think, however, that people had a right to speak for themselves—just as she was doing now—but she also thought everyone should care about what happened to people in the group.

I asked the others where they were. They agreed that people should be able to speak up for themselves and agreed that caring about everyone else in the group was a good thing—what the group was all about. "But," said Robbie, "caring about other people and trying to do something about it are two different things. I think we can care about each other and where they are but I don't think that means we have to do something about it for them." I asked what she meant, exactly. "Well, we were going along pretty well. People who wanted to talk were talking; people who didn't weren't. But, sometime or another, everyone was involved some way or another. We agreed in the beginning that if someone didn't want to talk or contribute in a group meeting, they needn't. I don't think anyone should try to speak up for them. I can tell when something we're discussing is too much or too close for somebody else and I respect that, just like I appreciate it when people respect where I am and let me talk or not talk, depending where I am."

Robbie had enunciated and reinforced one of this group's norms: letting people be where they are. Further, she had recapitulated the group's communication and interaction patterns: people had been talking when and as they could. "Then what seems to have changed?" I asked.

Paul ventured the suggestion that the closeness might be getting to people. "Are you saying that people are asking for more space?" I asked. "No, I'm really saying that I think people want to get close to others but that we only have our usual ways of doing that and those ways aren't so comfortable for us anymore—either getting close or having people be close to us. I think what's going on is that we're all somewhere on the verge of changing and it's scary so we keep using old scripts." The others seemed to agree with Paul but were not so comfortable or clear as he was, in expressing their feelings.

"Okay," I said. "What do we want to do, then, to make it possible for us to use new ways of relating to people rather than continuing to fall back into old habits? Does anyone want to suggest how we could follow up on Paul's insight?" There followed one idea after another; I let the suggestions flow uninterrupted for quite a while before I proposed that we begin to order their ideas.

This discussion produced a reaffirmation of the norms they had been employing and validated the roles that various members had been using. Their discussion also resulted in a new perspective on what they were there for and how they could go about helping each other get that.

●

Reinforcing Interactional Patterns

The worker will reinforce interactional patterns in a catalytic way; that is, the worker's interventions in the emerging group system will produce a new configuration. Until now, the group has been simply the sum of its parts, but as the members interact, a system is synergistically created. A dyad is more than two persons; it is the two persons plus the reciprocal interaction between them (Hartford, 1972). All larger systems are exponentially greater.

The worker acts to spark the relational mix. She or he may do this by pointing out the similarities or complementarities between people and the commonalities of their experiences or situations, and by passing on one member's communication to another member or to the whole group for examination and processing. At other times, the worker will align herself or himself with the members' own discovery of their similarities, complementarities, and commonalities as they more and more interact to form their own group.

In the divorce adjustment group, the worker helped the members find the commonness of their experiences. She drew attention to the feelings they were all experiencing, and she reinforced their reactions from a common base.

●

Judy brought up the fact that she was feeling very close to some of the members and very distant from others. I asked what that was all about. She said she wasn't sure but she felt like she had more in common with some people than with others, and that it was easier for her to understand where the people she was close to were coming from. Jo agreed. "I feel like I understand Troy and Brad for what they're going through, and it's just easier for me to want to give some feedback to them than it is to other people."

It seemed too early for the group members to be confronting each other, so I dismissed the idea that these two members might be commenting on the part the other members were playing (or not playing) in each other's progress.

I asked what others were feeling. Some understood Jo and Judy; others didn't comprehend their comments at all. Brad asked Jo for clarification. "I mean, this is a divorce group and I'm a man and you're a woman. My wife left me and you left your husband. I can't understand what you mean when you say that you understand where I'm coming from and what I'm going through. Our situations are just so different! I would expect two people, in our situations, to be at complete opposite ends of understanding." Others agreed.

Troy pointed out that he'd left his wife so he didn't see what he had in common with Brad and couldn't understand at all how Jo, who was in his situation, could understand both him and Brad. "What I hear," I interjected, "is that whether you left or were left, you hurt. You're feeling pain. It's not that everyone can jump into the shoes of the person who reminds them of the other person in their relationship, but I feel sure that everyone is feeling hurt and pain."

From there, they took off on their own discussion of feelings of rejection and guilt and uncertainty over whether they wanted their relationships back again. It was intense, with much deep feeling being communicated. It ended, however, with their expressing a great sense of relief over having been able to share at the level they reached. It was not that they could put themselves in the place of their former partners from hearing what others said; but they expressed that they were losing their feelings of being the only person in the world experiencing what they had experienced. They also expressed that they could understand that it was not necessarily easier to have been the one who left a relationship than to have been the one who was left.

•

○

Framework for Analysis of
Program Media

In the formation stage, the members need to strengthen their sense of the group as an entity. The analysis of members' needs and capacities should include consideration of their abilities to conceive of a goal and the steps necessary to reach that goal. Each of these abilities implies being able to imagine a future, to envision how they and others will be and what they will be doing in that future, to be able to identify with others and to think of themselves as belonging to a set of persons, and to be able to say what they want for themselves.

These requirements may impose limits on a worker's plan to get the people to become a fully functioning, self-directed group. Children, for example, are not able to perform abstract reasoning or to conceptualize the group as a collective entity. Children from early latency up to the age of adolescence belong to groups—some formal and organized and some informal and natural—but they do not engage in abstract thinking about them, either because the goals, means, and signs of membership are determined from outside the group or because no explicit agreement on goals, means, and signs of membership is necessary. Emphasis must therefore be put on cognitive operations.

People with certain kinds of intellectual limitations (which may be of organic, traumatic, or social origin) may have difficulty in conceptualizing and objectifying their experiences. Other people may have emotional or psychological limits that preclude abstract reasoning or group involvement. The cultural and socioeconomic experiences in a person's life may not have prepared her or him for making long-term projections and forecasting resource accessiblity. In such instances, the worker will remain more primary and central throughout the life of the group and will do more planning, initiating, and direction-setting for the group. The worker would plan a progression of activities designed to establish behavioral patterns for the members that are appropriate to the group purpose, whatever that purpose may be. The worker would take the initiative to introduce the activity into the group, monitor its progress and its effects on the members, and lead the group into its next activity when, for example, interest waned or members tired or the benefits diminished or the activity turned out to be beyond the members' ability.

The worker will use the information gleaned from the pregroup interviews and from observations of the group to determine what the members need and what their intellectual, physical, emotional, and social capacities are. Those determinations help the worker decide what the group should be doing when it is together.

The worker also analyzes the behavioral outcomes associated with certain kinds of program media. In the formation stage, the worker will seek behavioral outcomes that strengthen grouplike behaviors. The worker will look for media that lay down and then repeat patterns of behaviors associated with following a leader, watching for behavioral cues, providing for everyone's participation, noncompetition, various modes and networks of communication, doing things together, and sharing. These behaviors—done orally or nonverbally—are all in the range of normlike behaviors and may be useful to help members heighten their awareness of influencing and being influenced by the behavior of others. Behavioral patterns associated with role differentiation would include following a rotating leadership role, providing for everyone's participation, expression of feelings, and work on a task or tasks. These behaviors, when repeated and reinforced, will help members kinesthetically and emotionally experience differentiated roles.

The decision to use a particular medium may come from either of two directions. One direction would be to have a medium in mind and to analyze it for its appropriateness to the desired behavioral outcomes and to the members' needs and capacities. The other direction would be to delineate members' needs and capacities and the behaviors likely to strengthen groupness and then to see what kinds of media suggest themselves. Either approach is viable, and there may be merit in double-checking one's planning by doing the analysis from both directions.

The worker should ask herself or himself a series of questions about the members of the group, the medium or activity being considered, and the behaviors associated with group formation. The questions about the members focus on their capacities and needs:

What do they need physically, socially, emotionally, and intellectually
    in the long run?
    for now?
    collectively?
    individually?

What can they do
    physically?
    intellectually?
    emotionally or psychologically?
    socially?

What can they not do
    physically?
    intellectually?
    emotionally or psychologically?
    socially?

The questions about the activity itself cover all aspects of the medium:

What are the guides to conduct?

What is the source of these guides?

What kind and amount of physical movement is involved?

What level of skill is necessary?

What kind and amount of interaction is involved?

What kinds of rewards are there, what is their source, and what is the manner of distributing them (Crawford, 1957; Henry, 1964; Vintner, 1967)?

The questions about group formation concern the dynamics of norms and of role differentiation:

Is following a leader part of the group's repertoire?

Do the leadership roles rotate among members? Which roles?

Does the group watch for behavioral cues? With what response?

Is everyone's participation provided for?

Is interaction noncompetitive?

What modes and networks of communication does the group employ?

Does the group do things together and share?

Do members express their feelings? How?

Do members work on tasks? How?

Depending on the worker's approach in determining the program media to be utilized in the group—activity known but being analyzed for appropriateness, or activity unknown but being sought—the answers to two or three of the sets of questions should lead in the direction of suggesting what activity can be used.

When an activity seems generally appropriate to the group stage of development and to the needs and capacities of the members but does not quite fit what the group needs or is ready to do, the activity may be modified, as in the following example.

•

This was the fourth meeting of a third- and fourth-grade girls' group at a community center; the members are Anglo and Hispanic. The purpose of the group is socialization—learning to establish satisfying and productive social relationships. In the meetings prior to this one, the media had been mostly of the "parallel play" sort, providing opportunity for the girls to engage in something individually in the presence of others. Some efforts had been made to initiate group activities, but until now it had been necessary to keep the activities going without too much time in between, or else the girls wandered off into individual play. Given their age and the fact that this was the fourth meeting, it is not surprising that they had been pretty much individually oriented. At the meeting just prior to this one, some evidence of cooperation had been observed by the worker, and the elaboration of this was attempted in this meeting. We were going to make cookies.

I had previously divided the cookie mix into paper cups and set out spoons for each girl. There were only enough pans for the girls to work in pairs. When we reached the kitchen, I asked each girl to take a cup and a spoon, choose a partner and take a pan. They seemed to do this with little difficulty. Flora was left with a pan to herself. Then I explained to the girls about how much water to put in the mix and how to stir it up. They did very well. Janie and Laura worked together and when they had their share in the pan, they took the three extra cups of mix. Debbie and Margie worked together and Susie and Linda worked together.

The other girls noticed that Janie and Laura had taken more of the mix. I had saved some extra in case of emergency, so I divided it among the rest of the girls. They put their dough in the pans. I lit the oven. Some of the girls did not drop the cookies; instead they made a sort of cake. Flora made cookies. Each girl put her pan into the oven and when all were in, I asked if they would like to make their frosting now or play a game.

We played "I Spy" two or three times and then made the frosting. Instead of dividing, this time I let each girl take her own sugar from the box, add the milk and vanilla, and mix it. Of course, I told them how much of each before they started. They did very well and this time seemed to grasp the idea of sharing equally among all the girls.

During the mixing of the cookies and then of the frosting, the girls kept asking me if it was all right. They did show signs of being aware of each other at times during our cooking. It seems to be something new to them to share. Premeasuring the cookie mix and having the girls work together seemed important, to begin to give them the idea of cooperation; then having them mix their icing on their own let them pull back a bit to an individual activity. I could have divided up the tasks of mixing the icing and let them make a common batch, but their calling attention to

Janie and Laura's extra portions of the cookie mix made me think they had shared and cooperated as much as they could tolerate. So I chose the individual icing route.

●

To give another example:

●

This was a sharing group within the church; the purpose of the group was personal growth and forming new or more meaningful relationships with other members of the church. The group met for eight weeks, one and one-half hours each Sunday evening followed by informal social time for about one-half hour at which refreshments were served. Membership was voluntary.

A social worker who was a member of the church had volunteered to conduct the sharing group. Each week, group members were given an assignment to do during the week. During the next group meeting, they would focus on their reactions to the assignment.

The second meeting was late in starting, and several members came in after the meeting had started. Two new members were introduced to the group. The assignment was discussed with members making comments directed to the worker. Initially there was little interaction among group members. Ann began to emerge as a leader, making sure that each member was included in the discussion. Renee resisted Ann's attempts to involve her in the discussions. A subtle conflict ensued, concerning the setting of norms as to the degree to which group members would share their personal experiences and feelings. Some members were quite willing to share fully, while others were sending out strong covert "Don't push me" messages.

Rather than allow the meeting to slide into struggle and conflict, the worker suggested that people write down their responses and reactions to this week's assignment, pair off, and talk only with the person they had paired off with. People could share or not within the dyad; the dyad's report would later be the subject of a large-group discussion. Although this was not the optimal way of conducting a sharing group, it seemed the best alternative given the introduction of two new members and the resistance of some other members to participating in the large group.

●

Another example:

●

This senior citizen's group met every two weeks at the community center. One of the members was present when the worker arrived, having eaten lunch at the center that day. Mrs. and Mr. Field arrived next and I introduced them to

Mr. Hamilton. Mrs. and Mr. Julian came next; then Mrs. and Mr. Crist, Mrs. George, and Rev. Upham came. Then Miss Garcia and her mother. Miss Garcia said she had to bring her mother because she did not speak English. I said that I was glad she had come with her and invited her to sit down. Then Mr. Chappell and Mrs. Burns came in together. Mr. Gonzales came in after the movie had started.

The people were having a fine time chatting with each other, but I knew that they did not all know each other, so I asked each to make a name tag and pin it on herself or himself. Mr. Chappell does not write so I made one for him. Then I passed out the paper and pencils for Name Bingo and explained the game to the group. Before I started the explanation, I said that sometimes it was hard to get a big group quiet and suggested that we use the arm-in-air signal. They liked the idea and all agreed that we should use it. There was some resistance to the idea of the game—talking to people they did not know in order to fill in the bingo page—so I suggested that we go around the circle and say our own names. Before we could finish, some of the people were circulating among the group, so I just dropped the idea and let them go ahead. We finally got the names filled in and were ready to play real bingo.

●

Summary

The following profile of worker behaviors is described in this chapter. While the members' behaviors differentiate into role clusters and while the group's normative system is emerging, the worker will be monitoring and assessing the development. The worker will be prepared to encourage or discourage emergent norms or role differentiation patterns, according to their productiveness for members individually or for the group as a whole. The worker will be prepared to be the absent role taker, an action wholly consistent with the variable role and pivotal location of a worker vis-à-vis a forming group.

The worker will be leading the group in the transformation of the reciprocal contract into a mutual one and will let the members' growing self-determination and self-direction move the group as far and as fast as it can go in taking its own decisions.

Because the worker now has enough information in hand about the members' usual ways of relating to each other and of responding to stimuli, the worker will initiate, permit, or encourage the use of program media that help build and strengthen grouplike behaviors.

References

Benne, K., & Sheats, P. (1948). Functional roles of group members. *Journal of Social Issues, 4*(2), 41–47.

Biddle, B. J., & Thomas, E. J. (1966). Role theory: Concepts and research. New York: John A. Wiley.

Crawford, J. (1957). *Impact of activities on participant behavior of children.* Unpublished master's thesis, University of Michigan, Ann Arbor.

Garvin, C. (1969). Complementarity in role expectations in groups: The member-worker contract. In *Social Work Practice, 1969.* New York: Columbia University Press.

Hartford, M. E. (1966). Changing approaches in practice theory and techniques. In *Trends in Social Work Practice and Knowledge: NASW Tenth Anniversary Symposium.* New York: National Association of Social Workers.

Hartford, M. E. (1972). *Groups in social work.* New York: Columbia University Press.

Henry, S. (1964). *An exploration of the association between group interactional behaviors and four program activities.* Unpublished master's thesis, Western Reserve University, Cleveland, OH.

Henry, S. (1972). *Contracted group goals and group goal achievement.* Unpublished doctoral dissertation, University of Denver.

Johnson, D. W., & Johnson, F. P. (1975). *Joining together group theory and group skills.* Englewood Cliffs, NJ: Prentice-Hall.

Linton, R. (1936). The study of man. New York: Appleton Century.

Schutz, W. (1958). FIRO: A three-dimensional theory of interpersonal orientation. New York: Holt, Rinehart & Winston.

Schutz, W. (1966). Interpersonal underworld. Palo Alto, CA: Science and Behavior Books.

Schwartz, W. (1971). On the use of groups in social work practice. In W. Schwartz & S. R. Zalba (Eds.), *The practice of group work* (pp. 16–31). New York: Columbia University Press.

Shulman, L. (1967). Scapegoats, group workers, and the pre-emptive intervention. *Social Work, 12*(2), 37–43.

Taylor, M. (1970). The problem of salience in the theory of collective decision-making. *Behavioral Science, 15,* 415–430.

Vinter, R. (1967c). Program activities: An analysis of their effects on participant behavior. In R. Vinter (Ed.), *Readings in group work practice.* Ann Arbor, MI: Campus Publishers.

CHAPTER 6

THE CONFLICT/ DISEQUILIBRIUM STAGE

In the conflict/disequilibrium stage, the group enters a period of separation and distance. The alternating pattern of separation and union is not a movement back and forth but a spiral. In the formation stage, the emerging group system moves toward union; then, for a variety of reasons, it moves away from union; then its internal mechanisms motivate it to move toward union again, and it comes a bit nearer to that joined state before moving away again.

In this chapter, we are concerned with the products of the group's internal dynamics as it spirals away from union, through conflict or disequilibrium. Conflict is not a bad thing in itself. It is sometimes seen as the stuff from which growth occurs. The stance taken in this text is not "peace at any price"; but that undirected and unchanneled conflict is detrimental to the life of a group.

In this stage of group development, the dynamics are conflictual in tone; the affects that are expressed are conflict laden; the atmosphere of the group's life space is conflict ridden; and what people experience feels to them like conflict, and they are uncomfortable. In the course of this stage, members may acquire some skills in being able to tolerate and manage conflict situations,

127

not only in their present group experience but in other parts of their life as well. That may be, in some cases, an overt or covert goal.

For example, a group of people who experience unsatisfying interpersonal relationships or who suffer low self-esteem and inability to assert themselves might want, as their own objective and as their collective goal, to acquire the skill to manage conflict. Their conscious and public attachment is the overt goal; it is stated, agreed to, and affirmed. All of the members, as they were recruited, adopted this overt goal. However, not all of each person's individual objectives become appropriated into the reciprocal contract. The desire of some people to learn to manage conflict situations may be either unspoken or, even though spoken, not contracted for. The desire may then become a covert goal; some people may decide that, in addition to working on what they have contracted to work on, they will use whatever opportunity presents itself to learn to manage conflict situations. Whether the goal is overt or covert, the group worker needs to help the group clarify, handle, and move on from the conflict that it experiences.

To be sure, not every group passes through a clearly identifiable and demarcated period of conflict. There may be strong differences and even divisions within the group, but strong differences or divisions, or uneasiness with disagreement, do not necessarily constitute conflict.

Strong differences between people are naturally occurring, ongoing, and even essential dynamics at every stage of group development and in nearly every group. They allow the group members to retain their individuality and autonomy even as they merge themselves with the collective entity. Difference, uniqueness, and individuality are to be protected because, ultimately, it is each individual who is helped in and through the group experience. The philosophical stance behind this position is in accordance with the democratic values that underlie the practice approach advanced in this book: that the collectivity exists for the person, and not the other way around; and that the rights of minorities must be regarded and protected, even when the rule of the majority prevails.

Divisions within a group are also natural, and important, because they define the dyads, subgroups, alliances, and other subunits of the group entity. These represent the natural alignments of persons, expressing their identifications and orientation points. They constitute, at any given time, the relationship system within which the people who comprise them are able to function.

These phenomena do not constitute the conflict that is the subject of this chapter. Conflict is that which so profoundly affects the bond of the group that it appears to be in jeopardy of dissolution. Conflict is a level of imbalance that threatens to dissolve whatever cohesiveness exists, to derail whatever coordinated functioning has been achieved, and to impair whatever progress has been made.

The dynamics of the conflict or disequilibrium stage of group development are discussed in the first two sections of this chapter. The subsequent sections consider the mutual contract that is in effect at this stage, the worker's role and location, and the media utilized to enhance the social forces.

○

Dynamics of Conflict

The basis of the conflict at this stage of group development is who owns the group. Until this point, the worker has had a high degree of control over the life of the group. The worker had the idea to have a group, was responsible for identifying what kind of people should belong to it, talked to all the prospective members and decided who would be selected for membership, called them all together for their first meetings, initiated discussions of what the collective goal would be, and proposed the media that could help the group reach its goal. The worker has played a large part in the affairs of the group, and the members have gone along with the worker's having this much direction.

The members have collaborated with the worker's primacy and centrality by appearing for the pregroup interviews, sharing their personal information and consenting to the reciprocal contract, appearing at the first meetings, engaging in the discussions of the group's common and collective goal, and acceding to the worker's role enactment. At first they were trying out the group experience, suspending the decision to fully invest and commit energy. They were tentative—and even uncertain—about their future. The agreements they made were genuine, but genuine within the limits of their unwillingness to surrender parts of themselves in order to gain the greatest good for the greatest number. They formed themselves into a viable collective entity, and their issue then becomes an attempt to make the experience as fully satisfying and productive to herself or himself as possible.

When the group has formed, and the members have begun to take more responsibility for running it and are more active in saying what they want, the issue that surfaces is, "Whose group is this?" The desire to take charge and shape the group in the direction one wants is a strong one.

During the negotiation of the reciprocal contract in the convening stage, the members discovered, in a small way, that they could put forward their individual wants and needs and have them paid attention to. After that, the members' energies were directed toward getting on with the business of the help they came for. They also had the experience of determining how the group would be; in influencing and being influenced by the other members through the emergence of the group's normative system, the members began to learn what results occur when they assert their individual preferences. They have also seen the outcome of the division of labor and their relative status in the internal and external systems of the group. They have seen that some people have more power than others to lead the group in one direction or the other. Members also learn that group movement depends on agreement as to a common goal, and that differing amounts of energy need to be expended in order to get the group to move.

These lessons have not been lost on the group members. Although the primary expenditure of emotional energy has properly been directed toward the members' work on their own issues, they are aware (perhaps subliminally) that their force can move the group. When their connectedness to the group is fully felt, they are motivated to move the group their way. The meaning of this connectedness is that the members have committed themselves to the experience and to each other, have made some level of investment in the successful outcome of the group experience, and have registered some level of involvement with others in their interactions (Brager, 1969). Still, despite this collective orientation and despite whatever recognizable gains the members have made, the experience before them is unknown. Despite the trust level that has developed and the deeper levels of openness and sharing that exist by this time, the members want more. The question is how to get from this experience what they each need and want.

Consciously, preconsciously, or unconsciously, the mechanism exists within the mind of each member to trigger her or his desire to insure that the experience will be as she or he wants. When the member sees that most of the available time has already passed and comparatively little time remains to achieve what she or he wants, a strong effort is triggered, to own the group and to see to it that the group serves the members' individual needs. That member then takes on the worker and all the other members. The content of the challenge is that needs are not being met: the common goal does not serve the individual member's needs sufficiently, the chosen means are not contributing sufficiently to the individual member's goals, and neither the worker nor the other members are doing enough of what the member needs. "If only everyone else would get her or his act together and help me," goes the magical thinking, "this group would be worthwhile."

The magical thinking may be internal, but it motivates behavior, both verbal and nonverbal. The affects which accompany these behaviors are responses to perceived threat; perhaps the behaviors are hostile, or anxious, or withheld, or even inappropriately positive and compliant. Behind the sense of threat is the member's expectation of what will happen for her or him. In a sense, the emergence of these behaviors may be taken as an investment indicator—although it may be difficult to accept that these behaviors indicate anything so positive as investment! They look more like withdrawal.

Members typically enter this stage of group development by questioning what the worker has in mind for the group, questioning whether what has been going on and what promises to occur in the future has anything to do with their being helped, and questioning whether they are getting what they need. The worker is usually the first target because she or he is, in many ways, the most visible figure. The worker, after all, got them into this experience (goes their magical thinking) and is finally being seen to have feet of clay. The worker has no instant formulas to make them better; there are no magic cures. Getting well or getting better is hard work, and it turns out that they have to do the work. They may think the worker does too much, or the worker does not do enough; and whatever the worker does is done wrong!

•

At the fourth meeting of the ten-week sexuality group for adolescent girls, the members entered in a fairly agitated state. We were supposed to have made a field trip to the neighborhood health clinic to meet the health educator, Susan; but she had been called out of town because her father was critically ill, and the clinic didn't have anyone else to send in her place. I'd been able to phone the school and have messages delivered to all the girls to come to our regular meeting place instead of assembling at the health clinic.

They were very grouchy when they arrived. They came in, not speaking to me, whereas they usually greeted me warmly. They sat with their arms folded, legs crossed under them on the sofas, almost curled up in a ball. They were seething with enough tension that I'm sure if I'd touched them, they'd have uncoiled like a wound-up spring. Many baleful and hostile looks were being sent in my direction.

I started to explain what had happened. They ignored me, muttering and mumbling to each other under their breaths. I went on talking, saying that I knew they must be disappointed but that I'd gotten a film from the library that I thought might partly make up for us not being able to take the field trip. I asked if they wanted to see it and then have a discussion. Still no acknowledgement that I was even in the room. Now their exchanges with each other had reached conversational level; they were turning, in their subgroups and pairings, to face each other and put their backs toward me as much as possible.

I heard Tanya say, "Just keep talking; don't look at her. She'll get tired of talking to the wall after a while." The other girls giggled and snorted derisively and turned away from me even farther. I tried again, "Do you want to see the film? I'm sorry, too, that it turned out this way, but we can still make something of today's meeting." At this, they began to put their heads in the air and sing-song, "La-di-da-di-dum," over and over, getting louder and louder.

"Now, come on," I said, as pleasantly but firmly as I could. "You don't think I did this on purpose, do you? I told you that the woman's father got sick and was rushed to the hospital and she had to fly home and I just found out about it. You can't be thinking I could help that!"

Serena whirled around in her seat and said, "You! You're supposed to be knowing what to do with us! You're supposed to be here to be helpin' us. We decided we wanted to go to the clinic; you're supposed to help us do what we decide to do; you told us that the first day. You said you'd plan the first few meetings, and then after that we could decide what we wanted to do and you'd help us do it! You probably called up that clinic and told them we weren't coming 'cause you probably don't want us to meet anybody else who knows something. You're probably jealous that we might meet somebody who knows more than you do. You can't help us; you just don't know how to run a group. How're we ever supposed to learn how to do things if you won't help? Shoot, we'd be better off with somebody who knows what they're doin'!"

It was a direct attack from Serena, thrown out with much fire and feeling. She was egged on by the others who were huffing and puffing and bouncing in their seats, saying, "Yeah, yeah; you're right, Serena." Serena stood up and started toward the door. She turned back to the others and said, "Come on; I'm gettin' outta here. She calls herself helpin' us; she can't even help herself! Huh, roundin' up a dumb old movie; thinks that's gonna replace our idea!"

•

After the worker, the next most usual target is other members of the group. They, too, are confronted as being not much good; none of them really understands the problems the person is having; they are only looking out for their own interest; they have no commitment to the group or to each other; they have been selfish; they have demanded too much of the worker's time and attention; they have used up too much of the group's time. A member who asks for more structure is criticized for that; a member who asks for less structure is criticized for that. If, as happens on occasion, a member speaks up with a moderating or compliant attitude—perhaps as a way of dissociating herself or himself from the conflict in the hope of gaining favor and notice from the worker—that member may be taken to task for her or his failure to understand what the true issues are.

A group of girls graphically demonstrated the conflict over owner-ship of their group.

•

The purpose of this group was to help preadolescent and early-adolescent girls become aware of choices open to them for their lives and their futures. The girls were predominantly Hispanics.

I'd been aware that there was some kind of conflict simmering just below the surface for a couple of meetings, but hadn't been able to pinpoint the causes for it. It is obvious that the members do not see themselves as a group; they always seem to end up in two subgroups, with Barbara and Rosa each heading one.

At the sixth meeting, while I was waiting for all the girls to show up, I took advantage of the time to ask those present how they felt about the group. I thought they might be able to suggest ways to change it if they feel the group needs changing. Naturally, the girls were reluctant to say anything; they just exchanged glances with one another. The only comment came from Barbara, who said she had thought the group would be boring but it wasn't.

Since the girls did not give me any more clues that might explain the polarization, I left it for the time being. We had planned a field trip to a fast-food restaurant (to introduce them to future job opportunities). We took the tour and stayed afterward for complimentary french fries and cookies.

The girls had to sit in two booths, and it was obvious from their seating arrangement that there were two groups. Barbara and her followers sat at one table; Rosa and the others sat at the other. While they were having their snack, there was hardly any interaction between the girls at the two tables although they were next to each other. It is evident that these two subgroups are not mixing well at all. This division runs along color lines (not racial). The darker girls are in Barbara's circle and the lighter ones are in Rosa's. This may or may not be the cause of the chasm between them; I'm not certain.

When we reached the center, the two subgroups split along their usual line of division and went their separate ways. Debbie was hanging around for a bit, and I asked her if she could tell me why she disliked Rosa so much; she said she didn't know, she just did. I suggested she try to decide whether she liked or disliked a person for what the person was and not for her skin color. She shrugged at this and walked off after her clique. I decided to take this division up next time; but at the next meeting only Betty, Angela, and Cathie were present, and it was not possible to address the group split.

At the ninth meeting, six members were present and I decided to take up the issue of the split. I started by saying it seemed to me that none of them had missed noticing the fact that the group always seemed to divide off into two groups. I asked if they had any ideas about why that happens. Luisa and Doris both tried to say they thought we should all try to be friends and get along. Debbie jumped in right away to say it looked to her like I was always playing favorites with Rosa and "that bunch," and she just wanted everybody to know that she couldn't stand those girls.

I asked her if she knew why. She said she didn't really know for sure, but it just really irritated her that they were always being the "goody-goodies" and sticking real close to me and always suggesting things they wanted to do that they knew I would go along with.

She went on: "I thought this group was for all of us, but they're always the ones who get to make the plans and then the rest of us have to do what they say. Or else, if I suggest something, everybody says it costs too much and so we don't ever get to do what I suggest. It just makes me good and tired that they always get their way! They don't know how to share; they just decide what we're all gonna have to do. Talk about a group for learning to make choices! Seems to me some people need to learn how to share and let other people get their choice once in a while."

All of this was expressed with great feeling; the others fell silent. No one spoke up to support her, but neither did they protest.

•

Altogether, the climate at this stage is one of havoc and destruction. However well prepared the worker is, and however well aware of the naturalness of this stage of development, the onset of conflict is disorienting. Knowing that such an occurrence usually comes along in the course of group development does not always prepare the worker for the full weight of the event.

The most important intervention for a worker in this conflict stage is "containment" (Phillips, 1954; 1957, p. 148): containment of herself or himself by giving a nondefensive response, and containment of the unleashed forces by focusing and directing the energy. What the members express in their confrontational statements is true for them, at the moment it is uttered. The worker must try to understand what the person is feeling, without aligning herself or himself with the person's statements.

The need for the worker to be nondefensive is paramount. To the extent that the worker joins the fray, the possibility to help people deal with their feelings and resolve issues is lost. The worker needs to be prepared to reply to charges against herself or himself in a calm and rational way; the worker should not feel compelled to sit by impassively and accept as true any criticisms of her or his skills or style. The worker turns the matter back to the group, as in the following example.

•

The group of women and men patients in a psychiatric hospital met three times a week. During the 11th meeting of the group, a conflict occurred around issues of the hospital's and the staff's inadequacy.

At today's meeting, Marty was very agitated. He started off the meeting with accusations that the staff were incompetent, inconsiderate, uncaring, arbitrary, abusive, and critical. He included me in these charges. Wanda giggled nervously and said, "Boy, Marty, you're not handing out any Oscars today, are you? And here I was thinking to nominate these busters for the Nobel Peace Prize. Well, I guess I'll have to withdraw my nomination! Woo-ee, fella, somebody sure got you loaded for bear."

Pat, who usually tries to keep troubled waters smoothed because of her own fear of out-of-controlness, spoke up immediately and said, "I think Larry's doing all he can with this bunch of crazies. Let up on him, Marty. You're just going to make things worse."

"Talk about abusive and critical, buddy, you just did a job on old Larry," interjected Mike.

Marty turned on Mike. "Shove it, Mike. You think you are so high and mighty well in the head; you just can't face up to what's going on with you so you try to dump it on me. Listen to yourself! Instead of speaking up and agreeing with me that this place is run by a bunch of dum-dums who take delight in keeping us locked up, you start attacking me. Don't let me catch you in the john some night by yourself!"

By now Marty's eyes were flashing. He turned back to me. "You, sitting there with that smirk on your face, watching us chew each other up. You're supposed to be getting us off this jag. Just proves you're an incompetent who couldn't care less what happens to us as long as you get your little green paycheck every month. Nobody around here gives a tinker's dam about us. If they did, we wouldn't have to eat such slop three times a day and sleep on the same sheets two weeks at a time. And you think this getting together to talk three times a week is doing us some good! All it does is raise my blood pressure. You and all the other junior shrinks around here are the ones who ought to be locked up, not us."

Mike had retreated verbally, but I noticed that he was clenching and unclenching his fists. Wanda was still giggling to herself, but much more quietly now. Pat was clearly horrified by Marty's outburst. I was fighting down my gut response, which was to defend myself and the hospital. I recognized that this was not the time to discuss the institution's problems caused by a budget cut from the legislature, which had severely impaired our housekeeping budget.

I realized that I needed to address Marty directly and, by what I said, try to help them control the anger that was on the verge of spreading to all of them. So, I said, "Listen to me, Marty. You have these complaints, and they're important. I am concerned. But I can't take them all on at once, in the way you said them just now. I don't know what it is you want me to respond to. So, tell me about them, one by one. Maybe I can help."

•

There may be occasions when a group's conflict stage properly leads to the dissolution of the group. All guides to group composition are only guides and not predictors, and there is always the possibility that the assembled configuration of people will not be able to work together once they begin to meet and interact. Personality or behavioral factors may block the growth of cohesion or prevent the group from melding individual objectives into a collective goal. In such cases, the group ought to disband and the members be referred elsewhere. Nothing would be gained by keeping a mismatched set of persons together.

The following example illustrates the process of deciding that disbanding is the thing to do.

•

This group, a leadership development group at the community center, had just never been able to come together. Part of the problem was that, although the members all lived in the same neighborhood, the city's school busing program resulted in their going to two different high schools, and the two high schools were rivals. The teenagers had all grown up together, but they went in two different directions every morning when the school buses entered the area.

At the center, we had counted on their common identification with the neighborhood being enough to forge a bond of cohesion among them. But we had not counted on the conflicting loyalties and the turmoil the teens would be feeling over being the ones who helped integrate the predominantly white schools. The members had been screened and selected by us, and we had tried to honor their choices of others in the neighborhood with whom they wanted to associate. However, after seven meetings of the school-year-long program, they were no nearer cohesion than if we had picked people up off the streets downtown.

Among other things, members kept asking to bring friends to group meetings. During the pregroup interviews we had tried to make clear the basis for group composition, and we had set down ground rules in the first meeting. Because they spent so many hours of their day away from their friends, when they were back in the neighborhood they wanted to spend as much time as possible with them. Each time the issue came up, I tried to reiterate the basis of group composition (why they were the ones who were in the group and not others) and the purpose of the group related to that ("You're here because you've been identified as leaders and you've agreed to help us with the younger children's programs and to get leadership training along with that"); but their requests persisted.

At this particular meeting, the question came up again. Yvette asked if she could start bringing Marshelle to group meetings. I started into the usual rationale for this group's existence. At this point, Tony picked up the question. "Yeah, every time it's the same thing. Nobody but us can belong. Well, damn, I want to see my friends, too, and have time to spend with them. Between the hours every day I spend on that school bus and the time I put in here at the center with those snotty-nosed little kids and my homework, man, I just don't get to see my buddies and hang out with them like I want to." The others echoed Tony's remarks.

I said I thought we were smack up in front of a big problem; one that had existed from the very beginning. I said that I'd tried to explain the center's basis for establishing this group, but that it seemed to me that they were still having trouble with it. I reminded them of the process we'd gone through putting them in this group and that, at the time they agreed to join, they had each identified the others who were here as people they recognized as leaders and as people they wanted to be in a group with. They agreed that had been true earlier in the fall, but said that now that school schedules were a reality, they were having second thoughts.

"See, Kathy," said Silena. "I didn't know what it would really be like when I had to go to Roads High School and not see the friends I've had since grade school. Now that the school year is really here, I don't want to be a member of this group if it means I can't see Mona and Princess and Junie like I want to. I got nothin' against all you other guys; I been knowin' you ever since we moved here, but if bein' in this group cuts me off from my friends—well, I don't want it!"

I said I thought we ought to decide right now what we wanted to do. It was a rough time for them; they wanted the prestige and status of being identified with leaders and having the littler children in the center looking up to them; but finally, and not all that easily, they decided they would be better off if the group ended. So it did.

•

There may be other reasons for a group's dissolution. A worker's inexperience or incompetence may justify criticism by the group members. It is to be earnestly desired that such would not be the case, but it must be recognized that it could happen.

An inexperienced worker can gain experience, by working with a more practiced worker or by working under supervision. Incompetence is a more serious issue. After a time, the members would probably take the matter into their own hands and dissolve the group, either formally or by failing to appear. This could not long escape the notice of agency administrators, and administrative correction could possibly keep such an occurrence from happening in the future. However, that is not helpful to the members caught in such a situation, and other remedies should be available to them.

However, the basic concern in this stage, when the dynamic is conflict, is usually not the worker's inexperience or incompetence. The primary issue is the struggle of the members to possess their own experience, to shape the group in the image of their own definition, and to reduce the power differential they perceive between themselves and the worker. The members do not focus on an evaluation of the worker's competence, but rather on their individual and collective need to have the group be what they want it to be.

The worker should reply in a calm and rational manner to members' criticisms about the amount of control held by her or him, and should turn the issue back to the group. In doing this, the worker will ask how widespread the discontent is and what the group wants to do about the situation. It is essential for the future functioning of the group that its capacity to manage its own affairs be tried out in this stage.

Not every group struggles with ownership issues; yet there may be an uneven and spasmodic course toward integration and goal achievement. This process of fits and starts is the disequilibrium stage.

○

Dynamics of Disequilibrium

Almost without fail, the disequilibrium will be prompted by a member or members, as when ownership conflicts flare. This process of alternately working on task, stopping to reflect on performance and progress, moving on, rechecking, and so on is not the same as the periodic contract review and possible renegotiation, which will, in all likelihood, be initiated by the worker.

The dynamic and the climate of disequilibrium are more like floundering; temporarily, neither goals nor means seem to have staying power, as they do when the issue is conflict.

The emotional tone of disequilibrium is disorienting, disquieting, and balance-upsetting. The individual levels of commitment, and the resolution of the approach-avoidance dilemma, may not have been firm enough to power the forward thrust of the group toward coherence and goal attainment. There is a preoccupation with "How are we doing?" and "Are we going where we want to go?" This may reflect that the collection of people is unaccustomed to self-governance and is uncertain about proceeding. Issues that have been decided in previous deliberations may be reopened for further consideration.

Unless the amount of floundering actually overtakes the amount of connectedness that has occurred, the group is quite likely to weather this spell intact. The outward manifestations of conflict are not present in disequilibrium. There is no difference of opinion, competing views, opposing stances, or hostility. There is only a questioning of the group's functioning as a collectivity. The question seems to have less to do with the group's goal, its reason for being, and more to do with the group's operating procedures.

The two examples that follow illustrate groups floundering in progress.

●

The group for battered women meeting at the Safehouse Community Outreach Center had been together for six weeks, the usual length of time for women in the first stages of leaving the battering relationship. They decided that they wanted to remain together for a second six-week period. They stated that they wanted the composition to remain intact and to continue as a "first stage" group, meaning that the decisions about the structure of the group and the program media—topics, themes, activities taken up each week—would lie with the coworkers. First-stage groups typically address the women's need to understand that they had not deserved the treatment they received and that no one has the right to hurt another person.

In the second session of the new six-week period, the routine check-ins were completed, and the common theme deriving from them was identified. The group then started to address that topic. However, one member said, "I really need to talk about something else. I've been having flashbacks to my childhood and I think my dad sexually abused me. I need to talk about incest." The other members sat in expectant silence, glancing at the two coworkers.

"Well," said Mai, one of the workers. "We've always tried to honor the subjects group members bring up. What do the rest of you want to do?" A couple of members shifted in their seats and sank a little deeper into the corners of the sofa where they sat. Lauren put her hand over her eyes. Elly tried to speak but was choked with tears. "I can't," she said. "I can't talk about incest or anything close to it because all of that is too raw for me right now, since I'm trying to talk to my dad about my incest experiences with him and all he does is cry and tell me how he's got too many problems of his own to help me. It's just too close for me to be able to talk about it or hear anyone else talk about her experience." Jean reached over and put her arm around Elly. Ronnie looked straight ahead at the center of the room, with her ever-present enigmatic expression, half smile, half pursed lips. She made no comment.

Barbara, the member who had spoken first about her history of incest, said, with agitation, "I can't do anything else if I can't talk about this. I haven't slept for days; I drive and forget where I am and where I'm going. Sometimes I think I'm just going to lose control completely, and not ever come back to reality." For a long time, no one said anything and no one moved. Bet, the other worker, said, "What shall we do, then?"

Ronnie said, without altering her gaze, "I don't know. It never happened to me but it did to my best friend when she was eight. Then they moved away." Grace, the eldest member by 20 years, said, "My father never molested me, but he constantly ridiculed me. I was worthless, to him." Another long silence. Mai tried again. "Lauren, what's happening? You hid behind your hand when Barbara first spoke, and you haven't budged since." Still with her eyes covered, Lauren shook her head. "Go on without me," she said. "I'm not here."

Nan, who had been silent until now, said, "When I did my check-in, I talked about having met this nice geologist at a Super Bowl party and he likes me and takes me interesting places and really wants to keep seeing me. He is one nice guy, really, really nice. And I'm bored out of my skull! My head tells me I'd be very lucky to be with him, but in my heart I just can't see it. He wants to take me to a party with some of his friends, and I want to understand why I can't get up any enthusiasm. He's attractive; he turns me on. But I think going any farther with him would make me try to dump him, because he *is* so nice and there's no excitement. I want to try to figure out why."

Now none of the women made eye contact. No one spoke. Then Mai said, "Look, we only have 45 minutes left. That hardly seems time to deal with either topic. How do we want to handle this?" Ronnie looked at Nan and said, "I sure know how you feel about 'nice guys.' My boyfriend is still in jail for beating me up, and I haven't been interested in anybody else all these months." No one replied or commented.

After yet more silence, Mai said, "We don't seem to be able to decide. Everyone doesn't have incest issues; for some of you, it can't be discussed. Others want to stay with the original topic, but Barbara still is having her flashbacks. I think I'm going to have to make some decisions. We'll do the 'bad boys' versus 'nice guys' topic next time; during the coming week, try to think why this dilemma is true for you. In the meantime, Barbara, I can tell you I've heard other women talk about their flashbacks. They say they last about two weeks and the important thing is to try not to suppress them or force them out of your mind. They'll stop and you will gradually be less and less aware of them."

The other women were quiet; no one protested the postponement of the initial discussion topic, and no one specifically addressed comments to Barbara. They left rather more quickly than usual, not stopping to chat with each other or the workers.

●

The second example:

●

After more than a year of deterioration and collapse of an administrator's job performance, an interim administrator was appointed. During the time of the administrator's failing leadership, the professional workers had not become splintered and rancorous. In fact, as the situation continued to decline, the workers pulled closer together; they finally cast a united no-confidence vote in the administrator, resulting in that person's resignation. After such a painful time, there was agreement on the need to spend time together to heal and recommit to goals. So the professional workers in the organization decided to use a retreat as the setting for efforts to regroup.

An outside facilitator was retained. That person interviewed each member of the professional body and worked out a schedule for the retreat. The first evening session and the morning of the first full day went smoothly, according to plan. Work was done diligently and with a high degree of accord. After lunch, the agenda of the session was posted and work began. Things went well for about 30 minutes; then a couple of members sat back in their chairs and said, "Why are we doing this? I don't see where we're going to come out." Silence ensued.

The facilitator recapped the planning process and the shaping of the agenda, checking as he went, and asked if the group wanted to renegotiate its goal or means. No one did. They agreed that the facilitator's plan and planning process fit with what they sensed needed to be done. The problem, they said, was that they couldn't quite see where they would come out if they pursued the current activities. They agreed that the agenda item for the session was one that they had said needed to be addressed and dealt with. It was simply that the path to the goal was obscure to the whole group.

Someone proposed that they go back to work on the agenda item, and they did. Forty-five minutes later, the question arose again, "Why are we doing this?" The same processing occurred. Yes, this was an important piece of work; no, there wasn't a problem with the goal. There wasn't even a problem with the brainstorming and processing technique being used. It was a question about how the results of this agenda item's work would contribute to the general outcome of the retreat. Back to work went the group.

About an hour later, the question came up again: "Why did we say we needed to do this?" More discussion, more agreement to trust the group's original stated need for the retreat and its agenda. Yet again, back to work, conscientiously.

At the end of the session, with the work completed as planned and the product finished, the members all leaned back in their seats and agreed, "We didn't need to do this!" There was no blaming, no accusing, no apparent regret at the time expended. The group went off for dinner in self-composed small groups. The evening was unscheduled, and people were free to pursue their own interests. No late-night caucuses met, no skull sessions were held, no strategy designing went on.

The next morning, the group reassembled, addressed its agenda item, and worked effectively and efficiently, never referring to the afternoon session of the prior day. When the retreat ended, and for months afterward, the general feeling was that it had been a successful undertaking; there was a lingering mood of cohesiveness that greatly aided future decision making; and the awkward session has never been referred to.

●

Trying out its own capacity to manage its affairs is one of the ways a group reformulates itself as it passes through the conflict/disequilibrium stage. Although this stage represents the emergence of a new set of group dynamics (as each new stage does), the other three dimensions remain the same as in the preceding stage. The mutual contract is still in effect, the worker continues to occupy a pivotal location and enact a variable role, and group-sustaining media continue to be utilized.

If the group is to survive its conflict/disequilibrium stage and be in a state of readiness to work in the maintenance stage, it cannot stay in disarray. The contract, the role and location of the worker, and the program media being utilized lend stability and continuity as the group system reformulates itself. They build a kind of bridge over the conflict/disequilibrium stage. The members come to a structural arrangement whereby the group is able to run itself on its own steam. When the worker, acting from a stance of containment, defers to the group's emerging capacity for control of its own governance structure, the group's sense of its own identity is reinforced. The group's destiny is in its own hands.

○

Mutual Contract

In the conflict/disequilibrium stage, the mutual contract is in effect. The emergence of this stage is a natural time for referring to the contract, since the members are questioning where they are going and how they are getting there. It is usually the worker who brings up the reference to the contract, asking the group, "Are you wanting to take a new look at what we are doing and where we're going?" and keeping the ensuing discussion focused on the contract.

Much of what goes on, during this stage, is about the reformulation of the group system, on its way to its most mature form of functioning; so it would not be unusual for the statement of goals and means—that is, the mutual contract—to undergo more than one revision. This is true whether the group dynamics are those of conflict or those of disequilibrium.

•

It was the seventh meeting of the adolescent-family group at the community mental health center. The purpose of the group was to help parents and their adolescent children to communicate more clearly, to correct communication patterns that inevitably led to confrontational situations, and to establish family interactional networks that lead to more harmonious living.

At the meeting just prior to this one, one couple, the Bs, had questioned the other families present as to whether they were feeling that the group was helping them. They had not done this in a fault-finding way but rather in a way that seemed to communicate their need for information about how others were feeling. As the question had come near the end of the session, I proposed that we could begin with that question at the next session (this afternoon's).

So, when everyone was present, I began by referring to the Bs' question and asked the group to think about the question, "Are you getting what you're looking for here, or are there some changes we need to make either in where we're going or in how we're getting there?" There was silence at first, and then the parents began to talk to each other, softly, by couples. The adolescents, in each case, seemed not to be involved in the parents' conversations.

After a bit, I said I thought we needed to open up their conversations to a whole-group discussion and get the teenagers in on the question, too. I reminded them that we had agreed at the second meeting (when our group-level statement of their reciprocal contracts had been agreed to) that we would stop from time to time, to take a look at how we were doing. I pointed out that we hadn't done that since we arrived at our mutual contract three weeks ago. Perhaps this was the time, I suggested.

Ted shifted in his seat and said, "Well, the wife and the kid and I had quite a long talk going home after last week's meeting, and it came up again on the way here today. I don't know how all this is supposed to take place, this business of getting our family back on track and together again. I just know that Teddy, here, and I are at each other's throats most of the time. Everything he does just sets me off. I don't know; I thought coming here and talking to other families would help us figure out where we'd gone wrong and how we could straighten ourselves out. But to tell you the truth, besides just telling each other our troubles, I don't feel like I'm getting what I need." He glanced at his wife and son and sat back.

Herb spoke up: "Well, that's where Dorothy and I were when we came into last week's meeting; we were thinking about the same question." He turned to me. "We were agreeable to what you outlined about what this group could do for us; it sounded just like what we were looking for. But after six weeks, we're beginning to wonder if we're the only ones who feel like the progress is awful slow. Things are really generally better around our house, but that might not be too unusual; maybe we just haven't hit a big crisis lately. So we don't know whether it's helping us to come here or whether things have been quiet because we haven't had anything to blow up about since we started. Being so unsure, that's why we asked everybody last week whether they were satisfied with what's going on here."

From the reactions of the others, I felt as if a common chord had been struck. I reflected my feeling to the group and said, "Okay, it seems like you're at the point of wanting to reexamine what this group is all about, what you're doing here, and whether what we're doing is getting you what you want. Suppose we stop for a while and look at the center's purpose for having the group, your purposes for deciding to join the group, and what we're doing to help all of you get what you want."

I restated the center's initial purpose for offering the group and asked each of the families to state their reciprocal contracts. I then summarized our mutual contract and asked them to relate to that from where they are now.

●

There is often a kernel of truth in the members' statements that the group experience is not proving to be what they want individually. What they had previously said they wanted (in the reciprocal contracts) is now modified, and what they had previously agreed to do to achieve what they wanted may also be modified. This is therefore the time for them to reexamine what they want and how they will reach that. A deeper level of probing these issues should result in a renewal of their efforts and lead to a more enlightened and sophisticated agreement.

Before reaching that state, however, the struggle must be clarified, handled, and moved through. Focusing on the contract provides the mechanism for doing this. The worker focuses discussion by asking the members to recall what they initially said they were seeking from joining a group; then the worker considers with them how much of what they initially sought still applies.

●

As the discussion of the adolescent-family group's contract proceeded, it became more and more evident that people still wanted what they originally wanted from the group, and that they were generally satisfied with the way the sessions were being used. However, they became aware of the fact that they wanted to monitor and evaluate more closely and more frequently the progress they were making. They also became aware that more attention needed to be given to strengthening the couple communication between parents as well as working on the parent-teenager relationships. The outcome of this discussion resulted in the following rephrasing of the group's mutual contract:

"We want to meet every week on Wednesday afternoons from 5 to 7 P.M. to talk with each other and share our experiences about reaching family harmony and establishing good communication. We want to learn to communicate in a more satisfying and productive way as couples, and we want to learn to understand and communicate in a less confrontational way between parents and teenagers. To do this, we want to use exercises and role plays in group sessions as well as continuing our group discussions; we also want specific homework assignments to do between meetings, with time set aside at each group meeting to report the results of our homework to the whole group for feedback. At the beginning of every other meeting, we want to check our progress as families and as a group. We look to the agency worker for guidance and support and for help in defining the homework assignments we need to be doing. We will make our first check on our progress at the group meeting after next."

•

The group needs to address both its goals and its means for reaching those goals. The worker may direct the exploration by having the members consider the goals and asking them whether, if they continue to move in the direction they originally chose to go, their goals will be reached. The corollary is: given the goals they originally sought, will the direction they are presently moving in get them there? If not, what will the group now want to do either about the direction they are presently moving or about where they originally said they wanted to go? The answers to these questions need to be measured against original goal statements and a careful evaluation made of the strength of their need to alter their course or change their target.

•

As we begin to discuss the contract I focused on what Ted and Herb had said. I reminded the group that Ted had said he and his family weren't clear about what was supposed to take place in the group. I said I understood him to be saying that they had questions about the means and methods the group would use to reach its goals, and that he had thought just talking to other families would help, but that hadn't done the job for them. I also reminded them that Herb and his family had initially agreed to the outline for the group, but that they were feeling that the progress was slow. I suggested that we take those things up one at a time and add in anything that anyone else wanted to say, as we went along.

"What about it?" I asked. "Are you still wanting what you said you were when we started meeting? That is, are your goals still the same, or should we take a look at what we've said our goals are?"

In the discussion that ensued, the members of the group were unanimous in agreeing that the goals originally stated were still the primary and overriding goals: clearer communication between parents and their teenagers; correcting the communications that led to confrontations; and having a more harmonious family life. However, the parents had come to realize, in the course of our sessions, that they themselves needed to work out their communications as couples—not just the communication between them and their respective teenagers. So, although the original goal was still intact, they wanted to add to it working on couple communication.

Also, the feeling that the Bs and others were having, that progress was slow, needed to be taken care of by altering the means the group was using. Specifically, people expressed the desire for more structured use of the time in group sessions (their request for exercises and role plays came in here); for specific homework assignments both for the couples and between them and their teenagers; and for time set aside for monitoring and evaluating these structures or instruments as well as the group itself.

In sum, the group seemed to be saying that they were satisfied with the goals toward which they were aiming, with the addition about couples communication, but that they wanted to refine the means they were using for getting there and the procedures for tracking their own progress. These changes, they felt, would equip them with more problem-solving tools.

●

With respect to the means to reach the group's goals, the worker will ask the group to reflect upon whether those means are successive approximations of the goals they seek or whether the means, when viewed cumulatively, seem to land them at a different ending point from the one they set out for. Depending on the results of these reflections, the group may choose to select different steps for attaining its goal or it may choose to alter its goal to the one implied by the work it is doing.

The outcome of this review and evaluation will be a reaffirmed contract, perhaps in new language. The contract may be reaffirmed more than once. Clearly, however, it is still a mutual contract, still an agreement among the members, and between them collectively and the worker, to do certain things together in order to reach a certain desired end state.

When the notion of contracting is discussed, the question may arise of what or who the enforcers are. In this stage, it can be clearly seen that the enforcement mechanism is simply the people's intent to do something together. The force of the agreement is as strong or as weak as the intention of the people who made it. If for any reason the intention is not real or the choice not freely made, then it is likely that any penalties or sanctions to enforce the agreement will not carry much weight (Beall, 1972). Moreover, people may agree to something with only partial understanding of the implications and consequences of their agreement, and in the light of newer understanding they may choose something else. It is in the nature of human beings to change their minds, and the use of a contract needs to reflect that.

The mutual contract is a force for stability and continuity during the conflict/disequilibrium stage. The worker's behaviors with respect to the contract accord with the role and location of the worker vis-à-vis the group system. The worker continues to enact the variable role and occupy the pivotal location that she or he had during the formation stage.

○

Role and Location of the Worker

The worker's role and location have been successively defined by the process of contract negotiation, renegotiation, and revision. This successive definition has the effect of conditioning the worker's behavior in specific ways. A contract should refer to the behavioral expectations that the worker and the members hold for each other; if a worker intends to intervene in the event of a serious disagreement between members or in the face of possible harm or self-harm to a member or possible damage to property, then the worker needs to set forth that intention at the time that contracts are being formed. By the time a group reaches the conflict/disequilibrium stage, the worker's pivotal location and variable role ought to be both understood and expected by the members as they and the worker have helped shape them.

At this stage, the worker acknowledges the group's emerging capacity to be self-governing, and at the same time recognizes that the system has not yet fully reached autonomy. The worker stands ready to direct, steer, and focus the group's interactions when necessary and to let the group handle its own process as it is able to do so. The worker utilizes three basic skills at this stage: holding the system steady, turning issues back to the group, and creatively using the conflict or the disequilibrium.

Holding the System Steady

The worker holds the group system steady as the members vie and struggle with the issues of conflict or disequilibrium. This is done in several ways. The worker refers to the mutual contract and may initiate a review of goals and means; these actions represent stability and continuity. The worker tries to be as consistent as possible in the way she or he relates to the members individually and collectively. This consistency is not a matter of the worker's role; that changes from active to facilitative. Rather, it is a consistency in the feeling tones that the worker communicates: the degrees of warmth, firmness, acceptance, directness, empathy, regard, and so forth that the worker transmits to the members.

In the record excerpt that follows, the worker demonstrates the skill of holding the system steady by acting in a calm, nondirective, and non-judgmental manner.

•

The group consisted of 18 adolescent females, ranging in age from 12 to 16, who resided in a child-care facility. It was brought to the staff's attention that there was contraband in the house. The items were discovered, but it was not known who sneaked them in. There was a house meeting to find out who had brought the illegal items into the house.

I called the girls into the meeting room, which had two large couches and floor space for the girls to sit. They situated themselves in a circular formation, with no person in a more powerful position than any other. After making sure the residents were completely aware of the situation, I removed myself from the circle, but not from the room, to allow the girls to facilitate the group themselves. I hoped that the girls would be attracted enough to each other to bring about the desired outcome without me intervening.

The first thing I observed was that morale was low. The majority of the girls were angry and appeared to feel betrayed by the person(s) who brought in the contraband. Immediately, Stephanie demanded to know who did it. She expressed how unfair it was that whoever had done this was so selfish in not considering what would happen to the rest of the group. Several others clamored in agreement. Patty went on to say she overheard Sara and Joyce in the bathroom talking about cigarettes. Joyce became very verbal, stating she had no idea there was contraband in the house, and that Patty had no right to blame her. Patty and Joyce continued their arguing. Allysa, Carlie, and Joan all said how stupid this was and that whoever did it should just confess, because they did not want the whole house to be punished. Stephanie agreed with them and said, "If I get punished for something I did not do, I'm going to hurt someone." She looked directly into Carol's face. Meanwhile, those who were not involved in the discussion were fighting.

Janice, who had been sitting very quietly, stood up and yelled for everyone to shut up. She said there was no way they would find anything out if people didn't stop arguing. She sat back down. No one said a word. Cloe then turned to Angel and said, "You were going to try to get some on your home pass and bring it back." Mercy and Tara burst into tears, crying about how unfair everything was. The girls began to fight among themselves again. Wendy, who had used the house meeting as an opportunity to vent all her dislike for Georgia, stood up and said to no one in particular that she thought this was dumb and that she refused to stay. She stomped out of the room without anyone trying to stop her.

I had not been an active participant in the group's process. I remained more on the periphery, thinking the girls had a common desire and bond between them that would enable them to be protective of group norms and encourage the deviants to conform.

After a while, I said to the girls, "I am getting the feeling, from listening to you, that you are very angry with each other and with the staff." I realized I had their full attention so I went on. "I also get the feeling you are mad at each other because you all thought there was more trust in the house." I could feel the tension easing in the room. The girls were talking at a normal level instead of shouting and blaming each other. Even Wendy ventured back into the room to join the group.

The girls were talking about all the reasons why someone should admit to what they had done. They then began to discuss what they would do with the person or persons when they found out. After they had discussed this at great length, I asked, "What has been decided?" Allysa said, "We think it is important for the person to confess, because if they don't confess, the staff will give the whole house punishments, and when we do find out who really did it we will treat them really bad." I asked for a show of hands of all who agreed; almost everyone did.

After the girls had decided on how the culprit would be treated, and why she should confess, the only thing left was for the guilty party or parties to admit to what they had done. With the goal successfully reached, the residents were highly praised for doing such a great job working together, and the house meeting ended.

•

Turning Issues Back to the Group

In turning issues back to the group, the worker acknowledges that she or he is gradually relinquishing the power inherent in the worker role. The worker's power status is under scrutiny anyway, as the members question whether their experience, and the worker's contribution, has been helpful so far. The members see the power differential to be less than it was; the worker is now seen as being a little nearer their size, and this makes it possible for the members to criticize the worker. When the members are vying for ownership of the group, the wisest intervention for the worker is to join their struggle and to put issues and decisions back to them. The worker does not wholly give up her or his power, but holds back from what had previously been a more directive and active performance.

The precise meaning of being pivotal and variable is that the worker is ready to be more central and primary at times and at other times to move back from primacy and centrality. Turning issues back to the group exemplifies this role and this location in that, if the group is able to handle its own business, the worker does not need to focus and guide the group's processes. On the other hand, if the group seems to have no idea or ability about where to begin and how to address its questions, the worker will again be primary and central and answer questions directly or offer a couple of alternatives to the group to get started handling its issues.

The following record excerpt shows a group using its collective power to overturn a worker's decision, and the worker facilitating that by turning the issue back to the group.

•

When the members of the teenage group came into the meeting room, they were a bit slow in assembling. They were unusually quiet when I turned to their elected president and asked if she were ready to start the meeting. Rather than calling the meeting to order and starting their business session as usual, Michelle looked at Rhonda. Lois poked Rhonda with her elbow. Rhonda glanced around the room and then looked at me and then down at the floor. "That's just it, Nancy," Rhonda said. "We don't want to start our meeting yet because we have to say something." She paused and the others looked away, quiet.

"See, me and the rest of us, well, we were talking over the weekend and we decided that you should let us go ahead and plan to have the Valentine's dance for the other junior high clubs at the center. Two weeks ago, when you asked us what we wanted to do for the rest of the year, we mentioned that we wanted to put on a dance and sell tickets and use the proceeds for our club T-shirts. You said you didn't think we should do that because you hadn't seen any evidence that we were able to make plans and carry them out. Well, we went along with you because you're the adult and you're supposed to help us decide the right things, but it's the end of November already and our club will stop meeting over Christmas, and we want to have a party for Valentine's Day and we think we should be allowed to go ahead and put on the dance."

With the rushing end of what seemed to be a practiced speech, Rhonda let out a breath of air as in relief and sat back. The others said nothing but were now all looking at me to see what my response would be. What Rhonda had said was accurate: I hadn't any evidence that they were able to make plans. The idea of their organizing a dance, selling tickets, and making all the arrangements for the music, for chaperones, for refreshments, and so on felt to me like more than they could do while also making a profit to buy T-shirts.

I said, "You're right in what you're saying, Rhonda. I did say I thought you shouldn't try to put on a dance for Valentine's Day, and at the time I reminded you of how the planning had gone for the board dinner and for the trip to Saunders State Park. Putting on a dance is a lot of work—more work than you have done for anything else this year. But if you've been talking about this, you must have put together some ideas about how you could do it. Okay, tell me what you've been thinking and how your plans are at the moment. Let's see if you have your thoughts in shape at this point. Let's spend the meeting today, if this is what you want, going over your ideas. I'm willing to listen and help you decide whether you can realistically plan to give this dance. I'll be asking questions, though; be ready for that!"

From the discussion that followed, it was obvious that they had gone to work on their thinking. Amazingly enough, they had gotten very specific and detailed in their knowledge of what they needed to do, where they had resources or where they needed to go to get resources, and all the details that would need to be taken care of. Some of their ideas for the music, refreshments, and decorations were rather grand and elaborate, and I raised questions about those; and their ideas of their budget were quite out of line, but we problem-solved around that.

The way they went about listing the jobs and identifying who would do what made me believe that they had given some serious thought to their task, and it showed them working cooperatively and harmoniously. They checked each other out on their ideas, added information, restrained themselves from squabbling over small details, and talked each other out of disappointments when a pet idea was turned down.

When they proposed that I listen to their planning, and I did, they truly demonstrated that they could do the job and do it in a unified way.

•

Creatively Using the Conflict or the Disequilibrium

When the dynamic of the group is conflict, the worker needs to clarify the meaning of the struggle and help the members resolve the conflict. An issue that arises here is to what extent the members of the group ought to be made aware of the dynamics of the process they are experiencing. Some might argue that awareness of the stages of the group process is irrelevant; that people do not come to a group experience seeking such awareness but rather seeking help or change; and that energy and attention ought to be directed exclusively toward such growth. A worker adopting this stance would not call attention to or help the members interpret their social processes: "No need to process the process."

On the other hand, some may argue, consistent with this book, that people process information more usefully and advance more readily as they are conscious of what is happening to them. Bringing the process to people's awareness is consonant with the social work ethic of honoring client self-determination. Garvin (1969, p. 128) said that the use of a contract "has roots in social work's commitments to the self-determination of the client so that the client is not manipulated toward ends he [sic] does not seek through means he [sic] does not accept."

In clarifying the struggle, the worker helps the members focus on the means by which they are being helped—the group forces and processes being part of those means. The worker attempts to bring to people's consciousness the various processes and phases of their group experience. The worker not only monitors and assesses what the group is doing but also helps the members pay attention to what is going on. When conflict is being enacted the worker might put the question, "Does anyone want to talk about what they see going on in here?" This intervention does not necessarily interrupt the flow of the conflict; rather, it focuses it. It will help people be clearer about what their issues are, rather than continuing in an unbridled rejection of the experience, the worker, and other members.

At the end of a particularly conflict-filled episode (either at the end of a session or immediately at the conclusion of an outburst of charges and countercharges), it is a good idea to intervene with a proposal to process what has occurred, and to lead that processing. This is an instance in which the worker does not turn the issue back to the group and does not take a facilitative role or occupy a peripheral location. In this intervention, the worker opts for the primary role and central location.

The purpose of this processing is to help bring things to closure, to help clarify what information people carry away from the confrontation, and to see what level of discomfort people are experiencing. A person hearing negative criticism—or, sometimes, any negative expression at all—may experience a kind of system overload in which her or his receiving equipment shuts down. Nothing more can be taken in and the words that are being spoken sound like noise. Alternatively, the message that comes through, a negative evaluation from another person, may be turned inward on the self. Negative self-evaluation is reinforced, and seriously damaging consequences may result.

A structured process of bringing a conflictual situation to closure is often essential; for example, "To terminate a group session of alcoholics at a point of unresolved conflict could precipitate a drinking episode for some members" (Abrahamson, 1979, p. 7). It is not proposed that workers engage in rescuing behavior or excessive caretaking by trying to prevent conflict or by shutting it off too quickly. It must be allowed to occur when it does emerge (Bernstein, 1965). On the other side of this stage lies the period of the group's most productive work, the maintenance stage: and the group must move beyond the present stage if it is to be effective. Neither is it proposed that the worker try to save the group from its conflict by doing its work for it. The worker needs to let the process continue and not bring it to premature closure or clarify it too quickly. If that is done, the conflict will only go underground to reemerge at another time or in another form.

The worker's intervention may leave people with hurt feelings, but it helps provide information for them. In becoming aware of the manner in which they are being helped, they will be better able to tolerate conflict both within the group and outside it. They will be acquiring tools for use in future conflict situations.

In a group of adolescent males, the worker demonstrates the use of a conflict-resolution technique that might be generalized by the members to future conflict situations.

●

The conflict in the group had almost reached physical combat. Gene and Frank had been jockeying for ascendancy through the whole meeting, putting the other boys down, playing "one-up" about their school and work records, cutting in on my interventions and redirecting the discussion to themselves as models, laying down rules for others to follow but excusing themselves from compliance; in short, needling and taunting and lording it over the others. The other residents had had enough, and they tried striking back directly at Gene and Frank and appealing to me to protect them from Gene and Frank.

The major area of conflict was the double-standard rules Gene and Frank were trying to lay down. The more the other boys protested, the more the two young men announced bases for rule infractions.

I called a halt to this. "Look, we're not getting anywhere in this meeting. Gene and Frank, you're overstepping your place in the house. Rules are determined by the staff or by the staff and all the guys in the house together. I want us to do something different. I want us to take a different tack on working out relationships here. We're going to have Gene and Frank each state their position about what privileges should be given to guys who have reached a certain level, and then have the others restate those positions in their own words. Then you other fellows will state your positions, and Gene and Frank will have to put your ideas into their words. When everybody has had a chance to say where he stands and can say the other side's position, in words the other side accepts, then we can talk about finding a resolution."

I knew this was a technique of conflict resolution, and I hoped they would buy into it. I reminded them that they would not be allowed to evaluate, comment on, or alter the position of either side until all the points had been made.

In trying to get each side to put their opponents' position into their own words, my purpose was to get them to think about the other position and maybe begin to see some good points in it. Those good points could then be the ground for a discussion that might resolve the problem. It was time consuming and the meeting went on much longer than scheduled, but it did lead to a fruitful discussion.

•

In commenting on the dynamics of the conflict, the worker will be providing names for the members' feelings to use in future or outside-the-group situations. In naming and interpreting the steps taken to handle and resolve the conflict, the worker will be helping members develop conflict-resolving skills. In clarifying the meaning of this stage in the development of the group, the worker will be helping the members lose some of their discomfort in the face of difference, division, and disagreement.

These various ways of creatively using the conflict may affect the group processes or the processes that are going on within the members themselves and that will become skills available for their use in situations outside the group. When the worker comments on the dynamics of the conflict and the means of help being employed, she or he clarifies the sequence and instruments of the group form of service. The members can use this information to monitor and evaluate the effectiveness of the group's functioning and can use it as guidance in making system-correcting maneuvers. These worker interventions affect the group's internal processes.

When the worker comments on the steps being taken to resolve conflicts, members are being helped to acquire tools to employ in situations outside the group experience. Likewise, when the worker helps members bring to closure some particularly rocky episode, she or he is helping the members learn to stay with discomfort rather than avoid the situation. In these interventions, the worker takes on something of a guide or a teacher role, helping members be clear about what is happening so that the procedures of problem-solving can be made conscious and available for members' use outside the group.

In the case of disequilibrium, which may result from incomplete resolution of members' ambivalence about joining the group, the worker's interventions do not need to be as active or directing as when the dynamic is conflict. Questions should focus on why the members have agreed to belong to the group, what they seek in joining, and to what extent the chosen means are helpful for achieving the goals. Because the group's existence is not being questioned, the worker's activities need to be of the "How about it? Are we still together on this?" nature.

The mood is not conflict laden, and the questions and comments are not conflictual in tone. However, issues previously decided upon are reopened for examination. The clear path to the goal is not evident, and the group is, for the time being, out of kilter. Spurts of action and movement occur, and then the group lapses into disarray. The worker may veer toward the facilitative role and peripheral location. As the disequilibrium is not threatening to the viability of the group, the group itself may hold the system steady, with minimal activity on the part of the worker.

The example provided earlier, of a group of professional workers on a retreat following the collapse of administrative leadership, portrayed a worker being peripheral and facilitative in assisting the group to resolve its dilemma over its commitment to the task. That example depicted very well a worker's movement from the initially central location and active role to the peripheral location and facilitative role when the group confronted the recurring issue of investment in the session's agenda. That movement is exactly the nature of a pivotal location and variable role.

The worker represents stability and continuity to the group as it moves through the conflict/disequilibrium stage by holding the system steady, by turning issues back to the group, and by creatively using the conflict or the disequilibrium. The worker does this by occupying the pivotal location and enacting a variable role. The media utilized to enhance the group's process may also represent continuity as the group goes through the conflict/disequilibrium stage.

○
Group-sustaining Program Media

The type of media being used in this stage are group sustaining, as was the case in the latter part of the formation stage and as will be the case in the maintenance stage. Group-sustaining media have to do with those activities a group engages in to sustain itself as a system. Within the three phases of group development for which group sustaining media are appropriately selected—part of formation, all of conflict/disequilibrium, and all of maintenance—there will be some differences in the aim or use of media designated in that way. In formation, the media utilized will necessarily be those that nurture coalescence of the members into their collectivity. The group-sustaining qualities at that point need to be those that help to bind the members together and help to strengthen that bond so that the members emotionally adhere to each other. In the maintenance stage, the focus of the media utilized is to aid the group in its coordinated and integrated functioning. The group-sustaining qualities at that point need to be those that will support the group's decision-making processes, strengthen the members' feelings of security and belongingness, and, toward the end of that period, allow them the space to find and express their differences from each other, to individuate.

In the conflict/disequilibrium stage, some thread of continuity needs to be available to sustain the group through its disequilibrium. As the members emotionally and kinesthetically experience the dynamic tension of the stage, they will learn via the program media how conflict can be managed and resolved and how disequilibrium may be put right, and they will experience their growth and triumph in being able to say what they want and know how to obtain that collectively and individually.

In the conflict/disequilibrium stage, the following questions need to be addressed in the selection of media.

- Will each person have the opportunity to express preferences and point of view without being put down or discounted?

- Will each person have the opportunity for her or his time in front of the group?

- What instrument, structure, or mechanism will be adopted to regulate the behavior of members? By what means will the adoption occur?

- What role does the worker take with respect to the media? Is this appropriate to the group's need to acquire a sense of its own ownership?

- Is the activity medium a familiar one, thereby contributing to stability and continuity?

- Does the activity medium provide or require uniting behaviors or separating behaviors? Which behaviors are needed at each point in this stage?

The task of this stage of group development is to resolve the question of the ownership of the group, and to resolve it in favor of member control over the group's processes and structure, both internal and external. This resolution requires opportunities for members to have collective influence over the course and the outcome of the group's life while honoring each member's needs and preferences.

The members need to establish patterns of expressing and hearing points of view, patterns of allowing each person time and space, and patterns of togetherness and separateness. The members also need to experience the struggle of regulating the behavior of others and of having their behavior regulated. In this way, their expectations for each other and for the group as a whole will be communicated. Members need to begin to exercise more control over what the group does, and their involvement in determining the media will contribute to this.

The members need to correct the balance of power between them and the worker. The worker herself or himself will move back from primacy and centrality, will turn issues back to the group, and will engage in self-containment for the sake of member growth; in addition, the members need to confront the issue of worker power and put their needs and preferences into the central locus that the worker heretofore has occupied.

All of these things can be done by the use of media that establish these patterns of behavior. It is not enough for the selected media to be utilized once or twice. It takes practice and reinforcement and repetition for these behavioral patterns to be laid down. As has been wisely said, it is not that practice makes perfect; practice makes permanent.

The following examples illustrate the use of program media in the conflict/disequilibrium stage. The first example shows a medium helping latency-age children to deal with their own reactions to conflict.

●

The group was for preteen girls who were in foster placement. The agency had decided to try to work with them in groups to help them acquire feelings of belonging to a peer-support group, since their future—returning to their natural parents or staying with the foster parents—was so uncertain. The group worked fairly successfully, but some members soon discovered that they could put themselves into ascendancy by putting others down.

In one session, they were particularly hurtful, taunting each other about not being wanted and not belonging to anyone. This was especially hard on one child, who took the remarks very much to heart and grew quieter and quieter. None of my efforts to intervene verbally had much success. I decided to try paper-bag dramatics. I made up a paper bag for each girl and gave them time to prepare their skits. I suggested that each girl prepare to present her skit in a way that would let people know how she really is.

The girl who used attacking behavior most strongly presented a skit in which she was a wicked witch who had power of life and death over everyone. Anna, the one who was being affected by the teasing and taunting acted out that she was the Old Woman Who Lived in a Shoe, except that instead of "giving them porridge without any bread and spanking them all soundly and putting them to bed," she "gave them all jelly to put on their bread and kissed them all soundly and patted their heads."

At the end, everyone decided that Anna's skit was the best and that they would want to be one of her children.

●

    The second example shows a medium that provides stability and continuity for a group that became stuck.

●

In the multiple family group at the mental health center, the group seemed to get stuck at the point that we tried having parent/child groups communicate across family lines. Instead of each family working on an exercise to look at its own communication patterns, we were trying to have the fathers form one subgroup, the mothers another, and the teenagers yet a third, and try out communication between subgroups to try to defuse ambivalent family communications (such as saying "come here" with body language that shuts the other person out). It hadn't been working too well. Family communication lines kept creeping in, and sons and their fathers would get into conflict rather than keeping oriented to their respective subgroups.

I decided to videotape the exercise and then play it back so we could go over where things seemed to get out of hand. When we'd previously tried to discuss this, people's recall wasn't always consistent, and what they recalled was very much a function of which familial subgroup they belonged to. With the videotape and the capacity for stopping action and for instant replay, we could diagnose where the communication began to be mixed. The next step was to ask other members of each subgroup to role-play the conflict in a straight, rather than mixed, communication and to play back the conflict scene and then the resolved conflict scene.

●

    The third example:

●

The group meets as part of a service in the outpatient unit of a community mental health center; members are adolescent males, ages 16–19. They have been referred from juvenile probation, juvenile diversion, department of social services, and the schools. They are youth who are seen as out of control by their family or as being in need of supervision. Because of problems the group members are dealing with, the meetings have not always run smoothly; but this particular session was stormier than usual.

Andy and Bob really went after each other over who was taking up too much time and attention in the group. I felt they needed to understand each other better and to get some insight into their own behavior and the way others perceive them. If this could be done, I thought they might see more of a purpose in investing in the group rather than just putting in their time.

When the eruption occurred, I called a halt. I instructed Andy to take Bob's position, accusing him of monopolizing the group's and the worker's time and attention, and then asked Bob to take Andy's position. At first the heat didn't die down much; each seemed, in fact, to enjoy being able to put words into the mouth of the other. After a time, however, much of the heat dissipated and, although they went on using the other's phrases, they carried less and less strength of feeling.

Soon it became funny, as they dug for stronger and stronger terms to throw at the other but came up with absurd accusations instead: "Yeah, well, for attention next week, you'll probably show up in a pair of purple pants and a pink shirt!" Not only did Andy and Bob have difficulty keeping the stream going with a straight face, but soon all the boys were laughing.

After a while, I called a halt again and asked them what they'd gotten out of the role play. They both admitted that the chance to hear their own position coming back through the words of their opponent had given a different twist to their ideas, and that they could understand better where the other one was coming from. They'd also appreciated the permission to sound off without fearing that what they were saying would be cut off in midair, leaving them frustrated.

●

Summary

Conflict is a vying for ownership of the group, each member exerting as much influence as possible to mold the group according to her or his own needs and vision. This struggle may be read as an indication of the investment each member has in the group experience, because each person's degree of expectation dramatically affects the intensity with which the influence force is applied. In another reading, the group may be seen as dealing with its own life-or-death struggle: does it have the necessary vitality to grow beyond the internal threat to its existence and survive, or are its vital signs so tenuous that it will not recover?

Disequilibrium is a struggle to maintain some degree of balance and stability as the group moves through its course of development. Agreements once believed settled become fair game for redeciding. The progress is spasmodic, moving in fits and starts, but without particular contentiousness.

The group observes its functioning and makes attempts to keep its system on an even keel. There may be avoidance or withholding of full investment pending some sign of the value of making a complete commitment to the group.

The contract in effect at this stage is the mutual contract. It reflects people's recognition that their separate good is to be achieved within the context of the collective good. This agreement will be up for review—and possibly repeated renegotiation—during this phase, as the profound meaning of what commitment to the group experience requires spreads through the members' consciousness. As an instrument of the group's own making and an expression of the members' own intention to work together to achieve something important, the mutual contract helps keep the group system viable.

The worker retains the same role and location as during the formation stage. Thus, the stability and continuity of the worker's stance and performance are familiar. The worker, occupying a pivotal location, is ready to become more or less central, depending on the needs and capacities of the members. Taking a variable role, the worker utilizes three basic skills in the conflict/disequilibrium phase: holding the system steady, turning issues back to the group, and clarifying the group's struggle by creatively using the dynamics.

The media utilized to enhance the group social forces are those that help sustain the group while helping members learn to cope with the dynamic tension inherent in taking control of their group.

Most groups do survive their conflict/disequilibrium stage; it is a necessary phase in their development. However, not all groups experience such a phenomenon. There does not seem to be any difference between those that do and those that do not, in terms of the value of the group experience, its meaning, or its effectiveness; but there may be a difference in acquiring the ability to handle conflict or sustain a center in periods of disequilibrium.

A certain amount of regrouping has occurred in the conflict/disequilibrium stage; the maintenance stage picks up at the point at which some reformulation of the entity begins.

References

Abrahamson, L. (1979). "Termination as a stage of group development." Class assignment, Graduate School of Social Work, University of Denver.

Beall, L. (1972). The corrupt contract: Problems in conjoint therapy with parents and children. *American Journal of Orthopsychiatry, 42*(1) 77–81.

Bernstein, S. (1965). Group work and conflict. In S. Bernstein (Ed.), *Explorations in group work.* Boston: Boston University School of Social Work.

Brager, G. (1969). Commitment and conflict in a normative organization. *American Sociological Review, 34*(4), 482–491.

Fried, E. (1970). Individuation through group psychotherapy. *International Journal of Group Psychotherapy, 20*(4), 450–459.

Garvin, C. (1969). Complementarity in role expectations in groups: The member-worker contract. In *Social Work Practice, 1969*. New York: Columbia University Press.

Phillips, H. U. (1954). What is group work skill? *The Group, 16*(5), 3–10.

Phillips, H. U. (1957). *Essentials of social group work skill*. New York: Association Press.

CHAPTER 7

THE MAINTENANCE STAGE

The maintenance stage of group development may be thought of in two ways. In terms of the separation-union pattern, this stage represents one of the strongest periods of union in the life of a group. It is during this stage that groups are most coalesced and cohesive, that their internal and external systems are most integrated and effective, and that most of their work is done; in short, it is the stage when a group is most united and most productive. Another way of viewing the maintenance stage is as a transitional phase. The group's structure and functioning are reformulated as the conflict/disequilibrium stage is resolved and the maintenance stage is entered. Three of the four dimensions undergo change: the mutual contract is transformed into an interdependent one; the role and location of the worker shift from variable and pivotal to facilitative and peripheral; and the group enters a new phase—the maintenance stage. Only the program media dimension remains unchanged.

Even if a demarcated conflict/disequilibrium stage does not occur, there will be a transition from formation to maintenance, marked primarily by a redoubled commitment to the work of the group. This redoubled commitment would be seen in a spurt of energy, devoted both to maintaining the viability of the group's internal system and to holding firm the orientation and movement toward the group's goal.

The maintenance stage is presented in this chapter according to the four dimensions set forth in this book. First, the dynamics of this stage of group development are described. Then the contract form is discussed. This is followed by a consideration of the role and location of the worker vis-à-vis the group system, and the skills used in enacting that role. Finally, the media utilized to enhance the group's social forces are presented.

○

Group Dynamics in the Maintenance Stage

In the maintenance stage the social forces of role differentiation, norms, cohesion, and decision making come to full flower. These dynamics become the energy on which the group system runs and the glue that holds that system together. It might be said that the seeds of movement from a worker-intensive system to a member-intensive system flourish in the maintenance stage.

A dynamic that emerges during the maintenance stage is that of differentiation. The members find security in the experience of the cohesiveness of this stage, so that they are able to express their difference from each other. In this apparent paradox, the members are tightly coalesced into a mature group form, and that coalescence make it possible to emphasize their uniqueness and individuality.

This differentiation is different from role differentiation, though the dynamic is similar—individuals differentiating themselves from the mass. In the case of role differentiation, individuals sort themselves out on the basis of their typical patterns of behavior in order to create and sustain the group. In the case of the differentiation that occurs in the maintenance stage, members sort themselves out on the basis of their individuality. They are beginning to find their difference from the others. This is a precursor to the individuation that occurs in the termination stage.

Role Differentiation and Operation

In the course of the group's life, the roles (defined in terms of behaviors) continue to sustain the group system and move it toward its goals. In the maintenance stage, the roles shift from their function as creators of the internal and external systems to their function as sustainers of the two systems; the focus shifts from role differentiation to performance. In earlier stages, the worker encouraged social-emotional (or expressive) behaviors that contributed to the bonding among members and helped them use their interpersonal relations. The worker encouraged task (or instrumental) behaviors that kept the group on course with respect to its goals and helped members acquire a goal-oriented outlook. The differentiation into social-emotional and task-oriented roles has occurred and the roles would now be performed to fully maintain the group.

Now, in the maintenance phase, the roles—what some members do to express feelings for each other and what other members do to help the group reach its goals—are almost second nature to the actors. Ordinarily, the worker will not need to take the absent role because the members will be using all the necessary behaviors. Members may very well be initiating the group's business at each session, picking up where things were left at the end of the last meeting, putting agenda items forward, and shaping the content of each session. Members can be expected to attend to the mood of individual members and to the emotional climate of the group as a whole.

The following example shows members of a group beginning to manage the group's process.

●

This was a multifamily group at a community mental health center. The purpose was to correct the families' interactional patterns with their adolescent identified patients, who were being seen individually.

Mr. V was very discouraged and pessimistic about his role in the family; he was without much self-esteem. He felt that his only value to the other members of the family was as the breadwinner. His feelings often led him into deep depression, even to the point of suicidal thoughts and talk.

Mrs. V seemed not invested at all in the therapeutic process. From the beginning, her motivation for coming to the group was unclear, and we were not able to penetrate her wall of defenses. She was not following or participating in the process. If another mother in the group was talking about her teenager's problems and behavior at school, Mrs. V would deflect the conversation to ask what school the child attended, what extracurricular activities the child engaged in, or what courses she or he took. It seemed Mrs. V picked up on the most minute and farthest-removed aspect of what the other people said, and she took the discussion far afield.

One time, however, Mr. V began to invest himself in the helping milieu and began to work very diligently on his own feelings about himself and his role in the family. He began to change the way he talked about himself, his thoughts, and feelings within the group; he also, according to his and his wife's self-reports, began to change his behavior at home. Mrs. V remained distant in group discussions.

Because of the way Mr. V was changing and becoming more assertive, and because of the way the group itself was evolving so as to hold each other accountable for their behaviors in and out of the group, my role became less and less primary. I found myself holding back from intervening into the group's process. The members themselves had begun to confront Mrs. V whenever she began to stray from the discussion point.

One evening, when Mrs. V had picked up on another person's thought and started a digression, Mr. T said, "Wait a minute. That's off the topic; we're not talking about the teachers at Bob's school. We're talking about Bob's behavior at school that gets him into so much trouble. You do this all the time; you pounce on some little detail of what someone else is saying and try to lead us off the subject. It seems like you aren't tuned in on what the rest of us are working on at all; you treat these meetings like social events, talking about schools and sports and everything else under the sun except how we can help our families and ourselves."

Mrs. V began to defend herself, saying she didn't think she had so much to work on. Her husband turned to her and reminded her of his changes and how different their home life was now. "But," he said. "I feel like I'm having to do all of the work myself. It's funny; before, I thought I carried the burden of the family by working hard at my job and bringing home my salary and that's all I was good for. Now, it seems like I'm the one doing the work of changing. It'd sure be great to have you part of this, but like Mr. T, I'm tired of following tangents."

There was silence. Mrs. V was quiet for a time. "I hear what you all are saying. I know I'm not working in here as hard as my husband. I don't know why, and so I don't know what to do differently. I can't promise anything as far as changing my behavior. I have to think about it. I can't give you an answer right now."

"Well," spoke up Mr. E, "we're not asking you to make a sudden turnaround. But we are asking you to try to get involved with us and what we're working on. Think about it—that's all we want right now."

Mrs. P said, "I know it isn't easy to look at some of the things that come up in this group. Lord knows, I go home sometimes from these meetings with my head reeling! But I know I've got to stay with it. I hope you'll come around, too. Can any of us do something more to help?" Mrs. P turned to me and addressed the others through me. "Pauline says she doesn't know what to do differently. Could we take next week's meeting and have each of us state one issue we're blocked on and get feedback from the others? Sort of pooling our resources, I guess." She directed a question to Mrs. V. "Would that be a concrete starting place, Pauline? Maybe it would help all of us," she said, looking back at me.

"How about it?" I asked. "Does that sound useful?" They agreed to try this.

•

At this stage of group life, behaviors in the social-emotional arena often begin to dominate. Having experienced the struggle of the conflict/disequilibrium stage, members will find a way to establish, or reestablish, emotional equilibrium. They may devote considerable energy to the emotional ties among them.

Some members find the conflict/disequilibrium so threatening to their own equilibrium that they cannot mobilize to attend for a session or two. When they start attending again, they and the others will give some attention to their reintegration into the group system. For others, the realignment of the group's purpose to encompass the desires and wishes of all the members may provoke a need to reaffirm their commitment to the others individually and collectively and to the collective endeavor itself. What the members choose to do will thus be based more on their feelings for each other and toward the group than on their overt purpose for being together.

The phenomenon of goal displacement often begins to emerge at this point (Berlson & Steiner, 1964). The members feel so good about being together that they begin to propose additional goals to work on, as a way to insure their continued association. Sometimes at this stage of group development, being together may become an end in itself. Goal displacement becomes a more potent force in the termination stage, but its nascence is in this stage when people are feeling good about being together.

The more task-oriented persons in the group may see this emphasis on emotional ties as irrelevant to the original reason for the group's being together. A self-correcting mechanism is then set in motion, when members refocus the group's attention on its agreed goal. "Haven't we gotten off the track of why we're here?" they will say. Or, "I like all of you, and I like it when we are together as much as any of you do, but I really joined this group to work on some of my own stuff and I thought the rest of you did, too. I'd like for us to get back to that." It is not always a member who supplies the task or instrumental behavior; sometimes, even in this phase, it may fall to the worker to take that role and enact the instrumental behaviors. Generally, this is the one instance where the worker acts as the absent role taker in the maintenance stage.

Norms

Norms are implicated in role performance. In the formation stage, norms were beginning to emerge and influence member behavior toward conformity, which allowed the internal and external systems to be established. In the maintenance stage, the norms have become institutionalized and they regulate the behavior of members reasonably well. The seating patterns, speaking patterns, attendance and punctuality patterns, levels of sharing, amount of confrontation and/or support, and ways of expressing all reflect the operating norms and will be clearly recognizable in a group in its maintenance stage. The norms may be rarely mentioned, and recourse to norm-enforcing sanctions may be infrequent. The norms will just be there and be working.

The worker with the group of chronically mentally ill women living in Chipeta House made the following comments regarding the operation of norms.

●

Leann sometimes interrupts with her own observations about the topic at hand. As in tonight's meeting, she usually avoids eye contact with other group members. Her input, however, is rarely ignored and generally informs the discussion that ensures.

Ginny rarely speaks, and she does so only when asked a direct question. She is, nonetheless, an active participant in the group.

Because of Vicki's unusual behaviors, such as talking and laughing to herself, she has an important place in the group milieu. The group provides a wider degree of acceptance for Vicki than for some other members. It does not comment on her talking to herself.

At other times, the group becomes quite rigid in its enforcement of norms. This rigidity seems to be a response to a major infringement of group expectations that threatens the most basic of the norms (e.g., in tonight's meeting, issues of confidentiality and listening). The group appears to narrow its boundaries of acceptable behaviors in order to bring the errant individual back into line.

●

It is a mark of the effectiveness of its norms that a group has survived to this stage of development and is able to maintain itself. The group's viability depends on the degree to which people can act together in the service of their commonly agreed aim. The group's norms are a binding force in achieving this viability.

Cohesion

A group in its maintenance stage will probably have a higher level of cohesion than at any other time. The desire to be together, even as an end in itself; the early signs of goal displacement; and the push to reaffirm the value of the group experience and reestablish equilibrium are all signs of cohesion.

An example of high cohesion, which led to a group's considering continuing beyond the agreed time limit, is seen in the following record.

●

The women's student group had been meeting for two quarters (20 weeks). It was a problem-oriented discussion group structured as part of the requirements of a course. The problems addressed by this particular group were deviance and violence in society. Over the course of the two quarters, the women had examined various theoretical perspectives on those two subjects, had begun to identify the interrelationship between the two, had developed some interventive strategies in working with clients around the two problems, and had done a great deal of sharing of their own personal and professional experiences with deviance and violence.

A woman faculty member met with the group as part of the course structure. At the last class session before the Christmas break, they had devoted the time to examining their own group processes. They had used that information to be in touch with their development during the second quarter. A feeling of closeness and openness and sharing among the women had evolved. The formal group had become, in many ways, a support group to the women.

All of the sessions had been in a seminar room; but near the end of the two quarters, the group scheduled a session at the home of one of the members. The purpose was to summarize and synthesize their experience. A potluck meal helped contribute to the informal atmosphere. In the course of summarizing their experience, many of the women expressed a desire to continue meeting as a group during the third quarter of the school year, without the requirements of school assignments and expectations. Everyone, including the faculty member, would be expected to continue; they would meet in each others' homes; the topics would be identified by them; and no academic credit would be sought for the continuation.

The faculty member pointed out that groups often have these feelings of wanting to continue, especially when they felt so good about what had been accomplished, but that the momentum rarely held up. She proposed that they be very clear about the reason for extending the life of the group, clear about the topics they would focus on, and clear about their purpose for continuing: was it support, additional learning without having to produce an assignment, or just not wanting to give up being together in a group where good feeling existed?

They were sure that the reason they wanted to continue was their continued interest in the subject. On a high note of enthusiasm and commitment, they agreed to meet on the first Tuesday evening of the new quarter. A meeting place was agreed on, arrangements were made for providing refreshments, and the topic for the first evening was selected. The meeting ended with a strong feeling of closeness and support and identification with each other.

When the first Tuesday of the new quarter arrived, the women did not meet. An informal discussion among them had led to the conclusion that, despite the negotiations which had gone on during the potluck meeting, the proposal to continue had come in a burst of enthusiasm associated with their feelings of not wanting the group to end. They did not meet again.

●

The classic research definition of cohesion holds that it is the sum of the members' attraction to other members, to what the group does, and to the group itself (Cartwright & Zander, 1960). These attractions can be measured, and the degree of cohesion can be arithmetically computed. The math is not necessary; the indicators are evident enough.

When members return to the group sessions after absences following conflict or disequilibrium, it is a sign of their attraction to the group, to other members, and to what the group does. When the members regroup and reformulate their configuration and stay with that piece of work, it is a sign of their attraction to what the group is doing. When members notice the presence or absence of other members and ask the worker for information about the others, it is a sign of their attraction to other members. When people act to take others into account, seeking to be in their shoes when decisions are taken, it is a sign of their attraction to the group. When members take more and more responsibility for what the group does and where it is going and how it is getting there, it is a sign of the attraction that the experience holds for them. These cohesion indicators usually begin to flourish during the maintenance stage, although their roots may be seen before this.

Certain benefits derive from the cohesiveness of a group: communication patterns flow more evenly, and the information communicated is more readily understood by all, because cohesion creates a common frame of reference; and decision making is improved.

A question that often arises is whether cohesion can be increased by what the worker does. The answer is yes, if certain conditions are present. First, the worker needs to have done a thorough job of group composition; that is, there needs to be a reservoir of relational resources for people to engage with each other and identify with each other. Second, the worker needs to assess the social forces that are occurring so that productive connections can be made between the people. In doing this, the worker watches out for people who are unrelated to others and tries to get the others to relate to and include those people. The worker also looks out for subgroups of people who are too closely related and tries to expand their interpersonal network. Third, the worker needs to model cohesion behaviors. This is done by pointing out who is present and who is absent, by commenting on what the group is doing and how people are responding to that, by making reference to "we" and "us" and "our," and by including the group as a whole in her or his remarks in group sessions.

These behaviors of the worker will not guarantee the development of cohesion, of course, because cohesion is principally an outcome of the interactions and emotions exchanged among the members. They will, however, do much to encourage cohesion and demonstrate what it will look like when it is present.

Decision Making

The group's ability to make its own decisions by consensus is an indication of its mature functioning. There are several possible patterns of decision making; consensus represents the most mature type because it best integrates the contribution of all individuals on behalf of the collective whole. Other forms include rule by an individual with or without group discussion, persuasion by the group expert, averaging individual opinions, persuasion by the minority, or majority rule as determined by voting; these all depend on acquiescence, by some subunit of the group, to the preferences of another subunit (Johnson & Johnson, 1975).

Consensus does not necessarily represent 100 percent agreement of all the members on one position; it allows for accommodation to minority opinion, which is appropriated into the consensual agreement. Individual members' positions are heard, people accommodate to each others' positions, and a consensus emerges. People recognize that their individual good is best realized through the common good, and they are willing to give up some of their individual desires for the sake of the whole.

A group in its maintenance stage is functioning in its most mature fashion: its subsystems are well integrated and fully operating. It is not surprising, then, that a group in its maintenance stage, working at peak performance in its social-emotional and task aspects, would be taking decisions in a consensuslike pattern.

Because a group for therapeutic purposes is not usually thought of as being a deliberative body, the question arises of what kinds of decisions the group might make. There are three kinds. First, and most obvious, are decisions about the group contract in its changing forms. Members decide what the group goal will be and how their individual objectives fit into a common goal; they decide how the goal will be approached and what means they are willing to try in approaching the goal; and they decide what standards will be used in determining goal attainment and what corrective measures can be taken to bring closer congruence between reach and grasp. The following record shows a group making these types of decisions.

●

The agency's purpose for this group was to provide an opportunity for adolescent males in foster homes to get together and talk about problems they have in common concerning parental rejection, foster homes, and anything else they choose to discuss. The group met under the auspices of a county public welfare department.

In the beginning, the members' goals were highly individualized: "Try to figure out why we have problems and how to cope with them," "Try to straighten out my hang-ups," "Try to solve problems or get into my own mind and tell others how I feel," and "Find our identities." The first session was spent getting impressions of the purpose of the group. It was emphasized that this was their group and that the worker was there to provide insight and direction, as requested. By the end of the second meeting, some agreement (but not consensus, certainly) was reached on four general goals, to which everyone could relate some of his individual goals: to try to help each other while we help ourselves, to try to be as open as possible, to talk over our problems, to get to know each others' problems.

After several meetings, when the group members had begun to trust each other and the worker and had been able to get beyond surface issues, they spent a session focusing on their interdependent contract. When they had reviewed where they were going and how the group had been for them so far, the worker proposed that they try to summarize what the group was all about. He suggested that they search for a formulation that best summed up their understanding of what they were doing, a few sentences that each one of them felt they could identify with. After several attempts and many suggested changes, the group decided to phrase its goals in these terms:

"We're here to get support from each other in coping with individual situations and in understanding ourselves. We'll do this by keeping each other honest and on track. All of us, including Gordie, agree to keep communication open and to pitch in when we are getting off course. We're all agreeing to attend meetings and to come on time. If we can't come, we'll call someone else to say so."

●

The second kind of decision is individual decisions: the initial decision to come for a pregroup interview, the reciprocal contract, presenting oneself for group sessions, the coordination of individual objectives within the group contract, a determination to change behaviors in certain ways, choosing to do things differently as a result of the group experience; these and other individual decisions are taken in the course of the group experience.

●

At the session where the group of adolescents in foster homes came to the wording of their interdependent contract, the worker asked each member to talk about how he understood the phrasing that was finally adopted. One of the members said:

"I think we are all here to try to solve our problems together. I think we're trying to get a better relationship with our parents, the cops, and all the other people that have thrown us out or are rebelling against us. I think with people such as teachers, parents, and cops, they can't understand our point of view. In other words, we are trying to help each other live a better life. This group has helped me look at the world better. I once looked at the world and thought I understood it, but not any more. I hope at the end of this group I can look at the world better and it can look at me better."

Asked what he was willing to do to help himself and the group reach the goals set, he said he was agreeing to attend meetings, participate in discussions, give and receive feedback, and evaluate his own progress.

●

The third kind of decision taken in groups is decisions oriented toward group governance: norm emergence, development, enforcement, and compliance; the decision-making modes themselves; the means of goal achievement as those means have implications for how the group will function; and role differentiation within the group—which roles are encouraged or discouraged.

Decision making that reflects the strength of meaning of group membership is seen in the following example:

•

The preadolescent girls' group at the settlement house had set for themselves the goal of getting club jackets to identify the group as a club. Over a period of six months, various girls reported on bargains they'd seen in the stores. The cost estimates of these were higher than the group would be able to achieve within its one-year time span. As the club year moved into its seventh month, it became evident that jackets were not within the realm of possibility.

The girl who had the idea of jackets originally, and who had a very strong emotional involvement with the group, asked if it mattered if the club got something else "all alike," other than jackets. The girls thought it didn't matter what it was, as long as it was alike. Another girl suggested sweatshirts, which would be worn to club meetings and other occasions when the Dions were together. The girls responded favorably to this. They discussed colors, and settled on black with white letters, as they had originally planned to have black jackets with white lettering. A trip to a discount department store was scheduled.

We arrived at the store and went looking for sweatshirts. Even within this seemingly easy task, there were obstacles that called for on-the-spot decision making. Either there weren't nine items exactly alike, or the item didn't come in the range of sizes needed by this group, or they cost too much. As the girls met each one of these obstacles, their deliberation was always focused on the elements they considered would adequately meet their requirements for a symbol. They moved from children's sweatshirts to blouses to crop tops to boys' sweatshirts to men's sweatshirts. There, they found and finally settled on nine white sweatshirts; black had been modified to white because nine black ones in the size range were not available.

The process involved here is collective recognition of and commitment to a goal, various suggestions proposed for movement toward the goal, a narrowing of choices of paths open, and a final selection of the path which led to the goal. The suggestions were narrowed into alternatives by a process of sorting out what was possible in the light of reality factors: cost, immediacy of attainment, and substitute value. This latter variable is determined by testing the strength of feeling about an alternate suggestion against the strength of feeling about the original.

•

The maintenance stage is the strongest period of cohesive and integrated functioning; it is the time when the group is most united. It is the time of work. Members' objectives and group goals are blended. Decisions for members focus on the changes they are undergoing, the choices to behave in different ways, the contributions they will make to their own and the others' growth and change, the effort they will make and the part their behavior will play in the maintenance of the group's effectiveness and efficiency. Members are also deciding—and engaging in the group's decision-making processes—about the ways in which their individualized interests and investments will be surrendered or protected for the sake of the greater good for the greater number.

A research study showed that long after the names of other members and the details of group sessions were forgotten, the members recalled the decisions and the decision-making experience within the group (Bossman, 1968). This finding suggests that group workers should give close attention to the decisions and the decision-making process of groups. They should intervene so as to maximize both the process of making decisions and the quality of the decisions themselves. In this way, members will acquire greater skill in decision making; they will become better able to sort out the information used in making decisions and to test for the likelihood of being satisfied with the decision, and better able to mobilize action around the decision.

They will also have available a testing ground for trying out their commitment to the decisions taken. The group offers a forum for consensual validation of individual decisions to change behavior—that is, affirmation from the person's peers for who that person presents herself or himself as being. This affirmation will be helpful when decisions need to be taken outside the group and after the group ends; after the group experience, each member will be able to recall the group's feedback regarding her or his decision-making process.

One other type of decision taken during the time of an individual's membership in a group is evaluation of the experience. This will focus on the individual's progress toward goal achievement and the progress of the group as a whole toward the group's collective goal achievement.

The agreed goal statements of the contract may be fashioned into an instrument for evaluation (see Figure 7-1). The group members earlier declared their individual statements of the group's goals, using the Goals Questionnaire (Figure 4-2). These statements can now be amalgamated into a common goal statement. During times of contract review, renegotiation, or transition, something akin to the Goal Achievement Questionnaire shown in Figure 7-1 might be used to help group members assess the progress they are making toward achievement of each goal.

Individual members will regularly return to their reciprocal contracts and review their progress. Members may also want time set aside to focus on individual goal achievement. Some of this focusing occurs during the maintenance stage, as members orient their activities to the desired goal; more of it will occur during the termination stage, as members prepare for leaving or ending the group.

Figure 7-1
Goal Achievement Questionnaire

Some weeks ago, you said you wanted to accomplish these things together:

A. _____

B. _____

C. _____

Now, let's find out how you think you are doing on these. Think about the group. Read the sentences under each capital letter, below; decide which you agree with most; put a circle around the number in front of that sentence. Circle only one number for each.

A. _____

1. We finished working on this.

2. We are making some progress on finishing this.

3. We are right where we were when we started.

4. We are farther away from this than when we started.

5. We gave up on trying to finish this because it was too hard or because we decided to do something else.

[Repeat this scale for each goal, writing in the goal on the line at the top of the scale definitions.]

One more aspect of the maintenance stage remains to be addressed: the dynamic of differentiation that occurs at this point in the life of a group.

Differentiation

Differentiation is the process by which individual members of the group begin to find their uniqueness, their separateness, from the others. The maintenance stage sees people move toward union after their period of conflict or disequilibrium and sees them stabilize and do their work productively; it also sees them begin to make the transition to termination.

The closeness that characterizes the atmosphere of the maintenance stage also represents a safety zone for daring to risk differences, to express and manifest one's individuality. Just as an adolescent needs to find a separate identity after the closeness of the family of origin, and finds that identity by taking on forms of dress, speech, and behavior different from those of the family, so, too, do the individual members of a group emancipate themselves by beginning to dress, speak, or behave in ways different from the rest of the group. The underlying dynamic is similar: to become one's own person, people need to find and express their own uniqueness. The group experience and close emotional ties with the other members represent the backdrop against which each person begins to find her or his difference from the others.

Fried (1970) has stated that the purpose of all therapeutic encounters is the individuation of the clients; the aim is for each person to find a rootedness within herself or himself. The opportunity to express individuality, one's difference from others, is a vital component of the maintenance stage.

Differentiation can occur during the maintenance stage because the cohesion that exists at this stage provides a safety net for the members as they venture into their own space. Members feel accepted, included, and supported by the other members of the group and feel that their efforts in the direction of change are validated; they therefore feel free to risk being fully themselves. This freedom is not learned all at once or learned only once; but it does have a chance to be experienced and exercised within the secure environment of the group. This dynamic permits and encourages each member to be different and separate within the bonded-together group.

These are the social forces of this stage of group development. The group is closely coalesced and cohesive; roles are performed to sustain the internal and external systems of the group; norms operate to regulate the behavior of members; the social-emotional system of the group may be ascendant as members reformulate and reintegrate their group and themselves in relation to it; decision making is done on a consensus basis; and members find a zone of safety for risking the expression of their difference.

While these dynamics operate, the group contract undergoes a transition from the mutual form to the interdependent form.

◯
Interdependent Contract

Up to now, the members have agreed among themselves to stay together and to work on their collective aims by certain specific means; and they have made a similar agreement with the worker. Now the members and the worker agree together to pool the group's resources to sustain itself. The mutuality of the interdependent contract is seen in the dependence of all the persons together, including the worker. The structure of the mutual contract is shown in Figure 7-2; that of the interdependent contract in Figure 7-3.

The worker now depends on the members' collective ability to manage and sustain their group system and its business. The members depend on each other to enact the roles they have differentiated for themselves, which at this maintenance stage, sustain the internal and external systems of the group. Role differentiation, after all, is the manner in which the group's work is divided.

Figure 7-2
Mutual Contract Between
Members (M) and Worker (W)

Figure 7-3
Interdependent Contract Between
Members (M) and Worker (W)

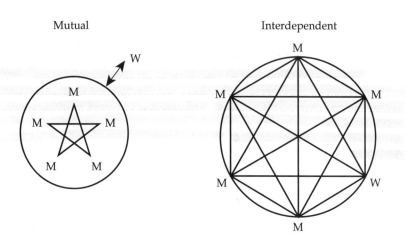

Every person in the group, including the worker, becomes a party to the agreement. Concomitant with the shift in who the parties to the agreement are, the matter of what is agreed to shifts. There is now an agreement among all parties, including the worker, that the system can maintain itself and get its work done. What is agreed to includes, for the first time,

reference to the group as a whole, to the intended outcome, to group content and to means of treatment. Member roles and worker roles are implicit if not explicit thus suggesting something of group structure, as well.

Clearly, the Interdependent contract is the common property of the group as a whole, since it contains all the purposes, goals, and objectives of the clients as individuals and as a collectivity. The contract also incorporates the therapeutic objectives of the worker for each individual..., those which he [sic] holds for the group as a separate entity..., and those new goals or objectives which have emerged either from him [sic] or other members as the group has progressed through various stages of group development. (Estes & Henry, 1976, pp. 619–620)

In recognition of the mature functioning that the group has now achieved and in keeping with the plan inherent in the use of a contract in its changing form, a decision to review and renegotiate the group's contract is in order at this stage. From the ensuing deliberation, the interdependent contract will emerge. The following record gives an example of an interdependent contract.

●

The county department of public welfare, children's division, established a group for girls aged 11 to 14 who had problems that caused the department to get involved: inadequate supervision by parents, parent-child problems, school problems, and emotional problems. The purpose was to help the girls learn to get along with peers, develop some social skills, find and practice alternative types of behavior, and improve their self-image. The group would meet for 20 sessions.

The interdependent contract, established at a discussion during the group's 11th meeting, was stated as: "To get together and share some of the things we have to show and tell, to help each other with problems, to get along with each other. We are going to accomplish this by treating each other well and helping each other not to make fun of other people and to get along with other people. We come to these meetings to make friends with the other kids who come. We are all here to be on good terms with all people. We will accomplish these things with George helping us say what we want and by all of us making plans for getting what we want. Every week, we discuss what we did at the meeting and decide what we will do next.

●

The Process of Transformation

The initiation of the review and renegotiation process may come from the worker or from a group member. A member who focuses on the social-emotional system may suggest that, since the group seems to be doing so well at getting along together and is making such good progress toward its goals, perhaps they should stay together longer and work on additional goals. A member who focuses on the task system may suggest that doing well at getting along together is secondary to the real reason for being together, and that perhaps the group should get back down to business.

Either suggestion would be the opening for clarifying that the group is ready to move on to its next form of contract agreement. The usual procedures for contract review would be employed at this point: a discussion of the goals toward which the group is moving and the efficacy of the means being used to move the group toward those goals; a critical examination of whether the means are taking the group toward goal achievement or toward a different end point; and a critical examination of whether the initial goal is still viable or whether a different goal is to be sought.

The following record reflects a group reviewing its goals and deciding to proceed on the course that had been set.

•

The adolescent boys' group at the community mental health center, working on power and control and responsibility issues, was in the 15th meeting of its 25-meeting time frame. The contract under which the group had been operating for four sessions stated that the group itself would be in control of planning and carrying out plans, and that the members would depend on each other rather than on the worker. As was their pattern, the members were evaluating their progress toward their goals. The means they had selected for moving toward goal accomplishment included role play, field trips, and discussions.

When the contract review began, David, one of the members, said, "I think it's time for us to see how we're doing. We've been meeting 15 times now, and we have 10 meetings left. We should see if we think we're progressing or if we should be doing something different. Charlie, what do you think?" Charlie, another member, replied that he felt things were going okay for him; he found the program media helpful, giving him things to think about and teaching him some new ways of doing things. Bill replied along the same lines.

Rich said he thought differently. "To me, it seems more like what I'm getting out of this is feeling better about myself. I think I see things from a different perspective now. It doesn't mean that I'm any more responsible for my behavior, but I don't put the blame of what happens to me on anybody else, now. I don't have more power than I did when the group started. I'm still a kid living at home with my folks and they still call the shots about things like my hours, and using the car, and where I go; but I feel like I'm different. That's what I've gotten from this group and that's what I'd like to spend more time on. Dan and I were talking about this before the group started tonight, and he thinks the way I do; don't you, Dan?"

Dan, a boy who usually acted out rather than verbally expressing what he was feeling, nodded and said, "Yeah." David said, "That's not enough for you to say, Dan. You have to tell the rest of us what you're getting out of group and what you want to change, if you want to change anything."

"Well, it's like Rich said. I don't have any more power now than I did last fall when we started, but I know I've changed. I don't have to keep getting into trouble with my folks and the teachers at school. I think it's because all of you guys are having problems just like me and you understand where I'm comin' from. You don't take everything I put out, but you let me be myself and I don't get too many hassles from you. Maybe, in the long run, I am learning something about control and responsibility. What I see is doing the most good for me is that I feel like I am somebody. Doing more things to keep me feeling good is what I think we should spend more time on."

Bob, who usually tried to mediate opposing points of view, asked why we couldn't work on Bill and Charlie's issues and on Rich and Dan's, too. He turned to me. "Can we do that, Joe, so everybody can get what he wants?"

"Well, you've got ten weeks left, and we have been working toward the goals you guys set when we started. Maybe the important thing is for us to decide what has priority for you, and whether you want to change what you're working toward or whether you want to change how you're getting where you want to go. Who sees what Bob is suggesting as something you want to try?"

Tom said he thought what everybody was saying was all the same, anyway. "Like," he said, "when you feel better about yourself, you do feel more in control of what happens to you and what you do. I think what we're doing and where our goals are going are okay; they're okay for me. But if some of the guys feel like they want to spend more time on how they feel about themselves, I think we can do that. In fact, I think we can go on doing what we're doing, but just talk more about how we feel, and we can accomplish what everybody wants."

I suggested that Bill and Charlie might think of something in particular they wanted the group to do to work on people's feelings about themselves.

"Okay," said Charlie. "One specific thing I want us to do is to spend one session giving feedback to everybody. Tell each other what our impressions were of each other when we started and what our impressions are now. Then each guy who's getting feedback from everybody else can tell the group which impression is the one that comes closest to what we feel about ourselves, inside. Or if we don't think we come across the way they're seeing us, or if we're trying to come across in a different way, we can say that. And then the rest of us can give feedback about that."

David spoke up to agree with Charlie, as did Bill. Bob said it seemed to him that Charlie's suggestion could satisfy everybody. Tom and Rich and Dan said that was okay with them.

I summarized the group's discussion before we ended the meeting: "It sounds to me like you think we're still moving in the right direction and using the right methods for getting there, but that you'd like to spend some time working on how you feel about yourselves and how that is changing. Maybe what you're suggesting is a small goal on the way to some of your larger goals. Anyway, you have agreed to use Charlie's suggestion of giving feedback on how you come across to people. Can we agree to do that next week?" They all agreed, and we ended the session.

•

Goal Displacement

The contract deliberations must pay attention to people's satisfaction with the way things are going and to the attractiveness of displacing the goal. The worker needs to clarify and evaluate the strength of the desire to select a new goal. This push toward goal displacement may be a sign of the members' attachment to each other, or it may reflect a need to redirect the group's energy. The worker must therefore be closely attuned to the meaning behind what is being said.

Sometimes what begins as a minority position actually reflects a shared sense that something needs to change. This sense may be held by a larger number of people but may not be expressed by them. In this event, the worker needs to stand firm, representing the original purpose in relation to which people were recruited and selected as members. The specific expression of the group's original purpose will have changed over time, but the worker should be vigilant to monitor the content of the contract, to make sure that what is being done and what end point is being aimed toward are still congruent with the initial promise and agreement.

Only in rare instances should the move toward goal displacement be carried to fruition. It is the worker's task to see to it that the group stays within the agreement boundary it began from. Conventional wisdom has it that displaced goals almost never have the staying power required for holding the group together (Hartford, 1972); so the worker should hold the group firm to its original purpose. The issue of goal displacement will reemerge during termination; for the time being, the group will most likely continue with its original, contracted goal and will seek only to reformulate it into the interdependent form.

In those rare cases when a change of goal is appropriate, the worker's role will be to test and clarify as strongly as possible what members now seek that is different from that to which they earlier committed, and exactly what they are willing to do to attain what they now seek. Only within such closely defined limits should the worker help the group move to a new goal.

In the maintenance stage, the members' ability to sustain their group system has become fully evident. The worker is now able to occupy a peripheral location and to enact a facilitative role.

○
Worker Role and Location

In the maintenance stage, the worker moves into a facilitative role and peripheral location. It should be noted that some approaches to group work designate the worker as a facilitator at all stages; the *Random House Dictionary* defines a facilitator as one who "makes easy" or "makes less difficult" some task (Stein, 1971). For our purposes, however, the terms *facilitator* and *facilitative* do not apply to the entirety of the worker role. They are used to indicate that, by this stage of its development, the group has become capable of self-determined functioning; the worker now moves back and does not put herself or himself into the center of the interactional field (Lang, 1972).

The worker does not undertake to do what the group does not do for itself, because the group can now sustain itself. Even when its self-management falters, it has within its make-up the resources to self-correct, and it will not fail completely. A premature intervention by the worker at this stage could shut off the group's development of its capacity for autonomy. Here is the time for the worker to be laid back; not to intervene is the best intervention. It is a time to trust the group process and to let it flow.

This noninterventive stance may be perceived as manipulative; people who are unaccustomed to being thrown back on their own resources often suspect the person who expects them to do that. Their behavior may reveal that they are waiting for the freedom to be taken away. However, when they believe that the worker's stance is authentic and that the worker truly thinks them capable of managing the group themselves, the effect is liberating. The worker's variable role and pivotal location during the previous stage have helped the members sustain their own system.

During the maintenance stage, the worker's location is peripheral: she or he is apart from the group and is not a member of it. From that location, the worker can see, more clearly than the members, the goal and the course of action toward that goal. With that perspective, the worker can guide and support the interactions of the members as they maintain the group for themselves. From this peripheral location, the worker can see the approaching termination and can prompt the differentiation that is essential to termination.

An apparent contradiction needs to be clarified at this point. The worker is in a peripheral location and is of the group but not in it. At the same time, the worker is an integral part of the interdependent contract, as shown in Figure 7-2. The explanation is that the worker is an actor in the system but is not a member of the system. In the agreement structure, the worker joins the group members in agreeing to commit energy toward sustaining the group; in this sense, the worker is an actor in the group system.

The interdependent contract spells out the role and location of the worker; the worker agrees to have no more and no less control than the members have. The worker still has a professional responsibility to see that no one is hurt, to see that people become as autonomous as they can, to see that ethical tenets are honored, and to see that quality service is rendered; but the ownership of the group has passed from the worker's hands. The work of growth and change and the work of sustaining the group is now in the members' charge; the worker becomes peripheral to the group system.

Worker Skills

The essential worker skills of the facilitative role in the maintenance stage are guiding and supporting the group, and encouraging expression of difference. Encouraging the expression of differences is included as a skill of this stage because it matches with the maintenance stage dynamic of differentiation. That dynamic is occurring anyway, in the normal course of group development, and the worker's role behavior can serve to encourage it.

Guiding

The worker skill of guiding consists of advising and counseling rather than regulating and managing. The worker, knowing the course of action to be followed, points out the way to follow that course. The course to be followed is not one that the worker alone knows but the one that the group has chosen. The course is contained in the group's contract; the worker's role is to remind the group of this course.

Because the worker is peripheral to the group system, she or he has a different perspective from the members who comprise the system. From that different perspective, the worker is better able than any of the members to see the course and to indicate what she or he sees ahead; the worker does this only when the members seem unaware of the implications of a particular decision. Guiding, in this sense, helps the group in its self-government and its self-direction toward goal achievement by means it has chosen.

Steering is an aspect of the skill of guiding. The group's contract identifies the goal and the course to be taken toward that goal. The worker then holds the group to pursuing that course of action in the direction of that goal. This is done by pointing out any deviation from the course of action that goes toward the chosen goal. As in steering a boat by a particular star, the point of orientation is chosen and the group is kept on course toward it. Most of the time the movement will be smooth sailing, and the group will need very little information from outside its own system to carry it along. When it does need information, however, the worker will be in a position to provide it; the worker will be ready to exercise guiding behavior from her or his peripheral location.

The following example illustrates a worker's guiding a group toward its goal.

●

In working with a group of mentally retarded young women, the worker actively promoted the maintenance stage. I selected serving refreshments as an appropriate way for the group to maintain itself. By having them responsible for the planning and preparing of refreshments at each meeting, I felt I could keep the members interested, as well as moving toward the therapeutic goals by encouraging decision making and responsibility.

I introduced the idea of their taking turns being responsible for refreshments, and I helped them work their way through the decisions that had to be made. I didn't suggest what they should serve; but once they had said what they wanted at the next meeting, I helped them figure out who would do what, how to get the supplies they might need, when we would serve refreshments, and so forth. Perhaps because the food they receive in the state home is fairly standard institutional food, they didn't have very exotic ideas for the kinds of refreshments they wanted to serve. Everything they suggested was available from the food service department, so I didn't need to help them plan realistically.

Returning to contracting issues is helpful in keeping the group together. I used references to their contract as a weekly reminder of why we were together, what we were going to accomplish, how we were accomplishing it, and how they were progressing toward their goals. I reaffirmed their worth by promoting the expression of feelings and actively supporting them.

●

Supporting

The skill of supporting consists of backing up the group's own capacity to maintain itself. A group in its maintenance stage is fairly well maintained by its internal structure of role differentiation, norm conformity, cohesion, and the like. The worker lends her or his strength in a variety of ways, but all of them are secondary to the internal strength of the group's structure.

One of the ways in which the worker lends strength is by representing the external force that balances the group's internal system. From the initial stage onward, the worker has been an actor in the group system but not a member of it. The worker has manifested her or his staying power and shown that she or he is there for the members and their collective system. For the most part, it is only in the beginning that the worker does some of the group's work for it (acting as the absent role taker, for example). Otherwise, the worker has acted according to her or his belief in the capacity of the members to do for themselves. Now, in the maintenance stage, the worker supports the group's self-governance and self-direction by being in a backup or secondary position.

In lending her or his strength to the group, the worker communicates her or his conviction that the group can, in the main, do the job itself but that the worker's resources are there to fall back on. If the members were fully capable of autonomous functioning, they would no longer need the group—they could leave the group or the group could end. Such is not yet the case in the maintenance stage, although that stage is approaching.

The following record shows a group of children learning to manage their group's processes and giving help to one member by helping her control her own behavior.

●

In the latency-age girls' group at the settlement house, one of the members, Angie, has more than usual needs for attention. She struggles to balance her impulse to gain attention and her nearly conscious knowledge that her society expects her to control this impulse to a certain extent.

Angie is the next youngest child in a large family; the youngest child (a year younger) is cerebral palsied. Often, Angie mouths food after the fashion of a person with muscle-control problems. When we play any game that requires the players to choose a number, Angie always chooses the number 6, explaining that her "baby sister" is six years old. Angie probably receives little attention at home, and imitating some of her sister's behaviors seems to be a way of gaining attention for herself. But this weighs very heavily on the goodwill and tolerance of her peers in the group.

Angie often thrashes about, kicking off her shoes, or runs wildly and randomly around the meeting room or out the door and through the building whenever her wishes to be central are thwarted. At first, I did not put all the pieces together. After one particularly prolonged and intense episode, I confronted her directly: "Why do you have to do this?" Angie reacted to this as a direct attack and fled. Members of the group were confronting her with much the same kind of comments: "You always have to have your own way," or "Angie's acting like a baby," to which Angie responded with her uncontrolled behavior or exploded from the room.

After one particularly disturbing experience, I followed her outside the meeting room to help her gain control. When we returned to the room, she was met with, "Why do you act like that?" (I noticed that this was very much like my own earlier question to Angie.) Angie replied that Janie had "started it." Maria said it looked to her like Angie started it when she didn't get her own way. Dori said, "When you start things like that, you upset everything the club is doing." Angie didn't reply. In this instance, the group, rather than I, held Angie accountable for her behavior and laid down some expectations for her. The encounter was possible, I suspect, because the group knew that a more intense attack would have been checked by me and Angie knew she had my support.

At first, when Angie fled the room I went after her, to get her quieted down and back into the meeting room. After a while, I simply let her go and turned to the rest of the group to say, "Well, it looks like Angie needs to leave for a while." Increasingly, she is able to remain in the room but withdraw from the group. The other members have come to recognize Angie's need to escape and are no longer bothered by it. This has been accomplished by their asking where Angie has gone and hearing from me that she needs to go off by herself to keep from getting too excited. They make such comments as, "If we go on to the meeting room, Angie will come in a while," or "Angie has to be the center of attention," as an explanation to me and a reassurance to themselves that anyone who needs help will find it in the group.

Recently, Angie has begun to incorporate the help available in this group. Janie had been reprimanded by Alice, another member of the group, and had dissolved in tears. Almost immediately, Angie and Josie surrounded Janie "to help her with her problem." They comforted her, protected her from further attack by Alice, and helped me ease Janie back into the group activity. This was a big experience for Angie, in that she was associated with another person in the cooperative venture of helping someone else.

●

Encouraging Expressions of Difference

The worker skill of encouraging expressions of difference helps members prepare for their exit from the group.

In the maintenance stage, the climate is accepting of the uniqueness and individuality of the members. A member may reveal a heretofore
hidden talent, or access to a resource that was previously believed inacces-
sible, or possession of a needed skill or perspective (Shulman, 1971). A
member may articulate a previously unspoken need, or offer an interpretation not thought of by the others, or pose a question that catalyzes or
synthesizes a piece of the group's work. People may now begin to emphasize
their differences from each other; this is necessary to the continued growth
of members.

The needs-to-resources equation has been present all along, but
relatively little emphasized since the convening stage. During the convening stage, it was a simple balance of needs and resources; the focus was
on members experiencing that they possessed the range of needs and
resources that would sustain the group's growth. In the maintenance stage,
the needs-to-resources equation is based on the members' experience with
each other and their ability to trust that they possess both the needs and
the resources for interpersonal relations.

The worker encourages expressions of difference among the members by attending to the spirit of differentiation. The worker's interventions
do not create these expressions of difference, but they stimulate or advance
them. In the language of the theater, on the stage set by the group's history
together, the worker prompts the members' expressions of difference when,
verbally or nonverbally, they manifest an inclination toward them. For
example, a problematic situation might arise in the group session, and a
member might start to offer a contribution but hesitate; the worker would
ask the member to go ahead, past the hesitation. A blocking-point might
be reached, and one member might look as if she or he had something to
contribute but not speak; the worker would state that observation and ask
the person to speak up.

In the following example, members are encouraged to participate
and express their individual needs.

•

The fourth of eight meetings of the church sharing group was attended by five
members. Two of the more reticent members were absent, and the members
most willing to share were present. I reminded the members that we would focus
on their experience with the homework assignment for this meeting, just as we
usually did, and asked them to start.

The group members discussed the assignment one by one until all but Laura
had taken a turn. Laura had been silent and seemed pensive. I asked her how
the assignment had gone for her. She spoke very hesitantly, with long pauses
between her comments. Frequently, I would say, "That's okay, Laura, go ahead;
we want to hear what you have to say." She expressed her feelings of inferiority
to the other group members. They were being very quiet in receiving this
information. A couple of them were glancing at me as Laura spoke.

Nita started to say something a couple of times but held back. During one of the periods of quiet, I nodded in Nita's direction and said, "You look as if you're wanting to say something, Nita. I think it could be helpful for Laura to have some feedback." Group members responded by trying to reassure Laura, describing problems they had faced that were similar to the ones she described. Laura said she thought she would leave the group and get into group therapy where she belonged. The group members told her that they did not want her to leave the group, that they were concerned about her and needed her in the group. Some of the members complimented Laura for putting herself in an extremely uncomfortable position so that she would have the opportunity to grow.

•

To summarize: in the use of the three skills of guiding, supporting, and encouraging expressions of difference, the worker in the maintenance stage is making less difficult the work of the group's self-governance and self-direction. In guiding, the worker helps the group along a course of action toward its chosen goal by advising and counseling. In supporting, the worker lends her or his strength to the group's action as a backup to the group's own force. In encouraging expressions of difference, the worker stimulates or spurs on the differentiation of members from each other by prompting individual contributions.

The final dimension to be considered is the program media utilized to enhance the group's social forces in the maintenance stage.

○

Group-sustaining Program Media

In the maintenance stage, as in the two previous stages, the program media to be utilized are those that sustain the group. At this stage, in keeping with the maturity the group has achieved, most of the control of the program media is in the hands of the group itself. The members have been highly active in assessing their needs and interests, planning and initiating what the group will engage in, and conducting and supervising the program media.

A member might suggest, for example, that the group try some kind of experiential exercise or engage in a certain activity; the member might receive encouragement from the other members; and the members might participate in the exercise or activity on their own initiative and under their own, internal leadership.

The following excerpt shows the members of a group having an influence on the choice of activities.

•

While the members of the junior high girls' club at the community center made taffy and were waiting for it to be pulled, I asked if there was something they would like to do at the meeting next Monday. Susie said she wished we could go into the gym and play, as her sister's club did. I said perhaps we could, and I asked if the rest of the girls would like to do that. They all agreed that they would like to play basketball next week. The second batch of taffy was considerably better than the first, and everyone had fun getting it stuck to their fingers. This batch was a violent blue color, which greatly enhanced the kitchen floor! The girls sang as they pulled the taffy, and there was generally a very happy air. When the taffy was pulled and half of it was eaten, Beth suggested that we go to the game room and play Ping-Pong or pool. I said fine, as soon as we cleaned up our dishes. Janie and Elaine were ready to go immediately, but all of the girls stayed and helped to clean up.

•

The group-sustaining media during the maintenance stage need to support or facilitate a consensuslike form of decision making, strengthen members' feelings of security and belongingness, support the differentiated roles, further norm-conforming behavior, and, toward the end of this phase, allow the differentiation process to begin.

The record that follows illustrates a group enacting its social processes as a fully formed entity.

•

Annie and Pam arrived early for the latency-age girls' group at the community center; while they waited for the others, they played jacks. The girls were quite interested in what we were going to do today. I had put the materials on the table but had not taken them out of the sacks. I asked if they knew what next Sunday was—most of them answered, "Mother's Day." I told them about the hankies and how we could decorate them, then I showed them some patterns. I told them they could use one of the patterns or could make up one of their own. Most of the girls liked the idea of the patterns. I asked all of the girls to sit down around the table before we started.

This is a red-letter day! It is the first time that all the girls have sat down together and have stayed seated—before, the Anglo girls would move away from the Hispanics.

I handed out the hankies, and we passed the patterns around. I made two of each so there would be plenty. At first, everyone wanted help at once. I started at one end of the table and worked around. After I had shown the whole group how to trace the pattern, the girls were pretty quick to select their own patterns and get to work.

We had only six pencils, but the girls who had to wait did so without any complaint; the others seemed to feel responsible for hurrying so someone else could use the pencil. There was quite a bit of grabbing for the textile paint at first; but the girls soon realized that they must take turns on the various colors. By the end of the time, they were saying, "I have the red, does anyone want it?"

Joanie did a very neat job on her hankie, and I complimented her on it. She decided to use some originality and put "Mother" across the center of the hankie. The others copied the idea. They worked along, chatting about this and that, and even though there was some wait for materials, they did not seem to get as disturbed as they have done previously. When a couple would be waiting, they would go over to the other side of the room and play jacks.

By the time they had all finished the project, it was almost time to go home. I had planned to suggest some games, but time did not allow. There was quite a mess from our crafts, so I asked Pam and Linda to go down to the shop and get some paint remover and rags. I asked the others to pick up the paper and the supplies. Everyone entered into the cleanup readily. We all had rags, and we scrubbed the table as clean as we could get it. Jean and Linda asked to take the paint remover and rags back to the shop. I asked Pam, Mary, and Bobbie to get some paper towels wet and wash off the table. They did.

The girls left as they had come, except that Linda and Pam lingered in front of the center playing jacks.

●

The worker needs to ask questions relating to the behavioral outcomes associated with a given medium. In the maintenance stage, this analysis enables the worker not so much to select media as to encourage or discourage the use of media proposed by members. The analysis might be as follows:

- What is the medium being suggested?
- Are the elements of the medium congruent with the stage of development of the group?
- What aspect of the dynamics of the group's functioning are addressed by the proposed medium?
- Does the proposed medium further those aspects?
- Who is suggesting the medium?
- Is the use of this suggestion helpful to the member's status and role in the group?
- Is the medium something that the members of the group have the capacity to participate in?
- If modification or substitution of some part of the medium is indicated, how can the changes be introduced?
- What function is served for the members or for the group as a whole by their participating in this medium?

This analysis may have to be on the spot. A group session might be under way and a member might ask, "Could we do the trust exercise we did two weeks ago? I'm feeling that we aren't sharing as openly as we did right after we did that." Or at the end of a meeting a member might say that, at the next meeting, she or he would like to lead the group in some activity focused on her or his own need or problem.

The worker needs to check the suggestion's usefulness both for the person proposing it and for the group as a whole. There will not be time for the worker to conduct a careful screening of the proposed medium, and it would not be appropriate for the worker to pull out a checklist and try to total up the pros and cons of the proposal. Two options are open: a fast mental check, or turning the suggestion back to the group to analyze. The second option honors the group's maturity of functioning, and is therefore more consistent with the practice appropriate to this stage of group development.

For example, the worker might say, in response to the proposal to do the trust exercise, "Danielle has suggested an exercise for us. What's your thinking about that? Is anyone else feeling that our openness in sharing has closed down? Let's take a look at what that exercise did for us. Are we all pretty much in the same place as we were when we did the trust exercise? Are we needing what that provided? As a whole group? Just some of us?"

This response engages the group in its own process of analysis. The guidance of the worker facilitates the group's management of its own affairs and acknowledges the group's control of its own functioning. The analysis by the group helps to increase the members' feelings of security and belongingness; if they can accept or reject another member's proposal in a supportive way, they communicate not only their collective strength but also their concern for the individuals who comprise their group. It also allows members to express their individual needs in terms of what they want from the group.

The worker's phrasing of the questions and comments, in the example above, demonstrates the worker skill of steering. The worker asks the group to orient itself to its understood goal and to analyze what course of action will aid its reaching that goal. The worker does not so much provide answers as check out the members' awareness of their goals and means.

The worker may have a private assessment of the appropriateness of the member-proposed medium; nevertheless, the group should be allowed to come to its own conclusions based on its own processing of information. To ask questions so as to subtly or openly lead the group to the worker's conclusions is to play "Guess What I'm Thinking" (Postman & Weingartner, 1969) and is controlling. The members should not be required to get inside the worker's head, or to struggle against subtle or open controls. They should be freed to act for themselves, to govern themselves, and to choose their own path, as in the following example.

●

A group of women who live in a housing project had been meeting under the auspices of a community agency for several months. The purpose of the group was to provide support for the women in their socially, emotionally, and geographically isolated life situation. They were all Black women, almost all of them raising a large family by themselves and either receiving AFDC payments or participating in job-training programs. They were seeking social outlets and self-validating activities, and time and space for themselves away from their heavy responsibilities to care for others.

After a period in which I had carried the primary role for planning what they would do from one session to the next, I began to offer a couple of choices. The women had chosen to do stained glass for four weeks; now they were finishing up their craft project.

It was drawing close to 9 o'clock, and the meeting was to end at 9:30. As we started to pick up our supplies and clean up the apartment, Mrs. T asked me, "What are we going to do next week?" I hesitated a moment and then said, "I don't know. What *are* we going to do next week?" The women were quiet, going on gathering up the materials and the coffee cups. I kept at my part of the cleanup, glancing occasionally at them and waiting, but not offering choices as I had been doing. After a bit of silence, Mrs. T, who was emerging as the task leader, said to the others, "Well, ladies, what do we want to do next?"

There were many fits and starts at suggesting possibilities, punctuated by silences and lots of "I dunno's" expressed in a laconic way. Finally, realizing that I was not going to ride to the rescue as in the past, they began to suggest, "I always wanted to . . . ," or "I think we should . . . ." They deliberated among themselves and decided that they would like to spend some time painting the apartment, which the project manager had donated rent-free to the agency for the group's use. They would also make new curtains and fix up the toys and equipment in the two child-care rooms upstairs.

I intervened only to suggest that, if they wanted paint, I could get some from the agency: I could try to get material for the curtains donated by a fabric mill in town; and I could try to get some toys and nursery equipment donated by some other clubs of the agency. They said that would be helpful. So we agreed to begin a paint-up, fix-up, clean-up project at the apartment for the next few sessions.

●

During most of the maintenance stage, a sense of collectivity and corporateness operates in the consciousness of the members. Shaw (1971) has termed this sense "veridicality"; that is, the awareness, in the minds of the members, of the group's existence. Persons who experience this sense of belonging are able to risk differentiating themselves from the others. So, even while the group system is sustained by the kinds of collectivity-oriented program media discussed above, the members also begin to exhibit their uniquenesses (Shulman, 1971). One member may ask for a particular exercise to be repeated; another may share a talent or resource of which the group had been previously unaware; yet another may reveal an area of self-perceived need of growth. As termination approaches, the members begin in various ways to sort themselves out from the mass.

In the following example, members of a group participate in an activity that encourages individuality.

•

This was the second to last meeting of the group focused on life decisions for girls in late latency and early adolescence. Since the program had been focused on helping the girls be aware of the choices open to them for their lives, we decided to use the last three sessions to summarize and identify some of the options open to the girls.

When the five members who were present had all gotten settled, I explained to them that we were going to play a bidding game, where they had to bid for those items they most wanted. Each girl was given $100 in play money and asked to pretend that this was the only opportunity, in their whole life, to obtain the things they wanted. I explained that each item would go to the highest bidder. Each girl was given a sheet with instructions and the following list of items.

1. A good, satisfying marriage
2. Lots of time to do what I want
3. To be able to help someone in need
4. To be a very honest person
5. A successful, satisfying career
6. A big, new car
7. Good, close friends
8. To be a very attractive person
9. To have children I enjoy
10. A nice, big home
11. To be able to travel to lots of places
12. To be accepted and liked by nearly everyone
13. To be confident and to like myself

I asked them to read the list carefully and perhaps mark those things they would like to have, in the order of their strongest wants. I told them they didn't have to bid on everything, and I advised them to watch their money carefully since they only had $100. Once they had read the list, I began the auction. After some initial confusion, the girls really got into the game, and there was much laughter and maneuvering as the girls tried to keep track of the amount of money the others had in order to make their bids.

The highest bid was for the car, $80 by Vonnie. The next highest bid was made by Beth, for $75, to have good, close friends. Margie thought she would like to have a good marriage, and obtained it for a $50 bid. Doris wanted to be able to travel to many places and got her wish with $45. A nice, big home went to Vonnie for $20; the rest of the items were more or less equally divided among the girls, the highest bids ranging from $5 to $15.

After the auction was through, the girls asked to play again. This time they did not immediately start to bid as I began calling the items. They were obviously waiting to see who bid how much for what item, in addition to saving their money for the things they wanted most. This time, the girls had apparently decided that the car, the house, and the opportunity to travel were the most desirable items. There were many attempts at compromise (you bid for the house, I'll bid for the car) and at guessing what the others wanted ("Margie's saving her money for the car").

Vonnie figured out that she could drive the bidding up so that the others would spend their money and she would have enough for the car. She admitted from the start that she was after the car, and she got it for $95. She spent her remaining $5 on an unopposed bid to be a very attractive person (Doris had obtained this for $15 in the first game). Margie got most of the other items, although when the auction ended she still had some money left over. Barb had her full $100, because she did not bid at all.

The girls wanted to keep playing, but now Doris suggested they make up other items they would like to have. We agreed, and I said they could write them on the board if they wanted to.

Margie went first; she wrote that she'd like to have a good boyfriend—not necessarily a future husband. Vonnie said she would one day like to adopt a kid, rather than have one. When we asked why, both she and Margie said there were a lot of kids who needed parents. I asked them if they meant adopting a Vietnamese child, for example, and Margie said, "Yes, but I'd adopt one from Honduras!" Doris and Barb would rather have their own kids.

Barb seems to feel she's destined for greater things; she wrote she would like to become president and stop taxes, to own a bank, to go to Africa, and to live in the White House. She's a very articulate girl who certainly seems to know her own mind.

The auction game went very well, and the girls enjoyed it greatly. I think they realized that in the course of their lives they will come across many desirable things and will have to choose among them. Also that in making this choice, they will have to consider things such as their real needs and how much they can afford to pay. In deciding which items they would each bid for, the girls were engaging in priority setting.

●

Summary

The maintenance stage may be viewed as transitional, with the group reformulating itself after the conflict/disequilibrium stage, and preparing for the termination stage. In the maintenance stage, the group's cohesion level is high and the differentiated roles of its members and their conformity to the group's norms strongly hold the system together. The decision-making form is consensuslike, even while the first signs of differentiation are seen.

The contract changes from mutual to interdependent as the members and the worker agree to be mutually dependent and to lend strengths to weaknesses in a concerted way. The worker occupies a peripheral location vis-à-vis the system and enacts a facilitative role. The shift from the earlier pivotal location and variable role reflects the group's newly mature level of functioning. The worker utilizes the skills of guiding, supporting, and encouraging expressions of difference.

The program media utilized at this stage are those that sustain the group system; they are more under the control of the group itself than at any previous time. Even while the media are sustaining the group, the opportunity is provided for members to differentiate themselves, in preparation for the group's termination.

References

Berlson, B., & Steiner, G. A. (1964). *Human behavior.* New York: Harcourt, Brace, and Jovanovich.

Bossman, L. J. (1968). An analysis of interagent residual-influence effects upon members of small, decision-making groups. *Behavioral Science, 13,* 220–233.

Cartwright, D., & Zander, A. (Eds.). (1960). *Group dynamics research and theory* (2nd ed.). Evanston, IL: Row, Peterson & Company.

Estes, R. J., & Henry, S. (1976). The therapeutic contract in work with groups: A formal analysis. *Social Service Review, 50*(4), 611–622.

Fried, E. (1970). Individuation through group psychotherapy. *International Journal of Group Psychotherapy, 20*(4), 450–459.

Hartford, M. E. (1972). *Groups in social work.* New York: Columbia University Press.

Johnson, D. W., & Johnson, F. P. (1975). *Joining together group theory and group skills.* Englewood Cliffs, NJ: Prentice-Hall.

Lang, N. (1972). A broad range model of practice in the social work group. *Social Service Review, 46*(1), 76–89.

Postman, N., & Weingartner, C. (1969). *Teaching as a subversive activity.* New York: Dell.

Shaw, M. E. (1971). *Group dynamics: The psychology of small group behavior.* New York: McGraw-Hill.

Shulman, L. (1971). "Program" in group work: Another look. In W. Schwartz & S. R. Zalba (Eds.), *The practice of group work.* New York: Columbia University Press.

Stein, J. (1971). *The Random House dictionary of the English language* (unabridged ed.). New York: Random House.

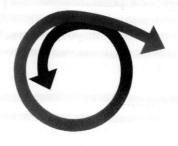

CHAPTER 8

THE TERMINATION
STAGE

Termination is an essential part of the helping process, and professional responsibility has not been fulfilled until a group has been seen through its termination stage. Energies need to be put to the task, as Hartford (1972) put it, of helping people tie up the loose ends of the interpersonal relationships that have been established in the group so that they can make new connections without a string of unfinished business running back to the past. The dynamics of ending need to be understood so that the social worker can help the members to move on from the group.

Although the theme of this phase is "ending," all four dimensions are undergoing transformation. The termination stage has its own distinctive dynamics and contract form; the worker returns to a primary role and central location; and group-ending program media are used.

○
Dynamics of the Termination Stage

Groups begin in separation and move, through the convening and formation stages, toward union. In the conflict/disequilibrium stage, there is

GREAT

FOREWORD BY BILL RICHARDSON

CANADIAN

BOOKS THAT SHAPED A NATION

BOOKS

VANCOUVER PUBLIC LIBRARY

OF THE CENTURY

another period of separation, followed by a time of strong union during the maintenance stage. That period of union is replaced by the final separation of the termination stage. The dynamics of the termination stage are connected with the expression of people's feelings about the separation they are facing, with the work that has to be done at this stage, and with the process of individuation that occurs at this stage.

Reactions to Separation

The emotions felt when a termination is approaching exhibit themselves in all three active agents in the group system: the members individually, the group as a whole, and the worker.

Members' Reactions The dissolution of any relationship is marked by a series of strong emotions, some of them positive and affirming, some negative and denying of the experience, and many of them contradictory. Members may feel ambivalent about ending the experience, just as they felt ambivalent about entering it. Some members may react to the termination with anger, some may experience relief that the experience is ending; many may feel a bit of both emotions, as they recognize the cohesion in the group and their movement toward health and also recognize the imminent withdrawal and disengagement from each other.

An imminent separation often evokes regressive behavior. People may move through a series of emotions not unlike the stages of the grief process as identified by Kubler-Ross (1974), or they may experience only one or two feelings around the termination. The whole group may be experiencing the same emotion at the same time, or the members may all have different feelings. Members may deny the reality that the group is ending, and may deny that they had any awareness that the group would terminate. Members often become angry that the group will end; angry that the worker recruited them into the experience and asked them to reveal so much of themselves, only to announce that the experience will terminate; angry that they are left with unfinished business.

•

When I arrived at the meeting place for the final meeting of the adolescent girls' group on sexuality, girls were already assembled and were eating a large amount of food they had brought with them. Nita reprimanded me for being late (although I was on time). This scolding expressed her anger and perhaps her feeling that I do not really care about the group or I would not leave them.

•

Members may deny the meaning or the value of the experience, deny that the other members or the worker have been helpful to them, and deny that the time and energy invested has brought any benefit to them at all. Others may become depressed that they will lose the relationships they had with each other and the worker, that the opportunity for more growth is gone, and that they did not invest themselves more deeply and work harder and take more responsibility for their own movement within the group.

●

Tina commented, "I didn't get anything from the group experience. It went in one ear and out the other." Another member: "Why does it have to end? I don't see why we can't keep meeting like we have been."

●

People's behaviors reflect these feelings. They may become passively aggressive toward the worker and the other members by failing to appear for meetings, "forgetting" to notify that they will be absent, or arriving late and asking to be brought up to date on what has occurred in their absence. They may forget to bring things they had promised to bring to the meeting or forget to do their homework. Then their forgetting, rather than the material they had agreed to work on, becomes the focus.

People may become very dependent, reverting almost to the dysfunctional, unsatisfying, or unproductive behaviors that brought them into the group in the first place. The latent content of these regressions is a demonstration of how much they need the worker and how desperately they need to continue in treatment. ("See how badly off I really am if you aren't around to help me? What kind of person are you to desert me at this point and leave me in this state?") Dependence may also be expressed in the opposite form: a member may suddenly become very much improved in her or his functioning. The latent content of this behavior is to persuade the worker to stay with them because the worker can make them so well so quickly. ("See how much improved I can be with you around? If you'll just stick around and stand by me, I promise I'll go on pleasing you by getting better.")

Members may become very compliant and conforming, even appearing early for sessions to try to convey to the worker the importance they attach to the worker and to the experience. It is as if they try to buy the continuation of the group by becoming very good members. They may bring gifts, make invitations to dinner or other social events, request a continued social relationship with the worker after the group ends, ask to become friends or offer their address, telephone number, and birthdate, hoping the worker will divulge the same personal information.

The doorknob phenomenon is not uncommon. The person terminating from the therapeutic experience may stand, ready to depart, figuratively or literally with a hand on the doorknob of the office or meeting room, and say, "Oh, by the way, something I didn't mention before is really troubling me...." The latent content is a bid to extend the time for working together by piquing the worker's interest and professional concern. Alternatively, the member may have avoided facing some particularly difficult issue, saying to herself or himself "If I don't talk about this thing that's bothering me, maybe it will go away." Now, in the closing moments of the group experience, the member discovers that this thing did not go away, and she or he wants it addressed. That is what occurred in the following example.

●

We were winding down to the end of the next to last meeting of the young adult group at the community mental health center. The group was for people who were having problems with their self-esteem and were lacking in social relationships. The evaluation discussion had gone pretty well, and I had just started to propose their homework for the last session: to think about what changes they wanted to make in their lives as a result of having been in the group. Dorothy spoke up, "I know I should have talked about this a long time ago, and I've been real uncomfortable with myself for not bringing it up. I'm afraid if I don't say it now, I won't ever say it; and I have to tell people." Dorothy was usually not very assertive and certainly never blurted things out; so her speech was a bit of a blockbuster.

"Go ahead, Dorothy," I said. "You're right, this is the time to say what's on your mind. The rest of us want to hear what you have to share."

She hesitated, and started to apologize for speaking up. "Oh, gee. Maybe I shouldn't have said anything. I'm sorry; here we were, ready to end for tonight, and I had to say something."

The others encouraged her to continue with what she had begun. "We're here for you, Dorothy. Go ahead." I said.

"Well, here's the thing. All these weeks, we've been talking about how hard it is for us to relate to other people and how bad we feel about ourselves and what we can do to change all that, and everybody seems like they've really been making lots of progress. But it's been harder and harder for me to go along with what we're talking about because I know I have a secret that I haven't been open about." She stopped. Everyone else was quiet, looking at each other, at Dorothy, and at me. Tears started to form in her eyes and she put her head in her hands.

"We'll wait for you, Dorothy. You know it's okay to cry in here. Let us know what is making you sad." I spoke softly and directly to her. Brad, next to her, put his hand out and held her arm.

Dorothy went on to report that she and her husband had decided to separate and to end their marriage, and he was moving out of town; but for the time being, they continued to live together. She was having great difficulty maintaining the appearance that all was well.

While she was talking, Dorothy was crying and pausing until she could continue. I noticed that others were very quiet and somber; a couple of the women had tears in their eyes, too.

"It must have been very hard for you, Dorothy, to tell about this," I said. "I want you to know that I value your courage and willingness to face up to the pain in sharing this with us. I appreciate that you decided to talk about this before the group was over. It's a rough experience you've been through; not just the past few months, but talking about it tonight, too. I give you lots of credit for that. I think you can see that the rest of us have been feeling your pain, too, and that we are really caring about you.

"We do need to go ahead with ending tonight's session and with ending the group next week, though. It's what we agreed to, and it's what we've been working toward. But I want to ask you to stay after the meeting is finished this evening, and we can talk about where you can go to get some help with all the feelings that have been brought up in you. There are organizations where people like yourself, who have been through this same experience, meet and talk and help each other. I'd like to talk with you about your getting connected with them. Will you do that?" Dorothy nodded consent. We all sat in silence for a few moments, people not looking at each other but looking at the floor, being quiet and reflective.

"Let's call it quits for tonight, then. See you all next week, when we'll write our future goals, okay?" The others got up quietly and, one by one, stopped to hug Dorothy or pat her shoulder on their way out of the room.

•

Group-as-a-Whole Reactions   It is not only individuals who appear to regress in their functioning when an experience approaches termination. Groups, too, appear to return to a previous level of functioning. The group's capacity to sustain its own internal system begins to diminish. With the approach of termination, members' energies go toward their own processes and are not so free as before to invest in the group's internal (that is, social-emotional) forces. Members tend to withdraw from facilitating each other's participation, from encouraging each other's expression of feelings, and from giving and soliciting feedback about emotions. It is almost as if, sensing the impending separation, the members begin to enact an ethic of "each one for herself or himself."

Conversely, reflecting the ambivalence that may mark this period of group life, cohesion may increase, and the members may become even more helpful and supportive of each other. In this way they can leave the group experience with good feelings toward themselves and each other for having given and received help, as in the following example.

•

At the beginning of the eighth meeting, group members were milling around, and there were conversations among dyads and triads. The assignment for the week was discussed during the first part of the meeting. Ruth and Laura were silent.

I then focused the group on termination. Each member talked about what the group had meant to her or him, with other members responding to these statements. Laura expressed her feeling that the group had changed her life and had meant more to her than being in therapy. She received praise for her participation and growth and many offers of continued friendship.

Members seemed comfortable with each other during the termination discussion, and there were many interactions between members. During the informal social time following the meeting, Laura went to each of the group members to give them a hug.

●

In the termination stage, the cohesion among the members does not simply evaporate; there continues to be a holding on to each other and to the experience. A good feeling, almost an aura of relaxation and comfort, may be felt in the atmosphere of the group session.

●

At the final meeting of the adolescent girls' sexuality group, the first thing I noticed was that all the members were wearing clothes in variations of green and brown. These are two colors that I wear frequently. I commented on the fact that they were all wearing the same colors. The girls claimed that this had not been preplanned, but there were nonverbal indications that some thought had been put into it.

The wearing of similar colors is significant for two reasons. First, it is a way in which the group members could establish a protective bond between them. Second, it indicates identification with me, because I favor those colors. In general, it is indicative of the importance of the group, and the relationships within it, to the members.

●

The indicators of the level of cohesion that were observable during the maintenance stage are not present with the same intensity during the termination phase. The group continues to be sustained by the momentum already built up; it carries out its functions using an accumulated set of familiar behaviors.

One worker commented, in discussing the termination of a group experience:

●

The group seems no longer the primary focus of the members' attention; they are beginning to look inward and contemplate their own uniqueness as individuals. They're beginning to seek outside sources for support. Ambivalence is evident, as members seem to want to move in other directions yet, at the same time, fear movement away from the group. I can offer them my support and my knowledge of community resources—other counselors and therapists and groups to network with, if they want.

●

The group's decision making may begin to deteriorate. Taking decisions in a consensus mode depends on a high level of cohesion among the members and a strong sense of identification with each other; as the interpersonal bonds are beginning to fade and as less energy is being given to maintaining the group's social-emotional system, the consensus form of decision making may not work so effectively in the termination stage. This is illustrated in the following record.

●

The seventh meeting of the church sharing group started with a discussion of termination. Group members were offered the opportunity to continue meeting for five more weeks.

Two couples said they were not interested in continuing. Laura said that she wanted very much to continue, and Bonnie told her that the church would be offering other groups that she could be involved in. Marian expressed concern that I might not have time to continue the group. After further discussion, in which some members did not express an opinion, Maria voiced her feeling that the group had expressed that it did not want to continue. A silence ensued.

After a few minutes, I mentioned termination and asked if the group wanted to discuss it further. After a few more minutes' silence, the homework assignment for tonight's meeting was discussed, until the end of the meeting. There were many short silences and only some interactions among members.

●

As members begin to be more preoccupied with their own issues about separation, the efficacy of the group roles evaporates. Now that members are returning to self-orientation rather than group orientation, some of the differentiated role behaviors may cease to be performed. A void appears, and to fill it the group may regress to a more primitive state of group functioning, as in the following example.

●

At the final session of the adolescent girls' group, one member said that she wanted to role-play. An attempt was made to get a role-playing exercise started, but nobody seemed very interested. There was much fighting, teasing, and cruelty among the members—very similar to the behavior during the initial stages of the group, with the same member bearing the brunt of the attack and many of the same remarks being made. During this time an incredible amount of food was consumed.

The suggestion to role-play during this meeting is an example of reenactment; role playing was an activity used in previous meetings. The regressive behavior the members displayed during this activity is indicative of Garland, Jones, and Kolodny's (1965) "regressive fugue," because of the great similarity between this and earlier behavior.

●

Worker's Reactions   The worker, too, may move back to an earlier way of behaving. This may be an appropriate professional response to what is occurring in the group, or the worker's own emotional repertoire may be influenced by the approaching end of the group experience. However much the worker has contained her or his personal feelings and shaped the expression of them to serve the group, the worker, too, is affected by the imminent ending. Feelings about termination come unbidden and express themselves in unexpected forms. The worker should be aware that her or his feelings about endings will be aroused and should be prepared to use those feelings, just as she or he has used other personal feelings in the course of serving the group.

The worker needs to be vigilant as to the surfacing of her or his own emotions, as in the following example.

●

I was preparing to terminate my relationship with the Dions, as their group at the settlement house was terminating. The club had planned its final meeting as an outing to a state park, and we had talked about how we would build in a ritualized end to the year's experience. The girls knew that that outing would be the last time they would be together and the last time I would meet with them.

The agency wanted to insure that the girls would have something available to them until next fall, when their club would be reconstituted. The program director met with me to get my input as to which girls might need support or service until fall. As we were talking, I thought about my Friday afternoons with them and remembered all the good things that had happened for them individually and collectively during our year together. "Well, listen," I said, "I'm not leaving town; I'll be here all summer. Maybe I could go on meeting with them in the evenings so they can stay together."

Needless to say, that led to a discussion of how workers' feelings get involved in the groups we work with and how important it is to let endings be endings for workers, too!

●

The worker with the adolescent girls' group on sexuality describes how she dealt with some of her feelings at the final session:

●

When Nita scolded me for being late, I felt annoyed. I knew that I was on time! They had all gotten here early and had started eating the food they brought. And I felt amused when they tried so hard to deny that they had preplanned wearing shades of green and brown to the meeting. I could see that they were all wearing those colors, a combination that I wear a lot. I was sure it wasn't just coincidence!

But I bit my tongue and didn't say anything to them. Their efforts to deny that there was any significance to the colors they had chosen to wear, along with what I understood as Nita's anxiety in remarking on my being late, made me aware that they needed to have their privacy to deal with the ending of the group in their own way.

●

In other circumstances, a worker might acknowledge her or his feelings to the group. The worker might say, "I'm glad you're feeling that this has been a good group experience, that you've changed in the ways you've wanted to, and that you're feeling satisfied with what has happened for you here. I'm going to miss our meetings, too."

If the experience with the group has been a particularly satisfying one for the worker, there may be a natural reluctance to let the group go. This may manifest itself as a too-sudden willingness to join the members in displacing the group goal, or as a suggestion by the worker that perhaps the members could benefit from an extension of their time together. The worker may like the members and wish to spend more time with them. Alternatively, the worker may feel that she or he has not been successful with the group and may wish to extend the group's life so as to have further opportunity to get it right. For whatever reason, a worker may manifest her or his feelings about ending in behaviors very much like those of the members.

The Work of Termination

Recapitulation and Evaluation   In the termination phase, when the group's life together is coming to an end, two pieces of work need to be attended to: recapitulation and evaluation of the experience (Garland, Jones, & Kolodny, 1965), and stabilizing and generalizing the change. At the end of an experience, there is often reflection on the value of the experiences for those who have participated in it. This is not the only time that recapitulation and evaluation occur; the contract provides regular opportunities for the experience to be reviewed and evaluated, and assessment has been a continuing worker skill. The termination phase, however, requires that recapitulation and evaluation be a major piece of work. The philosophy undergirding this book's practice approach holds that each aspect of the group process should be made conscious, examined, and made useful for the members of the group. In that way, they acquire mastery over the events of their lives, including their participation in the therapeutic experience. They are in more control of their own affairs, and the magic power ascribed to the worker is contained. When the members themselves can say, "This has been good," or "This is what I wanted and needed to have happen," then they will more confidently employ the tools and skills that they need to manage their own lives.

As the termination stage is entered, the worker will call attention to the approaching end and lay the groundwork for recapitulation and evaluation. The final meetings will come as part of the natural process;

there will be no surprise-party quality to the ending. The worker will keep the group conscious of its time frame.

Taft (1949) wrote that time is the dimension in which persons orient themselves to their existence. Time may be utilized in the helping process to enable persons to focus on the here and now, and to maximize their growth and change (Alissi & Casper, 1985/86). The worker should be aware of the "temporal goal gradient"—the fact that work and productivity tend to increase as the amount of time allotted for the work diminishes (Reid & Epstein, 1972). A knowledge of this "I work best under pressure" theme can help the worker orchestrate group processes against a backdrop of time constraints.

The following example illustrates how a worker helped the members be aware of the time span within which the group would do its work.

•

In the group of mentally retarded women preparing for community-based living, the termination process was built in from the beginning. We started with a plan for the group to last 20 weeks; I knew that I would be leaving at the end of that time. I tried to focus them on the number of times we would meet together. Since I wasn't sure how much they could conceive of the idea of "20 weeks," I got a large wall calendar. I put red lines around 20 Wednesdays and suggested that at the end of each meeting, we cover that Wednesday with a gold star. In this way they could see how many times we had met and how many more meetings we had to go.

I wanted to deal with this in a way that was sensitive to the fact that these clients have a lifetime of unresolved terminations: their families come and go, on visits; they come and go, on home placements; staff members all over the institution come and go; and they may have had several institutional placements. So the issue of time was brought to the members' attention throughout the 20 weeks. As the stated termination point grew nearer, more time was spent on references to what they had accomplished, their feelings, and their goals for the future.

•

When the worker announces, "There are four more sessions after tonight," or "The week after next will be our last session," then the work of recapitulation and evaluation can be addressed. The members may choose to spend the next to last or the final meeting looking at the experience and its value for them. The format for this activity may also be planned by the members. They may have a preferred style of giving and receiving feedback, of expressing emotion to each other, or of accessing verbal and nonverbal participation. Within one ruling principle, that the activity be a common and shared one (Middleman, 1968), the members ought to be fully engaged in determining in what way and by what means their group ends. (This is discussed further in the "Group-ending Program Media" section of this chapter.)

During the process of naming and assessing what has happened, where the group began and where the members are now, feelings about separation may start to emerge.

As they leave the experience, members will revert to a self-orientation and be less oriented to the group as a whole.

•

To recapitulate the group experience, I restated the group goals and asked for feedback about whether they had been accomplished. A few of the members talked about how much they had gotten from the group. Juanita said, "When I started I didn't think I had anything to learn, but I've learned so much." Some members expressed complete—even extravagant—satisfaction, some expressed anger, and some denied the ending.

Their answers were so individualistic that I almost felt as if each one was reporting on a totally different group!

•

The following example illustrates several methods for aiding recapitulation and evaluation of help received through group involvement.

•

The ending activities of the multifamily group were geared toward revealing the structural changes that have taken place in the family through group involvement. The families took turns sculpting themselves as they were in the beginning and as they are now.

Another exercise was simple feedback from all participants of the group. First, each family gave and received feedback among its own members. Then we had the fathers as a group, the mothers as a group, and the children and siblings as a group give feedback to each other. Finally, we had the group as a whole give feedback to each member. This exercise gave the opportunity for each family to process its own experience, since they would be continuing their interactions without the group as support. It also gave members the opportunity to relate to their peer group and to finish with the group in its entirety.

•

During the termination phase of the physical fitness group for adolescent women and adult women serving as their mentors, the worker wrote this about evaluation:

•

I do not think a written evaluation is appropriate for use with all groups, but I think it is useful with this one. I will also have a group discussion on ideas for improving the program. As an oral evaluation often focuses more on change than on judging the effectiveness of the just completed program, I will have the written evaluations completed first.

I also use attendance and drop-out rate as tools of evaluation. A group that has strong cohesion and is meeting members' needs will have a high attendance and a low drop-out rate. By monitoring these details throughout the program, I have been able to intervene early in the process so the group can meet members' needs.

Follow-up on members' continued athletic participation after the group ends will also be a valuable evaluation. Since the major purpose of the group is to establish lifelong healthy habits, the success of the group will be measured by the number of participants who continue to eat healthily and continue in some type of physical activity after the group ends.

Evaluation will be part of the termination process, but I do not want it to be the major focus. As the program gets closer to the end of the 16 weeks, time will be taken in the Monday night meetings to discuss ending activities, and also individual feelings about termination of the group. I would consider the group a success if, during the evaluation, the group decided to stay together as an informal exercise group that would meet at scheduled times. This would allow the members to reinforce their new attitudes and maintain or continue to improve their fitness levels.

●

Stabilizing and Generalizing the Change   When a sequence of events is conceived as a planned change process, it is important to help people stabilize and generalize the change that has occurred (Lippitt, Watson, & Westley, 1958; Pincus & Minahan, 1973). The stabilization of change begins at the termination stage. A general rule of practice is that everything occurring in a group—behaviors, emotions, expressions—should be handled as if it were termination-related once the impending termination has been announced. From that time, the group is no longer on its way into its experience; it is on its way out, and the individuals in the group are working toward completion. New issues and new material can no longer be brought to the group, despite the tendency for the doorknob phenomenon to appear. Growth and change do occur during termination, but the change that comes during this stage is more a consolidation of previous changes than a generation of new issues.

The consolidation or stabilizing of change comes about as the worker helps the members claim for themselves where and how they have grown as a result of belonging to the group. The generalization of the change occurs as the worker helps each member project herself or himself toward the future and into new relationships, events, and situations (MacLennen & Felsenfeld, 1968). Part of this projection toward the future is done in the independent contract, discussed in the next section of this chapter. Generalizing the change may also involve the members' becoming resources to each other, as a way of elaborating the growth that has occurred. When this is an appropriate extension of the group experience, it may be planned for the termination period, as in the following example.

•

In order to help the individuals move away from the sexuality group, I provided them with the names and phone numbers of appropriate resources and contacts. In this way I attempted to show them that the termination of the group signaled the beginning of further growth and development. I felt this would help the members to let go, with the realization that there were other resources and experiences available to them. At this time I clearly stated that although the group would be ending, the members could continue to use each other as resources, and in this way continue to make use of the support system formed in the course of the group experience.

•

Individuation

The primary task of the termination stage is what Fried (1970) called individuation. This process is more than each member finding her or his way of leaving the group system with feelings of strength and confidence to face the future because of the benefits of having been part of the experience. Individuation has to do with the ultimate goal of all therapeutic encounters, which is to help people find "a rootedness in the self." (Fried, 1970). The dynamic of individuation involves finishing any unfinished business with this set of persons, so that new situations are entered with a clean slate and no strings left dangling back to this experience. That process is helped by recapitulation and evaluation and by stabilizing and generalizing the change, so as to leave the members rooted in themselves and confident of their capacity to meet, face, and handle future situations.

In the following example, a worker uses self-portraits to promote members' sense of the changes they have made and to encourage them to see their differences from each other.

•

The group ended with the drawing of self-portraits and a discussion of how these compared to those drawn in the first group meeting. On the basis of this, I could say that besides the growth of the group as a whole, personal growth also seems to have taken place for each of the group members. This individual growth is apparent in the self-portraits. In the case of the five group members who completed both drawings, there is a significant difference between the first and second drawing. This may indicate growth and development of the girl's identity and an improvement in her self-concept through her membership in the group.

Tina's second drawing has the addition of jewelry and more women's wearing apparel, giving a more mature appearance. Her second portrait is also larger than the first—an indicator of growth.

Nita's first portrait is a stick figure; the second is a full-body drawing of a much larger woman. In the first drawing, Nita simply used dots for eyes; in the second drawing the eyes are wide open.

Juanita, Tina, and Rose drew breasts in their first portraits but not in their second. This may indicate that they are more comfortable and less anxious about this mark of female identity and are asserting their identity in different, more mature ways.

In a feedback session I had with the school nurse, I received further indications of the individual growth that took place during the group. She said that the girls were no longer coming to her office so frequently; when she did see them, she was surprised at how good they looked. She said that their physical cleanliness and neatness had improved, and that they looked happier and healthier.

Further indications of growth and change came from the members themselves, in their feedback to me about the value of the group experience. Each member said that the group had been a positive and worthwhile experience. This was reinforced by my own perception that the girls who attended the final group meeting were different in many ways from the girls who came to the first meeting. As the girls left the group I observed more self-confidence and a greater degree of self-esteem, a clearer sense of identity and a more mature level of communication.

•

To summarize: the dynamics of this final stage of group development reflect feelings about separation and behaviors associated with those feelings, as manifested by members individually, by the group as a whole, and by the worker. The work to be accomplished in this stage is centered on recapitulation and evaluation and on stabilizing and generalizing the change. The process of individuation is at work, leaving each member rooted in the self as she or he moves out of and on from the group experience. With the ending comes evaluation and a projection of the self toward the future; these two things are embodied in the independent contract that emerges during the termination stage.

○

Independent Contract

In the termination stage, as the members prepare to terminate with the group and separate from the other members, each person makes a promise to herself or himself of what she or he will do as a result of having experienced this group. The independent contract embodies this promise.

•

It was the last meeting of the group—time for the members to write their independent contracts. Dorothy and I had had a conversation after her revelation about her separation and divorce, and she had followed through on my suggestion to contact the local group for people who are going through divorce. At tonight's meeting, Dorothy wrote and read aloud the following independent contract.

"I've learned in this group that I am a person of worth; that I am not bad because of what has happened. Finding that I could trust people enough to tell them about all of this is one of the most important things that has ever happened to me. From this group, I have found the courage to start to take my life into my own hands. What I will do, from here, is begin to attend meetings of the divorce support group. I have already talked to their worker, and she asked me to come to their next meeting later this week. I'm going to do it, and I expect to find support and help there, just like I found here."

•

A research study found that the factor most contributory to the ability of people to recall a group experience after a period of time was their participation in decision making (Bossman, 1968). The independent contract represents a decision to do certain things because of what resulted from the person's involvement in the group. The self-oriented, change-oriented decisions made by the members of the group will endure as a change-determining force after they leave the group. The negotiation of an independent contract also strengthens their rootedness in the self.

As the person establishes an independent contract, she or he creates a feedback loop for that aspect of herself or himself that aspires toward the goals embodied in the individual contract. The individual contract still exists—only some aspect of it was taken into the group experience—and the person's life goals still apply. Now the person has the changes experienced in the group to merge with her or his individual contract, and system-correcting information is available to help the person continue in the direction implied by the individual contract.

The relationships of the various types of contracts are shown in Figure 8-1. The output of the system—the independent contract—is fed back as input to the original entity, the individual contract. Thus, the person's individual contract (her or his life goals) is changed by the independent contract that issues from the person's experience in the group.

The negotiation of the independent contract in a formal and structured way occurs as the worker engages the members in generalizing their changes. The independent contract is preferably a written one, which represents something tangible for each member to carry away from the group experience. There is no intent to bind the person for all the years ahead. That would fly in the face of the idea of change and growth as dynamic life processes. An independent contract is more on the order of a tradition sometimes used by youth groups, in which young people write their hopes and aspirations for the year ahead on a slip of paper that is collected by the staff and mailed to the young people at the first of the next year. (Perhaps writing on paper that self-destructs after six months or using vanishing ink would not be too far-fetched!)

The only party to the independent contract is the person herself or himself; that is, people enter into an agreement with themselves. The subject of the agreement is a change-based projection toward the future that orients the person to the significant others, values, and institutions that make up her or his social milieu and constitute the arenas of her or his social functioning. The independent contract is shared orally with other members of the group, so that the promise is made in the presence of the helping community that has fostered the growth (Estes & Henry, 1976).

Figure 8-1
The Five Forms of Contracts

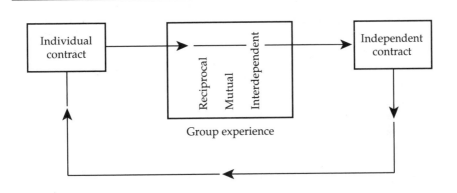

The process of transforming the interdependent contract into an independent one is a natural process. The social forces and dynamics of the termination stage are laying the groundwork for the loosening of ties, for a loss of cohesion, and for individuation. In their interactions, people are pulling back to a focus on self and away from a focus on others and the group entity. The process of transforming the interdependent contract into an independent contract is also a radical one. It moves directly from the most mature form of collective contract to the most individualized form. Whereas the previous contract forms had been built up incrementally, the independent contract shifts back to one person in one move.

The ongoing focus on contract review and renegotiation can help to keep people attuned to their own progress toward a projected goal, as in the following example.

●

This was the last meeting of the group for young men working on control and responsibility issues at the community mental health center.

I began the meeting by saying, "I guess you all know that this is our last meeting. Remember that last week, we evaluated the group and talked about what we had accomplished in the past six months. We agreed that this afternoon, each of you would write down what changes you're planning to make in your lives because of being in the group. You were each asked to think about this as your homework for today. What we'll do is take some time, now, for each of you to write down what changes you've been thinking about. Then I'll ask each of you to share what you've written with the whole group, and we'll give each other feedback."

The boys went to work, with some pausing to reflect and then energetic writing. After twenty minutes or so, I asked them to finish up so we could start. I asked for someone to lead off, and then we would just continue around the circle. David, who had emerged as the task leader in recent weeks, offered to begin.

"Well," said David, "I think the thing I want to do most for myself because of being in this group is to give straight information and straight answers to my folks. I used to think, before I started in this group, that I'd be better off if my folks didn't know what I was doing. Sort of a 'what they don't know won't hurt them' idea. But I found out that I was spending a lot of time keeping my stories straight, and my folks knew all along that I wasn't telling them the truth. So they kept cracking down on me harder. It just got into a no-win situation. But thanks to you guys and Joe and this group, I learned that I'll be trusted, I'll get more privileges, I'll have more control over my life, and my folks will let me have more responsibility if I'm straight with them."

The other boys spoke up to support David, referring to specific situations in the group when David had tried to justify his evasiveness with his parents and they had confronted him about that. Charlie, sitting next to David, went next.

"My goal is to stay out of the hair of the teachers at school. It's not going to be easy because I still get a charge out of watching them get all flustered when I put them on, but I know that just gets me in hot water and keeps me there. So, what I want to do is put my energy somewhere else. I only have some half-way ideas about what else to do, but I've really started seeing in this group that hassling the teachers is a dead-end street, a one-way ticket to the principal's office every day. I've been suspended twice this school year already; one more time and I have to stay out of school for a whole semester next year. I'm not that crazy about school, but if I don't finish I'll have bigger troubles from my dad. So I guess the percentage is in cleaning up my act at school."

The others were very supportive of Charlie. They all went to the same high school and were aware of Charlie's reputation. They gave him good feedback on his honesty and lots of encouragement for his new efforts.

Bob offered to be Charlie's checkpoint: "If you need to touch base with somebody for strokes or just to blow off steam, buddy, look me up. I'm going to need somebody to do that for me, too; maybe we could team up." Charlie enthusiastically accepted Bob's offer.

"Bob," I said, "why don't we hear from you next and see what your idea is?"

Bob started: "My folks put a down payment on a new car for me on the condition that I would pay for gas, their increase in insurance rates, and the car payments, out of what I earn in my part-time job. But the job's such a drag I cut out two or three evenings a week. I mean, the chicks are out there waiting for me and I hate to let them down! The problem is, I'm going to have the car keys confiscated if I don't shape up. So, what I have to do, from now on, is get to the job every day and get to school all the time and see the girls in between. It's a bummer; I hate it. But I want those wheels! So I don't really have an option.

"When I told Charlie I'd be his check point if he'd do the same thing for me, what I meant is that I know the pressure is going to build up and some lady is going to let me know that she's available some evening and I'm going to want to ditch the job. I want to be able to talk to somebody who'll help me get my head straightened out and get on back to work. That's what I mean."

The rest of the group reacted sympathetically; they knew very well the pull to be out and about, especially if they had a flashy car like Bob's. But they all seemed also to be responding to the reality of the choices he was going to have to make. They endorsed his proposal for a buddy system with Charlie and thought there could be some benefit if they all tried it. The rest of the meeting went on in this fashion, with each boy stating his goals for after the group ended and proposing to link up with another member of the group.

●

○

Role and Location of the Worker

In the termination stage, the worker returns to the primary role and central location that she or he took in the initial and convening stages. There are several rationales for this. First, the individuals are preoccupied with their own feelings about ending. Second, just as they had questions and issues as they came into the group experience, so, too, they have questions and issues as they leave it. Third, the worker's tasks at this point are to help the individuals clarify and focus on what they want to take with them from the group and what they have gained through belonging to the group.

The worker has a part to play in helping the members individually arrive at their independent contracts, just as she or he did in helping them reach their reciprocal contracts. However, the movement of the initial and convening stages was toward union, whereas the movement here is toward separation. The worker helps people disconnect from each other by assuming a more central location, redirecting people's energy away from the collectivity and toward themselves separately.

○

Worker Skills

In the termination stage, the worker takes the lead in preparing the group for separating. She or he keeps the approaching ending time before the group's awareness, directs and focuses the expression of feelings about terminating, and facilitates the ending by helping keep the business directed toward finishing well. These are the essential skills of the worker at this stage.

Preparing for Ending

The worker prepares the group for the approaching ending by keeping it before the group's awareness, by using "time as a medium of the helping process" (Alissi & Casper, 1985/86; Taft, 1949) and by activating the temporal goal gradient. Prior to the final meeting, there needs to be sufficient time for the group to plan its last session together, to work through and master its feelings about terminating, to prepare and share the independent contract of each member, and to engage in recapitulation and evaluation (Hartford, 1972).

There is no hard-and-fast rule as to how much time is needed for ending. Some groups are structured to last only a specific period of time; such groups will be aware of the schedule, and may even have a week-by-week agenda. In other cases, the number of sessions will be incorporated into the group contract. Three sessions would be sufficient if all the work that needs to be done is finished. One session needs to be given to a clear announcement that the last meeting will be the meeting after next, and a guiding of the discussion toward recapitulation and initial planning for the last meeting. The next to last session will probably need to focus on people's feelings and the management of those. This could be the meeting in which the group experience is evaluated and the elements of the independent contract are discussed so that members would come to the final session ready to share their independent contracts. The final session will consist of each person sharing her or his independent contract and receiving feedback, the ritualized ending that the members have planned, and some final common activity that enables people to finish any unfinished business (Middleman, 1968).

If the group has been structured over three months or more, the termination phase could extend to four sessions, with the independent contracts shared in a separate session, leaving the last session for the other activities suggested above. This could be left to the discretion of the worker, depending on her or his assessment of the time the group usually takes for processing information.

Focusing the Expression of Feelings

The worker reassumes the primary role and central location after announcing the ending, as the members' feelings about separation begin to emerge. As in the conflict/disequilibrium stage, the worker needs to be contained with respect to the force with which members' feelings are expressed. When feelings begin to spill out, the worker needs to acknowledge the meaning behind the expression, relate it to feelings about termination, and help the members vent those feelings.

The worker directs and focuses feelings by using such phrases as, "It seems to me that the idea of the group ending is pretty scary for you. Can you say what's scary about it?" or "George, you're being pretty hard on yourself and the rest of us with your comments about this group not giving you what you wanted. Is it hard for you to think about losing the support the members of this group give each other?" or "I know that it's sad when we come to the end of important relationships." Any intervention that puts the member's contribution directly within a "feelings about termination" frame.

The use of this skill reestablishes the worker as the center of the structure of communication and interaction. The worker becomes like a discussion leader again, much as she or he was in the convening stage. The worker should try to channel communication through herself or himself and monitor that communication process with each member, so that each person's issues are before the group.

In the following record excerpt, a worker structures and encourages member communication so that each person has a chance to express feelings.

●

I facilitated the group's working through the separation by acknowledging the feelings that often occur during endings and helping the members to express those feelings. In this way, the members were able to verbalize their feelings and deal with them rather than denying them.

I started by reminding them that it was our last meeting and that we had talked, at last week's meeting, about how we would spend our time this afternoon. I suggested that we take turns, going around the circle, with each one of them saying what had been the most important thing she had gotten from being in the group and what the lesson was that she wanted to take away with her from the experience.

After each of the girls had spoken about those topics, I asked them to speak again, not in any particular order, about their feelings about the group coming to an end. When they had shared their feelings, I asked them to try to summarize the general feelings, and we talked about how these are the things people usually feel when something ends.

●

The communication and interactional structure, the relationships among the members, the climate and atmosphere of the group sessions, and the cohesion level of the termination stage will resemble those of the convening stage, with two exceptions. First, instead of focusing on connecting people into relationships, the worker will focus on disconnecting the relationships and centering people back on themselves individually. Second, the members will be involved in planning for the final session and will have the interactional, decision-making capacity to do that.

Unlike in the formation, conflict/disequilibrium, and maintenance stages, the worker will keep a hand in the group's planning in the termination stage, so as to help people end the experience well. The worker will help to keep plans within realistic and appropriate bounds. There is a tendency toward overkill in some ritualized endings, and part of the worker's task is to keep the level of sentiment proportionate to the level of cohesion within the group during its working period. If that level is considerable, the ending may be highly emotional; however, the worker needs to direct and focus the expression of feelings so that it is authentic and commensurate to the real level of feeling among the members.

Facilitating the Ending

The worker may moderate the trauma and disruption of termination by helping members express their feelings, talk about them, work through them in verbal and nonverbal ways, and, finally, master them so that they can be effectively and productively channeled in future relationships. Although there is no way of alleviating entirely the feelings of sadness, loss, and grief associated with termination, those feelings can be made easier to bear.

The worker can facilitate the termination by emphasizing the naturalness of the ending point of a process and by making the ending point an inherent part of the whole helping sequence. An essay by a social work educator expresses this idea in its title: *Endings as Related to Beginnings* (Weitzel, 1961). The center of this idea is that the ending is part of a process, and it should come with preparation and not as a surprise.

An instructor of a class in groups uses a student's experience about termination to demonstrate how to help people deal with imminent endings:

•

At the class session before Thanksgiving break, I reminded the students that when we returned from the holiday, we would have three weeks left. The classes on December 5 and 12 would be scheduled for student presentations of their semester's projects; the last class, on December 19, would consist of a discussion and exercises related to termination.

"Omigosh!" said Karen, one of the students. "That's not enough time to get everything in. I didn't know the semester ended that soon. Can't we schedule some extra class time?" I said it sounded like a surprise to her that the semester ended on the 20th, but if she checked she would find that made 15 weeks, and we had mapped out the class sessions early in the term. I said the class meeting time (11 A.M. to 1 P.M.) made it difficult to extend hours, because of conflicts with other classes and the classroom.

"Let me suggest," I said, "that your question is very much like the one raised when termination is approaching in any group. We will take these issues up and deal with them at our last class session, okay? In the meantime, after Thanksgiving break, we'll have two sessions of your colleagues' presentations and then a focused termination session."

•

Another way the worker facilitates the ending is to help the members interpret the source and meaning of their feelings as the end approaches. A practice ethic in much of contemporary social work is to help people be as aware as possible of the process they are experiencing, to give names to the events that are occurring, and to help people talk about their feelings rather than simply act them out. With this "raise to the conscious level and verbalize" approach, a premium is placed on being able to handle feelings with words rather than actions. So the worker should help people put their feelings into words, by supplying the words when a member cannot, checking that the member accepts the supplied word, and prompting the member to use the words until they have incorporated them.

The worker also facilitates the ending by acknowledging her or his own process of handling termination feelings; this is parallel to the modeling of entering new situations that the worker did during the convening stage. The focus and purpose of self-disclosing is always on the side of what will be beneficial for the clients to take from, learn from, and use. In a very real sense, this is the meaning of containment as that worker characteristic has been used here. By sharing her or his feelings in a self-contained way, the worker helps people finish the experience well. It may also help the worker to finish the experience well, as the following extract suggests.

•

I chose not to make myself available to group members after termination, because I felt this might prevent them from freely moving on to new life experiences. I did share some of my own thoughts, feelings, and experiences with the group; this helped my ability to empathize with the group members. In reflecting on and revealing some of my own previous endings, I became more aware of what the group members might be experiencing and more able to feel with them.

•

Finally, the worker helps to facilitate the ending by joining the feedback that the group members give to and receive from each other as the group draws to a close. Whether the worker also prepares an independent contract to share with the members will be a matter of the worker's professional judgment, and perhaps personal preference. If the worker does decide to prepare and share an independent contract, the cautions about self-disclosure and containment, and about the professional role of the worker in the group, should be observed. It should be remembered that the worker is not a member of the group; her or his position and responsibility set the worker apart. Whatever the resolution of that question, the worker may nonetheless join in the giving and receiving of feedback as the group ends. That worker behavior communicates very clearly the worker's involvement with the group.

A common way of finishing any unfinished business consists of each person, in turn, going up to each other person, looking at them directly, and saying, in a few short phrases, "What I really liked was the way you ... (supplying a specific behavior exchanged between the two persons, such as 'always gave me positive strokes when I could finally say something that was hard for me to say')," and then, "But I wish we ... (supplying a specific wish for a behavioral exchange between the two persons which did not occur, such as 'had made more opportunity to talk to each other more directly')." This exercise need not be prolonged; the purpose is not to raise new issues but to bring closure to the present situation. Other such exercises are discussed in the "Group-ending Program Media" section of this chapter.

The worker's primary role and central location in the termination stage have some similarities with those of the convening stage, as these two records concerning the same group illustrate:

●

In the convening stage, I came to the group with the realization that the initial period would be a time filled with uncertainty and ambivalence. By acknowledging that it is natural to have these feelings at the beginning of a new experience, I feel that I alleviated some of the anxiety of the members and helped them to begin to move into the group experience. After recognizing and commenting on the fear and uncertainty that is a natural part of beginnings, I attempted to lessen these inhibiting feelings by making the unknown known. One way I did this was by restating the goals and purposes of the group that we had discussed during the individual sessions; at the same time I asked the members to talk about their own goals and expectations for the group. This helped to begin the movement of the group in a purposeful direction.

I also used structure to alleviate some of these feelings. We set a specific time and place for the group, and enunciated certain group rules such as respecting each other's time to talk and keeping confidential what goes on during the meetings. This helped the members to be more certain of what was expected of them, and at the same time to feel safer about becoming involved in the group experience. I also did much planning of activities and topics of discussion that would enable the members to become involved at a safe and comfortable pace without requiring a great amount of investment.

During the approach of termination, I facilitated evaluative processes by asking for feedback concerning the meaning that the group had had for the members, and the changes that had occurred for the members since the beginning of the group. In this way, the learning and growth from the group experience was put into words and made more real for the members. I facilitated the group's working through the separation by acknowledging the feelings they were having and helping them express those feelings. I asked them for feedback concerning the value of the experience; I restated the group goals and got them involved in determining whether they had been accomplished. I also provided them with the names and phone numbers of appropriate resources and contacts so they could leave this experience with a sense that there were other resources and experiences available to them.

●

In addition to the shift in contract from interdependent to independent, and in addition to the movement of the worker back to a primary role and central location, there is a change of program media from group sustaining to group ending.

○

Group-ending Program Media

The characteristics of group-ending media need to be those which afford the opportunity for bringing closure to the experience, for finishing unfinished business, for helping members leave the group as individuals, and for helping them move toward their future.

Middleman (1968) has identified the most important quality of group-ending program media as being a common and shared activity. It is the group as a whole that is ending, and the group as a whole should do something together as it finishes. For example:

●

The members decided to go to dinner in Chinatown after the last group meeting. This was a formal way of marking the end of the group experience.

●

Another example:

●

At the end of the meeting, the group decided to accept the task suggested by the minister; that is, to write a litany relating to the group experience for use during a Sunday morning service. Each member was asked to write a sentence or two on their experience in the group or their feelings about it. The details of the task were worked out by the group.

●

When the final activity is a common, shared one, all the members can see each other go, hear their words of farewell, say their own good-byes, and feel that closure has been reached. (It should be noted that the establishment of members' independent contracts is more like parallel play—people doing things individually in the presence of others—than a shared activity. However, although the members do not work on their contracts collectively, they do have independent contracts in common and they will share them with the other members of the group.)

The guiding questions for selecting group-ending program media are:

- Has the group participated in this program medium before? With what results? At what point in the group's development?
- Are the behaviors and capacities required by the activity appropriate to the termination stage? Do they require separating kinds of behaviors rather than uniting?
- Does the activity provide an opportunity for all the members to be doing the same thing together as well as to be doing individual things singly?
- Can the members express feelings verbally as well as nonverbally? Which mode of expression do the members use most comfortably? Do the members desire or need to adopt the other mode and be comfortable with its use?
- Is an opportunity provided within the structure of the program medium for members to express their individual uniquenesses? To participate regardless of skill level?
- Does the program medium focus more on the future than on the past?

The members themselves may be involved in the planning and even the analysis of the ending program media. The worker, of course, retains a veto power, a gate-keeping function, by virtue of her or his role and responsibility with the group; the worker's professional responsibility for quality of service cannot be abdicated.

The program media available for use in the termination stage are multitudinous. Experiential exercises such as fantasy trips, symbolic gift giving, group hugs, group rounds (the leave-taking exercise described earlier), and many others are useful to help people both verbalize and act out their parting. For example:

•

The group consisted of 14 social workers, youth leaders, and other human service professionals from abroad; they were all participants in the local affiliate of the Council of International Programs. They were finishing a five-week orientation to American society at a school of social work. The end of this five-week period signaled the end of their daily association; from here, they would each go to separate social service agencies and organizations for ten weeks of practical experience. They would also be moving from the first American home where they had been staying to the second. So they faced one termination and two transitions, all at once.

Several of the group members were manifesting signs of feeling these changes very deeply. One sign was a reluctance to think about changing families; another was requests from some group members and their first American families to extend the stay for another five weeks; another was anxiety about whether they would be able to handle conversational English well enough to be effective in their agencies. On the other hand, some members denied the importance of these changes altogether. I decided to spend a morning focused on termination.

Many members arrived late; as the session began, they were showing prints of photos they had taken and talking among themselves. One woman turned to me and said, "Maybe we don't want to deal with termination!" I said I understood that, but I said, smiling, "We're going to do it, anyway!" I explained the process we would use this morning: we would spend part of the time focusing on the change of host families and part of the time on the ending of the group.

I handed out slips of paper called memorygrams. They looked like small memo sheets. I explained that each person was to write a memorygram to each other person. They would put their own name and the name of the person to whom the memorygram was addressed and then write two things: what they had appreciated about the person in the five weeks they'd known each other, and something they wished had happened.

There were expressions of perplexity, resistance, and reluctance. I knew it wasn't a matter of their not having understood my English! Some of them giggled in an embarrassed way; they looked at each other with wonderment and then there was silence. Then they began writing, and they seemed to be sincerely working on what they would say. As they wrote, they looked at each other in a thoughtful way, smiled at each other, and went back to writing.

The ones who finished first began handing out their memorygrams; the recipients smiled in response. When everyone had finished and all the memorygrams had been distributed, they began reading them. Then they shook hands with each other, embracing, patting others on the shoulder, and smiling warmly. One of the men observed that they had ten weeks in front of them to do the things they said they wished had happened between them. The others enthusiastically agreed, and they decided to meet together once a week to catch up on their colleagues' experiences. Altogether, there was a very nice atmosphere.

One man commented that he was very uncomfortable with the idea at first, because it is difficult for him to express feelings and he's not too used to doing it; but he said he felt much better now. A woman said she'd been reluctant to participate, but now she felt good about it.

●

Arts and crafts may be employed to portray people's feelings at termination or their evaluation of the whole experience. They may also be employed to produce some object to take away when the group ends or to be displayed by the agency to say, "We were here."

●

I borrowed a page from *The Together Book* (Affective Education Office, 1975) for the last session of the adult group. I dittoed the free-form design and distributed it to the members, explaining that they were to think about the various emotions they had felt during their membership in the group and now that the group was ending. They should assign a color to each feeling, decide how much of that feeling they had felt, and color in the section of the free-form design that corresponded to the time they experienced the named feeling. When they were all finished, they would be asked to evaluate their experience in the group, using the colored free-form design to talk to the other members about it.

●

Members may write poetry; they may assemble a group-composed poem or a collection of poems written by each member.

●

At the end of the four-week training school for professional workers in the national agency, a choral reading had been prepared using humorous references to the group's shared experiences. The choral reading was interspersed with singing and modern dance interpretations set to the language of shared events.

●

Food seems to take on special meaning when it is shared and symbolizes the group's variety and unity. Some groups go out for a last meal together or plan a potluck or prepare a common meal.

●

When I arrived at the meeting place for the final meeting, the girls were eating a large amount of food they had brought with them. During the chaotic attempt at role-play, an incredible amount of food was consumed.

The great amount of eating that took place during this meeting is symbolic of the need for emotional support and nurturance at a time when feelings of sadness and loss are prevalent. The decision to go out to dinner after the meeting is a significant step in moving away from the group and out into the world where new contacts will be made and new things experienced.

●

Another example:

●

The sectarian agency had a six-week group for prospective adoptive parents. At the last meeting, when practically all of the parents had received their babies, we had a party to celebrate the adoptions. During the social time, many of them decided that the sharing had been too good to end. So they devised a plan to meet once a month—for as long as they were all interested in continuing—for a potluck, taking turns at each other's homes.

●

Whatever program medium is selected, it needs to be a shared activity and a launching pad for the future of each member.

Summary

So the group ends. With the close of the last meeting, the set of persons comes to the end of their time together. The dynamics of this phase of group life are such that the individuals and the group as a whole express their feelings about separation, based on previous experiences with endings and based on the meaning the group experience has had for them. There is an element of regression in the way these feelings are expressed; the latent content of the regression is to bid for continuation of the experience. The terms of the group contract may be employed to hold members to their originally agreed time frame and also to do the kind of recapitulation and evaluation implied by an ending time. From the security of the interdependent contract that was in effect in the preceding period of the group's life and in the face of the imminent termination, members negotiate an independent contract with themselves individually. This is a way of projecting themselves toward the future by a promise to generalize and stabilize the changes that have occurred in relation to the significant others, values, and institutions that make up their social environments.

Both because the group is ending and because the dynamics of individual and group functioning dictate it, the worker returns to a primary role and a central location vis-à-vis the group system. The worker employs three essential skills in relation to the group's termination: preparing the group for its separation, directing and focusing the expression of feelings about termination, and facilitating the ending. Group-ending program media are employed to help the members experience emotionally and kinesthetically their separation. The media have the properties of being common and shared activities and of being a launching pad for the future of each member.

The most important ingredient not only of the termination process but of the whole group experience as well is the drive toward individuation, in which each person finds rootedness in the self.

With the end of the group experience, the chapters of this book that discuss the four-dimensional approach to group skills in social work come to an end, too.

The practice depicted in these chapters is that designed for direct service, helping purposes. It has been assumed that there is a solo worker with the group, not coworkers; and that the groups are closed in membership and limited in time.

In the next chapter, these assumptions are discarded. Three major aspects of social group work practice are taken up: open versus closed groups, solo worker versus coworkers, and the recording of group practice. The final chapter discusses the use of the four-dimensional approach with groups for other than direct service purposes.

References

Affective Education Office, Philadelphia. (1975). *The together book*. Board of Education, Philadelphia. Mimeographed.

Alissi, A., & Casper, M. (1985/86). Time as a factor in groupwork [Special issue]. *Social Work with Groups, 8*(3/4).

Bossman, L. J., Jr. (1968). An analysis of interagent residual-influence effects upon members of small, decision-making groups. *Behavioral Science, 13,* 220–233.

Estes, R. J., & Henry, S. (1976). The therapeutic contract in work with groups: A formal analysis. *Social Service Review, 50*(4), 611–622.

Fried, E. (1970). Individuation through group psychotherapy. *International Journal of Group Psychotherapy, 20*(4), 450–459.

Garland, J., Jones, H., & Kolodny, R. (1965). A model for stages of development in social work groups. In S. Bernstein (Ed.), *Explorations in group work*. Boston: Boston University School of Social Work.

Hartford, M. E. (1972). *Groups in social work*. New York: Columbia University Press.

Kubler-Ross, E. (1974). *Questions and answers on death and dying*. New York: Macmillan.

Lippitt, R., Watson, J., & Westley, B. (1958). *The dynamics of planned change*. New York: Harcourt, Brace and World.

MacLennan, B. W., & Felsenfeld, N. (1968). *Group counselling and group psychotherapy with adolescents*. New York: Columbia University Press.

Middleman, R. (1968). *The non-verbal method in working with groups*. New York: Association Press.

Pincus, A., & Minahan, A. (1973). *Social work practice: Model and method*. Itasca, IL: F. E. Peacock.

Reid, W., & Epstein, L. (1972). *Task-centered casework*. New York: Columbia University Press.

Taft, J. J. (1949). Time as the medium of the helping process. *Jewish Social Service Quarterly, 16*(2), 189–198.

Weitzel, K. (1961). *Endings as related to beginnings*. Western Reserve University, Cleveland, OH. Mimeographed.

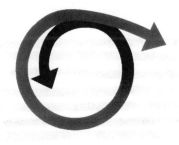

CHAPTER 9

COWORKERS, OPEN GROUPS, AND RECORDING

Three pieces of business regarding direct service to groups remain to be addressed: coworkers with a group, open groups (people entering or leaving the group at their own pace), and group recording. The first two of these touch on value stances that, with other assumptions, form part of the boundaries of this approach to social work practice with people in groups. The third is a continuing practice behavior and transcends the separate stages of the approach described in this book (a worker activity that occurs at each stage of group life, as well as at the end of the group's experience). Each of these will be taken up in turn.

◯
Coworkers

The question of whether to use coworkers or a solo worker with a group does not have a clear right or wrong answer. The choice is based on a number of considerations: a preference for one way of working over another, administrative and management concerns, or theoretical questions. Points of view may be taken on both sides of the issue.

Arguments for a Solo Worker

Con's

In this book, a solo worker has been presented as the preferred arrangement. There are several reasons for this.

First, a professional worker is expected to be able to utilize the necessary range of instrumental and expressive behavior and to be the absent-role taker, according to the group's needs. Each person has a dominant style, but it is an assumption of this practice approach that workers with groups are able to enact either style with some ease, relative to group members' needs and capacities to perform roles. Sometimes the decision is taken to choose coworkers because one worker will have predominantly an instrumental style and the other, an expressive style. Part of a group's purpose is to help people become whole and integrated, capable of choosing how they will relate to others and capable of a range of relational skills and styles. If two coworkers always act in their respective styles, members might conclude that they should strive to be like one or the other. For members to catch the idea that one relates only from one state seems to sabotage the stated therapeutic aims.

Second, a solo worker presents the members with only one power figure to deal with. The power differential between the group members and the worker is strongly felt by members, regardless of the worker's attempts to minimize it, and presenting two such power figures could overwhelm members' efforts to speak up for themselves. Compliant behavior could result; members could attempt to accommodate to the workers' agendas and cease working on their own issues.

Third, time is saved when planning, coordination, and evaluation are done by one worker only. In a period of high cost-benefit and cost-efficiency awareness, time translates to money considerations. One worker serving a group is less costly to agency budgets than two. The time that coworkers spend in working out arrangements for communication and coordination is time away from direct service delivery to clients, and this too is costly.

So, in accordance with the value premise of this practice approach, a solo worker is favored because (1) it is expected that one worker is able to be both instrumental and expressive in relational style, (2) group members should have only one power figure to relate to, and (3) logistical problems of managing time, cost, and communication are increased by having coworkers.

Arguments for Coworkers *Pros*

The reality of practice is that workers and agencies often choose the coworker pattern. Several reasons are offered for this choice.

First, assigning an inexperienced worker as the coworker of a more experienced worker will help her or him gain experience. This use of coworkers for training purposes is frequently used in field instruction with social work students. The use of one-way mirrors for observation of a worker's practice is an equally viable option and is less obtrusive than having students and field instructors as coworkers (DeMarche & Iskander, 1950; Haley, 1976; Montalvo, 1973).

Second, it is believed that with a coworker, more of the individual and group dynamics will be dealt with. Individuals notice different things; one person's figure is another person's ground, to use the language of Gestalt therapy. Having noticed different things, people then proceed to do different things about what they have noticed.

Third, coworkers can give each other backup. While one worker follows a potentially fruitful pursuit with a group member, the other worker can attend to the emotional climate associated with the other members' presence in the working milieu. This avoids the problem of dividing the worker role rigidly among instrumental and expressive lines, and it allows workers the freedom to focus on one member without fear of losing the others or of doing work with individuals in the presence of others. The observing worker would signal to the first worker when group-as-a-whole issues were ready to be addressed.

Fourth, a coworker arrangement gives workers the opportunity to model interpersonal relationships with another person of equal status and position. By seeing how the two coworkers communicate, arrive at decisions, resolve differences, agree to differ with equanimity, and support each other, the members will learn a range of behavioral options for their own interpersonal relations.

Fifth, some workers may feel more secure with a coworker. A coworker can step in if the worker falters, and can prompt the worker if she or he does not seem to know what to do in a given situation.

So the coworker pattern may be chosen to give experience to inexperienced workers, to give greater certainty that the group and individual dynamics will be attended to, to offer the opportunity to model interpersonal behaviors, or to give security and support.

Using the Coworker Pattern

Once the decision is taken to use coworkers, there are several points to be regarded. Communication is necessary on a variety of matters; there is a need to match the coworkers; and there are pitfalls to be avoided.

Communication   There needs to be communication between the coworkers about three vital topics.

First, the coworkers need to communicate about planning. They should both be involved in mapping out the initial purpose for the group, in recruiting, and in thinking through how the group might reach the end point envisioned in the initial stage. They could divide the pregroup interviewing;

in this case, the coworkers would need to consult and agree before an interviewee is selected for membership. They would also need to insure that each could accurately represent her or his partner's working style and inform prospective members of the coworker structure.

An alternative pattern would be to share the pregroup interviewing, with both workers meeting each prospective member. This might afford a fuller view of how the interactional network will operate in the group. However, this shared interviewing would be costly and might overbalance the interviews with too much worker power.

The following example illustrates some of the problems of having only one coworker conduct the pregroup interviews.

●

A graduate student in field placement was designing a group for women in life transitions; the student's coworker was to be one of the faculty members from the local school of social work. They agreed to conduct pregroup interviews. As the group assignment was part of the student's field work, it was decided that the student would do all of the interviews, and then the two of them would consult about the appropriateness of each interviewee for the group.

Several problems ensued. Each person who became a member had an initial connection with only one of the workers, and in the early meetings of the group it was difficult to create a connection with the other worker. In the pregroup interviews, the relational style of the faculty member could not truly be represented by the student; it could be described, but the prospective members could not truly experience who this other social worker was. Likewise, the faculty member was unable to get a sense of who the prospective members were and how they would connect. No matter how fully and accurately the student took down the information following each interview, the members were basically unknown to the faculty member at the outset.

●

Second, coworkers need to communicate about evaluation. They need to exchange feedback on how group sessions went and how each worker carried her or his aspect of the worker task. They also need to discuss the progress being made by the group as a whole and by the members individually. This evaluation will be concerned with the goals and objectives of the group, an assessment of member progress, a comparison of progress made to agency and worker purpose for offering the service, consideration of potential resources to meet the group's needs, and the reporting of members' progress to any referral source. Planning is sometimes called prehash; evaluation may be called rehash or posthash.

Third, coworkers need to communicate about their relationship to each other and to the group. They need to talk over as fully as possible what they know about their respective styles (instrumental or expressive), what each predominantly attends to, what each tends to pick up or to miss, under what circumstances each is likely to modify style or strategy, how they wish to handle coworker differences or disagreements in front of the group, and how to signal each other. All of this requires a high degree of self-awareness and a willingness to be receptive to feedback, as the following example illustrates.

●

The group was at a residential facility for adolescent males on the way to emancipation. The male coworkers were both conscientious, self-aware, and skilled workers. They met before each group meeting, checked each other out during meetings, and met afterward to process and evaluate how the session had gone. They made a point of spending some time together each week away from the facility, to get to know each other better; they felt that these occasions enriched their working relationship.

Skip was especially skillful in following task-oriented lines of discussion. His interventions were instrumental to the group's goal achievement, keeping members focused on the business at hand, bringing the discussion back to the point, moving in to ask how issues would be resolved. Marc, on the other hand, followed the social-emotional climate. His interventions were empathic, affect-focused, and expressive. He could speak with warmth and sympathy to the members having difficulty expressing feelings, and he could encourage them to stay with their feelings and express them. He made space in the group's sessions for the young men to struggle with emotions.

The two men had worked out that these were their personal styles of working with people and had reached an understanding that these would be the ways they respectively related to the group. It was working out very well.

But one evening, the group session grew quite heated with conflict over one member who the others said was "not working" in the group. Skip suddenly took on the expressive role. Marc signaled him: "Skip, I'm not following where you're going. Are you wanting to stay with Tom's business of getting his feelings out? I'm lost here!" Skip looked blank. The members stopped their discussion to watch the exchange between the workers.

"I've lost where you're going," Marc repeated. Skip didn't understand what had happened and what he had done. He asked for clarification. Marc pointed out what he had done: "I was with you when you were asking Tom what he planned to do about getting down to work, but when you shifted gears to go after his feelings about what was getting in his way, I didn't see your plan."

Skip then understood. "Okay, I know what happened. Tom and I have been talking about this in our individual sessions, and he struck a chord. I went on with that and lost the group focus. Let's get back to where we were, Tom, in terms of what you're going to do about getting down to work, here in the group, and leave the other business for our session tomorrow."

●

Being in a coworker situation also requires time and a commitment to working at the coworker relationship. I once had a coworker who preferred to hold back on interventions early in the life of the group, to see where the group members' own interactions took them. My style is to be active, primary, and central in the beginning, and to move back as the members' abilities to manage their interactions strengthen. One consequence of these mixed styles was that the group was never without an active worker; this sort of coordination is crucial between coworkers. If the choice is made to have coworkers, the agency needs to provide the time for coworker communication.

The following description, excerpted from the record of one coworker with a support group in a safe house for battered women, portrays some of the practical and philosophical matters that require attention by the coworkers.

●

Fortunately, there are two coworkers for this support group. "Sharing the power of leadership can present a strong model to women in the group by showing that mutual respect and support are attainable goals in a close relationship," said NiCarthy, Merriam, and Coffman (1984, p. 51), and it's been true here.

It has been very important for the coworkers to meet before the support group in order to share information about the composition of the group that evening. We have a superficial familiarity with most of the members, since case supervision is held earlier in the day on Tuesdays; only women who have entered the safe house since Tuesday noon will be unknown to us.

The coworkers also met before the group began, to discuss our individual styles of facilitation, the structure of our shared responsibility for the group, and the flexible agenda for the group. We followed NiCarthy, Merriam, and Coffman's (1984) suggestion to rotate the primary leadership role on a weekly basis and found it a good way to proceed. In this plan, the primary worker for the week decides on the content for the meeting and is also the one who might completely change or abandon this plan in response to the group's needs. The coworker assumes the task of giving attention to members' well-being and their responses to content. She tracks the process of meetings when she isn't the primary worker.

After each session, the coworkers meet to evaluate the session and plan for the next one, as well as to give each other feedback. Mutual support and positive feedback between coworkers is especially important in this context, since burnout is a common phenomenon in crisis work of this sort.

The completely unpredictable nature of this support group presents a worker with a challenge that must be met with flexibility, patience, and creative spontaneity. In the absence of cohesion, norms, group culture, and possibly even communication, the worker must be more ready than ever to respond to the moment in a way most helpful to the other actors in the real-life drama.

●

Matching   The match between the two workers depends on such factors as age, gender, race, theoretical orientation, and style (as discussed in the previous subsection).

The importance of age in matching coworkers depends on the purpose of the group. With groups of adolescents working on their self-identity crises, coworkers who are both very young adults may not be the most fortuitous match. Although some advantage may accrue in diminishing the age gap for purposes of role modeling, few young college graduates have resolved their own identity questions enough to be able to represent adequately the "adult in relation to youth" figures. In groups focused on particular life-cycle crises, coworkers who are themselves resolving such crises may not be advisable.

An important consideration in making the match would be not to pair coworkers whose age difference is complicated by other differences such as status or level of experience. Large gaps between coworkers may affect both their relationship with each other and their relationship with the group.

Age is perhaps less a factor in matching coworkers than gender. For example, women in a shelter for battered women may not be receptive to the presence of men workers (at least, this is the stance taken by the staffs of many shelters). Agencies and workers need to be clear as to the purpose of assigning coworkers across gender lines; sometimes there may be good reason to do so. For example, Emprey (1977) found that groups of one gender who had workers of the same gender had more difficulty moving into the work phase of their group experience.

Race is an issue, too. A growing body of literature (Davis, 1984; Feldman, 1968; Goodman, 1973; Lewis & Ho, 1975; Lum, 1986; Mangold, 1971, 1976; Martinez, 1977; Ryan & Gilbert, 1976; Symposium, 1975) points to the need for clear thinking on this issue. Decisions about cross-racial assignment of workers should be guided by sound professional judgment based on an assessment of the purpose for making these assignments. It is preferable to let the difference make a difference, rather than affect a color blindness that is artificial; and to raise to a therapeutic issue level any questions, comments, or behaviors related to the racial or ethnic identity of a worker when it is different from that of the coworker or different from that of the clients.

Differences in theoretical orientation present a more complex problem in matching coworkers. Agencies tend to hire workers whose theoretical orientation accords with that of the agency, as reflected in the way it defines its functions and projects its programs. Nonetheless, even when people of closely congruent orientations are employed, they might draw upon different methods or techniques. Communication between workers is therefore crucial, regarding both their orientations and the underlying assumptions of their respective disciplines.

The following example illustrates some of the problems that can arise between coworkers.

●

A 25-year-old woman graduate student was assigned in a VA hospital as a coworker with a group of male World War II and Korean War veterans who were alcoholics. Her coworker was her field instructor, a man nearly 20 years her senior. When she arrived for field placement, she had been introduced to the group as a student, and the field instructor had identified his role relationship to her.

As time went along, the group raised questions and challenges about her youth and inexperience. She was alternately ignored, criticized as naive, put down for her enthusiasm, scorned for empathic statements, and generally rebuked for her efforts. The field instructor tried heading off or blunting some of the comments, but in conference with him, the student stated that she needed to speak for herself in the group and that she could not establish herself in the group if she appeared to be under his wing. He admitted that he had been overprotective. He said he had intervened to try to prevent her being attacked because he felt a responsibility for her learning experience and because he felt protective toward her since she was a woman and younger. She asked him to let her handle the situation.

The next time the put-downs began, the field instructor started to intervene, but the student said, "Wait, Ed. I want to say this to the men myself." She turned to them. "Do you wonder what I'm doing here? Are you doubtful that I know anything about alcoholism because I'm not an alcoholic? Do you question what a woman is doing in this group of men? Are you thinking I'm 'just a kid' because I wasn't even born when you were in the Army, fighting?

"Well, it's true I'm not an alcoholic; in fact, I rarely drink at all. And it's true I'm a woman and that I am younger than all of you. But I do know something about how groups work, because I've been working with groups for three years. And I do believe in people's ability to change their behavior, because I have changed as I have grown and I have seen change happen with other people, and I think that I have that to offer you: a belief in your ability to change if you choose to and a belief in the possibility of this group to be the place where you begin to choose to change."

The men's acceptance of her was not won instantaneously; the challenges were repeated from time to time. But her field instructor ceased his overprotective interventions and began to relate to her both in the group and outside with more equal regard. Gradually, she became a valued coworker with the group and throughout the agency.

●

The choice to use a coworker arrangement should take into account not only the need for communication and for matching but also the pitfalls to be avoided.

Pitfalls   There are five possible pitfalls facing coworkers with groups.

First, the group may divide and conquer the coworkers. Some members may identify with one worker, some members with the other worker, and the two factions may play against each other. This can happen very subtly in the beginning and stay below the surface for some time before it erupts. Some of the signs of divide-and-conquer behavior are: some members habitually turning to one worker for information, feedback, and support while routinely ignoring the same from the other worker; checking with the preferred worker anything suggested by the other worker; agreeing with one worker and not the other; praising one and, by implication, criticizing the other; and accusing the "not preferred" worker of favoritism toward members who favor that worker.

The workers should check with each other to see if these warning signs are present, and they should plan ways to circumvent the divide-and-conquer behavior, by confronting it, by reiterating their support for each other, and by addressing directly the need for them to work together. They could also clarify how they consult with each other, the content of their communications, the areas in which they have agreed to differ, and how and why they sustain the working relationship despite those differences. A head-on approach is the best way to prevent divide-and-conquer efforts.

The second potential pitfall is the absence of one coworker. When an unavoidable absence is to occur (such as a conference attendance, vacation leave, or a court appearance), the session before the absence should have some time set aside for announcing this and dealing with it by reassuring the members that it does not reflect abandonment or rejection. The worker who remains should be prepared to handle the members' feelings about the other worker's absence. The members may feel rejected or abandoned, despite efforts to reassure them prior to the absence. They may bid for the remaining worker's favor by making favorable comparisons with the absent worker's way of practicing. They may try to solicit the remaining worker's agreement to an innovation in the way the group is going or to a contract renegotiation while the other worker is away.

The worker should respond to these efforts by restating the reasons for the coworker's absence, reiterating the coworkers' solidarity, declining to participate in comparisons, and keeping the group focused on its business of the day. The worker may need to fill both coworker roles, and that may require explanation; for example: "I think Jeff would have asked you, about now, what the benefits of your statements are for you."

There are times when a coworker appears for the group meeting but is not well or is preoccupied with something external to the group. That ought to be communicated to the other worker, and some agreement worked out—that the coworker will explain the situation and leave, or that the coworker will remain but will not participate fully. Otherwise, unusual silences or unexpected interventions could occur that would have to be handled before the whole group.

(If there is only one worker and she or he must be absent for a group session, the session should be canceled. Far better for the worker to return and deal directly, herself or himself, with the members' feelings of rejection and abandonment than to send in a substitute who does not have the history with the group or the individuals who comprise it.)

The third pitfall is that the group may become more interested in the coworker relationship than in group-oriented issues. This can happen for a variety of reasons: it is a way for members to postpone working on their own issues, and it reflects a kind of curiosity, not unlike the curiosity children often have about what adults do when they are not around. This curiosity may be expressed as suppositions ("I suppose the two of you have cooked something up for us in those conferences you have between sessions") or as innocent-appearing questions ("Do the two of you ever get together for drinks when you are not working?"). There is no way, really, to satisfy this curiosity, however much straightforward information is given. The best response is to answer appropriate questions, such as, "Have the two of you worked together before?", and to explore their latent content ("I wonder why you're asking that.")

Group members have a particular sensitivity to the nuances of the relationship between coworkers. If the coworkers are social friends, or have (or had) a more intimate relationship with each other, or have a disagreement or faulty communication that has not been resolved, the members may pick this up. Coworkers should try to resolve differences before they spill over into the group, should agree on what they will disagree about in front of the group, and should be prepared to respond from a common stance about any other issues. Keeping the group focused on its own issues is the best way to handle this pitfall.

The fourth pitfall is sex-role stereotyping. Whenever coworker patterns are contemplated, the tendency is to think of a woman-man team. The rationale usually given is that a woman-man team will afford group members the opportunity to see a healthy female-male relationship, and to learn from it appropriate sex-role behaviors. However, Broverman and Broverman (1970) found that "healthy adult" and "healthy adult male" were defined by similar behaviors. Nothing since that time has shown such sex-role stereotyping to have changed. Rather than assuming that female-male coworker duos will model suitable sex-role behaviors, group workers should exercise their assessment and analytic skills to create alternatives.

The fifth pitfall is using a coworker as a security blanket. This may be a genuine reason for choosing to use coworkers, though practitioners might not name it aloud. No one should take someone to work with her or him in order to feel better and more self-confident on the job. There is support in having another worker present, but if that is what motivates the choice, the decision is flawed. This pitfall is avoided by taking the need for security to where it can be dealt with appropriately: to a supervisor and not to a peer.

Summary

A coworker pattern may be chosen so as to give experience to an inexperienced worker, to insure that more of the group's dynamics are attended to, and to afford a broader range of interpersonal behaviors to be modeled for the members. When coworkers are used, the coworkers need to communicate about planning, evaluation, and the coworker relationship, and the agency needs to provide time for this communication. The coworkers should match with each other and should be on guard for pitfalls (Papell & Rothman, 1980).

O

Open Groups

An open group is one that people enter and leave at their individual pace of growth; a closed group is one in which persons begin their experience together as a set of people convened by a worker, move through their experience together, and end their experience together at a predetermined time (Ziller, 1965). The approach to practice written about so far has focused on closed groups, for two reasons. First, it was thought that the model could be grasped more readily if presented in a pure and fixed form, showing each stage of group development separately. This does not mean that the model is linear or mechanistic; the whole process has been taken apart for examination and discussion, but the entity is really fluid, matrixlike, and spiral in character. The second reason for choosing closed groups as the model type is that a closed group represents a more consistent system and provides a better opportunity to observe the dynamics that occur in a group.

Arguments for Closed Groups

A closed group affords a better opportunity than an open one for members to identify with a constant set of others, and this lends stability to the helping milieu. Cohesion will develop more solidly and will serve its function more productively when the same others continue to be present as attracting forces. The stages of group development evolve more forcefully when the same others are part of the movement between separation and union. The amount and intensity of commitment is greater when the same others continue to be available—when a member can count on the presence, week after week, of the familiar and trusted others.

Closed groups avoid the shifting or blurring of roles that might occur when an original member of the system is replaced by a new member and the behaviors associated with the performances of a role by the original member are spread among several people (Wilmer & Lamb, 1969). Role differentiation, communication patterns, and decision-making processes are all affected in a closed group. (Norms, values, and culture may not be changed so much by members' coming and going as would be the other group social forces.)

In an open group, depending on the rapidity with which new members enter and old members go, the question could arise as to whether a continuous entity exists. If there is too much turnover in the group, the bond may not take hold. The possibility for maximizing time as a medium of the helping process may be forfeited (Taft, 1949). Time remains a factor in open groups; but the focus shifts from group-as-a-whole processes to individual members' processes. In that shift, some opportunity to use group social forces to help individuals may be lost. The entity will be less cohesive and possibly less available as a therapeutic means; what remains will be the others as a context for help to individuals.

Finally, in an open group the anxiety level of those who do not progress rapidly enough to leave the group at an early point may prove to be immobilizing, as in the following example.

●

Members of the alcohol education group at the community mental health center were there as part of their probation. Membership was open, but each member was required to complete a cycle of meetings and homework assignments. The group was ongoing.

After several sessions of attending the group, one member had not spoken. One evening, another member commented on this. Barry, the worker, turned to the silent member and asked, "Did you hear what Pat said? What do you have to say about that?" Tony replied, "I see others leaving here with their certificates for having completed the cycle; I'm not. They're doing their homework; I know I'm not. I guess I'll be here through I don't know how many cycles. I'll never get rid of probation. I'll never get my driver's license back."

Barry said, "Look, people move and grow at their own pace. Do this program on your own time frame and don't try to do it on other people's. If it takes you two weeks to do something, take two weeks!" He turned to the others. "How many of you take two weeks to complete some of your homework assignments?" Everyone chorused, "I." "Me." "I do." "We do."

The worker turned back to Tony. "See? Nobody is knocking himself out rushing around to complete the work. Take your own time. It's worse for you, as you just said, in the long run, for you to do nothing."

●

The immobilizing effect can be moderated, however, as discussed later in this chapter.

Arguments for Open Groups

The decision is often taken to structure groups in an open form. There are three main reasons for this decision.

First, individuals learn at different rates. When all persons in a group are treated as if they have the same rates of growth, there may be some harm to both slow movers and fast movers. Slow movers may struggle to keep up, perhaps losing some growth experiences as the collective pace goes faster than they do. Fast movers may be held back, may become bored or impatient, may not be satisfied, and may leave the group or otherwise act out their frustration. On the other hand, members will encounter slow movers and fast movers everywhere in the world outside the group: in workplaces, social situations, community associations, and the like. Learning to accommodate to different rates of change, finding a grounding in one's own pace, and becoming more tolerant of differences between people are valuable outcomes for members of closed groups.

Second, an individual's growth should not be sacrificed to the good of the whole group. However, the position taken in this book is that the group entity is both the means and the context for help to individuals (Vinter, 1967a). The social work principle of individualizing the client is the key. The nature of the various contract forms, in particular, insures that the needs of each individual are focused on. Never does the individual negotiate away her or his unique needs and aspirations, even in the interdependent contract. In a closed group, the worker keeps one eye on the needs and growth of the individuals in the group while keeping the other eye on the evolution of the group as a whole.

Third, if the ultimate goal of all therapeutic encounters is, as Fried (1970) says, individuation, rootedness in the self, then group members should not be held together in a mass. Open groups are advocated as being the form which best insures respect for individuality and provides opportunities for individuality to be expressed.

Practice with Open Groups

The decision having been taken to make an open group available, four areas of practice need to be regarded: the worker needs to help the group recycle through the stages of group development as new members arrive and old members depart; to handle the arrival and departure of members; to decide the timing of arrivals and departures; and to sustain the continuity of the group as its membership changes.

The Recycling Process   Necessarily, a group reformulates itself whenever a new member joins or an old member leaves; a change in one part of a system causes change in other parts of the system. When a new member joins the group, the internal structure realigns to take the new person in.

From the time the initial set of people was convened, their interactional patterns have created roles, alliances, and subgroups—all the arrangements that hold people together while they work toward their goal. Although these arrangements have changed over time, the change has been mainly in the direction of maturity of functioning and self-governance. The roles performed by members have been given value, and a status hierarchy has developed. A new member will bring certain typical ways of behaving, which the group needs to accommodate. The new member must also accommodate to the already existing system; she or he cannot enter like a wedge driven into the system, pushing all others aside, and hope to be accepted and integrated into the group.

When a new member enters, the group cycles back to the convening stage, takes the new person in, accommodates her or him into its functioning, and reformulates its reciprocal contract to take the new member's needs into account. The group adjusts its proprietorship structure in a brief reenactment of the conflict/disequilibrium stage, and absorbs the member as it moves back to maintenance. When a new member has moved through these stages with the group in its recycling, the maintenance stage will look much like that of a closed group. Whether a group is open or closed, the maintenance stage represents the most integrated group form.

When an old member departs, her or his leaving creates a gap in the system's structure. The group then must realign itself to fill that gap. The remaining members will assume some of the behaviors of the person who has left; other behaviors may not be picked up. Some compensatory action may need to be taken: equivalent behavioral patterns may be substituted; the worker may supply some of the absent behaviors; or the group may realign itself around the vacant space.

When a member leaves, the group will find itself functioning partly in the formation stage and partly in the termination stage. The formation dynamics—those connected with role differentiation, decision making, and communication—will be manifested in the actions taken to compensate for the vacancy. The termination dynamics are those concerned with recapitulating and evaluating the experience and stabilizing and generalizing the change, both for the person who is leaving and for those who continue. The individuation dynamic will also be operating for the person who leaves, while those who stay represent the core from which the departing member separates herself or himself. An open group usually does not reach a collective termination phase; instead the termination dynamics are seen when a member leaves.

It should be remembered that people are not interchangeable parts. No new member, and no compensatory action by the group, can replace exactly a departing person's function in the group system. At best, the open group system is a fluid association with a central core—which is the essence of the group—composed of the initial purpose, the normative structure in relation to that purpose, the group's history, traditions, and culture, and the worker. An open group is a kind of pass-through system in its structure, but not in its process, because the essential elements are unchanged (see Figure 9-1).

Figure 9-1
The Core of an Open Group

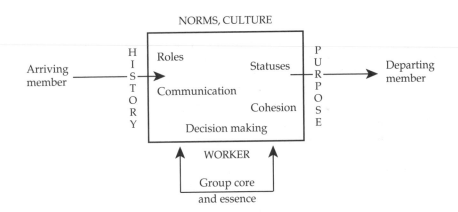

Handling Arrivals and Departures   The worker needs to do individual and group preparation for the arrival of new members and the departure of old members. The recruitment and selection of members for an open group is similar to the activities of the initial stage of a closed group. Pregroup interviews need to be held and reciprocal contracts negotiated. The most striking difference between that situation and this one, however, is that, in describing to the potential member how the group operates, the worker will describe the actual group rather than a projected one. Otherwise, the same procedure should be followed as for a closed group. The group needs to be prepared for the appearance of a new member.

It should be part of an open group's contract that there will be new people added from time to time. Then the worker would inform the group when a new person is about to join. The worker should, if possible, prepare the group two sessions before the newcomer appears, to allow time for the members to become accustomed to the idea and begin to adjust to the change, and to provide an opportunity to discuss how the group is to be presented to the new member. A technique used by many workers is to ask the members to describe the group at this meeting where the addition of the new member is announced, as a preparation for describing the group to the new person at her or his first meeting. This provides an excellent opportunity for the members to reflect on their experience and to recapitulate and summarize it for themselves, and for the worker to learn how the members see the group. Some workers also ask the group for suggestions about what the prospective member should be told in the pregroup interview.

At the new member's first meeting, she or he hears the description of the group, asks questions if she or he chooses, introduces herself or himself, and says anything else she or he is moved to say. The anxiety of facing an already existing group may be high, and at the first session the new member should be allowed to say as much or as little as she or he cares to.

●

As the meeting began, I reminded the group that we had talked earlier about the fact that a new member would be joining the group. "Tonight, she is here for the first time. I'd like all of you to make her welcome!" Turning to the new member, I said, "Polly, why don't you introduce yourself to the group? Say whatever you'd like. You know what the group is for, and the others are here for the same reasons you are; so say whatever is on your mind."

Polly gave her name and said she'd been glad to be accepted for the group. "I can't say I know a whole lot of what to expect because I've never been in a group before, but I'm looking forward to getting some help. I guess that's all I want to say." She ended nervously and looked at me.

I asked the others to introduce themselves by name to Polly. When they'd done that I turned to the group. "When we talked about Polly joining us, we talked about the fact that I would ask you to let her know how the group operates, some of what she'll find when she comes for meetings. Who will summarize the group for her?"

Annie volunteered. "Well, I guess the best thing is to say that we're all women and we're all working on establishing our identities as separate individuals from the men in our lives. When we're working on something, we usually go around the group and find out who wants to talk about some issue, and then we decide which issue we want to focus on. We try to give each other positive strokes and not put each other down for the choices she's made in her past life. Sometime or other, all of us have probably made the same decisions, so we each know where the others are coming from. If someone doesn't want to talk, we let it go until she is ready. We try to keep track of each other so no one goes lots of sessions without contributing anything."

She stopped, and Mimi picked up. "Yeah, and we always go around the group again at the end of each meeting to see if anyone has anything burning that didn't get taken care of. Mostly, that's the way our meetings go."

Polly was asked if she had any questions. "I don't really, I guess. I think I'll just have to see how it goes and try to get in on the action. Thanks; I'm really glad to be here."

●

Some people advocate adding two or more new members at once, rather than one (Rose, 1977). As the system will undergo change anyway, the disruption of adding more than one may not be any more traumatic than that of adding only one. Moreover, the new members may feel more comfortable not to be the only new person, and they may be able to move into the group more smoothly than if they were alone. The decision should be based on an assessment of the group's capacity to absorb new elements and sustain itself.

The contracts for members of an open group are different from those of a closed group. The reciprocal contract will refer to each member's own time frame, and the mutual and interdependent contracts of the group as a whole will not refer to a common time frame. Thus, two contract tracks will be running simultaneously in an open group. One track will follow the evolving contract forms as described in chapters 3–8; these contracts will refer to all the same terms as for a closed group, except for the time frame. The other track will be specific to the time frame for each member's tenure in the group. Monitoring and contract review and renegotiation will always have to take the two tracks into account. When the contracted goals for any member have been reached, she or he is ready to terminate from the group. This would be acknowledged in front of the whole group, and preparation for the member's termination would proceed from that point.

This preparation is akin to what is done with a closed group when it is to terminate. The group is encouraged to give feedback to the terminating member on her or his growth and change, the member is encouraged to recapitulate and evaluate her or his experience in the group, and the departing member and those who will remain should all address ways in which the person can stabilize and generalize the change. During this process, the worker may return to the primary role and central location; she or he will then revert to the role and location appropriate to the level of functioning of the residual group. In the final session attended by the departing member, many of the exercises and media described in chapter 8 for group termination may be used.

The worker will need to devote attention to the members who do not terminate, and help them deal with their continuation. Sometimes anxiety rises when the remaining members conclude that they are not making progress if they cannot leave the group. Unfavorable comparisons between themselves and the departing member may be made, and this can have a discouraging effect on those who remain. The worker needs to help the remaining members differentiate themselves from each other and from the one who is leaving, and help them interpret for themselves where they are in relation to where they want to go. Probably some time will need to be spent on this at the next meeting after the departure of a member.

Timing   A worker with an open group must determine when, in the life of the group, new members may successfully be added and old members terminated. There are no hard-and-fast rules, but some guidelines may be offered.

It seems advisable not to add new members during the conflict/disequilibrium stage. Many things are up for grabs in that stage, and the addition of a new figure could prolong the struggle. For the new members, it would surely be threatening to walk in on group turmoil; and, for the group, the arrival of a stranger could prematurely close off pursuit of its task of gaining ownership of its experience.

Likewise, it does not seem advisable to introduce a new member in the group's termination stage. If no new members have been added by the time the original group as a whole reaches termination, it would be better not to do so then. It seems pointless to add a new person when all the others are about to terminate; one person could hardly be the nucleus for continuing the group. Moreover, the members would be far too involved with their own process of getting out to want to bring someone else along. The most propitious times for adding new members would be during the initial, convening, formation, or maintenance stages.

It seems inadvisable to terminate a member during the formation stage or the conflict/disequilibrium stage. In the formation stage, the departure of a member could delay the group's coalescence and affect its capacity to become fully integrated. In the conflict/disequilibrium stage, the level of struggle and of uneasiness about struggling could be increased if a member were to terminate, and this could jeopardize the continuity of the group. The time is anxiety-ridden enough and sustaining the group system is a delicate enough task without members leaving the group. The abandonment and rejection that people fear when they assume ownership of their group would be acted out many times over if members also were to terminate at that time. Sometimes, however, people's circumstances change and, for whatever reason, they are unable to remain in the group.

In the initial and convening stages, persons may choose to discontinue if the match between their objectives and the way the group is shaping up is not a good one. In that case, the person should be terminated with careful interpretation to her or him and to the group. Preferably, the member who is leaving would return for one final, farewell session. The most acceptable times, then, for a member to leave the group, would be the initial convening, maintenance, or termination stage.

The worker should avoid introducing a new member at a departing member's final meeting. That would present too much emotional material for the core members to handle. Entering and leaving should be handled separately, to give each the emphasis it requires.

Sustaining the Thread of Continuity   Four elements help to sustain continuity in an open group: norms, goals, the worker, and the history of the group.

Norms become effective in the formation stage, but the ground has been laid for their functioning from the earliest times; they are therefore available as one of the constants of the group system. Norms can be used to induct new members into the group, and they help to sustain the thread of continuity.

The goals serve the same function. Even though the contract form changes and even though two tracks of goal orientation are running simultaneously, the initial purpose for the existence of the group remains intact. As each prospective member is interviewed prior to joining the group, the interview would necessarily begin from the original purpose for having this group. That initial purpose stays as the point toward which individual and collective efforts are directed. It is appropriated into the reciprocal contracts and the group's mutual and interdependent contracts.

The worker is another strand of the thread of continuity. The membership of an open group changes, but the worker remains. A member who left the group for a period and then returned could expect to find the worker still there even if a total turnover in membership had occurred. The worker's continuing presence is one of the factors that would make this still the same group.

Worker turnover might occur, however, particularly if the group continues for a year or more. In this case, the worker should prepare the members for her or his departure in much the same way as for the departure of a group member. The worker should recapitulate and evaluate, focus on stabilizing and generalizing the group members' changes, deal with own and others' feelings, prepare the group for the entry of the new worker, and engage in some ritualized ending. The members will have gone as far as they are going with the departing worker's help; they need to claim their growth with the person who has aided that growth, and put new issues on hold pending the arrival of the new worker. The advent of a new worker is a time for regrouping and adjusting to her or his ways and style. With a new professional person, the group (whether open or closed) will cease to exist in exactly its original form.

The fourth element of continuity is the history of the group. This history fixes the group in its time and space and relates the changing entity to something stable. It enables new members to attach to the roots of something that has existed for some time. It is a security anchor; it communicates stability and durability, whether it is told by the worker or the members.

Maximizing the four strands of continuity in an open group lets members who come into the group know they are joining something that has stability, that has a reason for being, that has a way of regulating the behavior of its members to realize its goals, and that has a constant helping professional available. The new membership will not need to reinvent the wheel or make things up as they go along.

Some groups meet for only one time. These might be one-day or half-day training sessions or workshops; orientation meetings for clients new to residential facilities; or what have been called "vestibule groups" for people on waiting lists for service at agencies. Some groups are fluid in membership and attendance; these might be groups in drop-in, partial-care, or day programs like those available in many mental health centers. The group meets at a regular time, but the membership varies from week to week. Such a group might be referred to as, for example, "the Tuesday support group."

The record excerpt that follows, from one of two coworkers with an in-house group in a safe house for battered women, describes an open group of this discontinuous kind.

●

The members of the support group are battered women of all different ages, ethnic backgrounds, social classes, and special populations.

Because cultural factors play such an important part in intimate relationships and may figure strongly in women's decisions whether to stay in those relationships, it is essential that the group workers maintain an awareness of the ethnicity of the members and not do anything to separate them from their culture. This may be particularly important when the group membership is so transitory; the workers need to work within a culture and not against it.

Some members may be women in Lesbian battering relationships, women with multiple problems, women with physical injury, women in emotional shock, women with serious disturbance or psychosis, or severely depressed women. All of them are battered women who have sought refuge in the safe house, where they may stay for up to six weeks.

Since the membership of this support group can be different from session to session, the group exists totally in the present. Each session is a discrete entity with a distinct beginning, middle, and end. If a member should be present who was at the support group the week before, then she is a possible bearer of group culture along with the two coworkers.

The constant fluidity of membership makes the support group unpredictable, and this shapes the workers' roles. Preparing for each group meeting requires great patience and flexibility on the workers' part. It requires being very much in the moment.

•

Summary

Some workers and agencies choose an open group format. This format can more effectively accommodate differential patterns of growth and change, and traditional social work values favoring the uniqueness of the individual argue against submerging the person into a collective mass. Those who favor open groups argue that they are the best means to achieve the ultimate goal of all therapeutic encounters: the individuation of clients into a rooted-ness in self. When an open group form is chosen, four areas of practice need to be attended to: the group's recycling through stages of group develop-ment as new members come and old members go, the coming and going of members, the timing of arrivals and departures, and the continuity of the group.

○

Recording

It is good practice for workers to keep records of group sessions. Unfortu-nately, few workers do so once their professional education is completed; often the only record kept is the statistical attendance record. Various reasons are given for not recording: that there is not enough time; that narrative process recording is a too long and involved procedure to go through; and that no satisfactory format for recording group sessions has been developed.

Records form part of the focus of supervisory conferences, they aid the service decisions that agencies take, and they help form the basis for worker evaluation and planning. They also contribute to knowledge building and the development of practice principles for group work. As Hollenbeck (1954, p. 13) observed, "Social group workers, for years, have been working with people in groups, analyzing what they have observed, formulating new concepts of the group process and methods of leadership." It is regrettable that the knowledge accumulated in the field tends to remain at the point of its origin: in the minds of group work practitioners and, when they do record, in their files. Other purposes for recording were listed by Wilson and Ryland (1949).

Narrative Process Record

Anne Lindsay (1952, pp. 1–15) conceives of the narrative process record as being concerned with "the step-by-step development of groups... the processes which are occurring within the group." Wilson and Ryland (1949, p. 70) consider that its utility lies in its "revealing the interaction which took place in the meeting."

In this form of recording, the worker writes a narrative, as soon after the session as possible, of the process of member interaction that occurred: what happened, the members' relationship to each other and to the worker, and their responses to the activities. The worker performs a dual function throughout the session: while performing her or his helping role, the worker makes mental notes of her or his observations and of the members' responses. Shortly after the session, these mental notes are transferred to paper, and then expanded into a full narrative record with an analysis of the observations and a plan for the next session.

Wilson and Ryland (1949, pp. 76–77) describe a narrative process record as follows:

> As nearly as it is possible to do so, the record should describe chronologically the interacting process of the members, as the process actually occurred, without reference to the logic of the content.... The sequence of events, remarks and reactions as they happened is more important than their subject relationship. The purpose of the record is to understand the interacting process between the members; the subject matter is secondary because its significance is discovered in the way people feel about it rather than what they say.

The advantage of this kind of record is that it may be used to compare changes over time, to see the structure of the group and the relationships and influence patterns among members, to see the worker's interventions and their results, and to define the stage of group development at any given meeting. In supervisory conferences, the record provides a picture of the group session and the worker's activity, to be used as a teaching tool. When a worker has before her or him the precise procedures performed, the performance can be seen most clearly. By comparing similar situations, skills can be gradually integrated.

There are some disadvantages to this form of recording. Despite Wilson and Ryland's (1949) observation that the subject relationship is secondary to the sequence of occurrence of events, much that is written into the record may be extraneous. If a record is to have any usefulness, the material which goes into it ought to be carefully selected. Social workers with groups need to develop a disciplined way of looking for specific predetermined phenomena rather than attempt the very difficult, wasteful, and confusing task of observing all individual and group behavior.

Non-narrative Process Record

An alternative to the narrative process record has been developed. It focuses on the group social forces and the individual members' behavior, and on the worker's goals for future sessions and future interventions (see Figure 9-2). This format aids in the planning aspects of group practice; prior to the next group session, the record may be reviewed and goals and interventions for that session specifically designed and framed. Over the long term, the accumulated records will reveal evaluative material by which to assess group growth and movement.

The records of a group, in the format presented here, may be summarized to create an evaluation over an extended period. Statistical data can be obtained by counting attendance at each meeting. Group attendance figures and individual members' attendance patterns could be used to establish possible associations between behaviors and group dynamics. The descriptions of group dynamics could be used to formulate practice principles. If phrased in the form of working hypotheses ("If I make this intervention, then that happens"), the results of worker interventions may turn into future practice principles.

The effectiveness of worker interventions could be evaluated by reference to cumulative summaries of these records. Goals established by the worker on the basis of what occurred in one session, in any group dynamic, may be compared to the behavior in succeeding sessions, to assess the adequacy of the chosen intervention. The effect of each intervention on any given group dynamic may be seen by observing what is happening in a group session before and after the intervention. Changes in that dynamic, from before to after, could then be assessed to determine whether intention and outcome are in accord. Some of the material drawn upon for the program media dimension in this book was developed by studying the association between group interactional behaviors and four program activities, from before to after the introduction of each activity in a group. Although the recording format presented here was not utilized in that research; an adaptation of Bales's (1950) Interaction Process Analysis was used.

The effect of the group experience on individual members' functioning may be assessed by looking at various aspects of the group social forces. The member's role functionality or dysfunctionality, participation in decision-making processes, leadership-followership patterns, task or social-emotional arenas of functioning, status, interpersonal alliances (subgroups, dyads, triads) and ties (positive, negative, "star," isolate, etc.), norm conformance, and norm enforcement behavior—all of these elements may be tracked over time for each member, observed in any one session, or compared to goals to measure progress. Goals for individual members may be revised, on the basis of this information.

Figure 9-2
Process Recording Form

Name of group: _____ Date: _____

Meeting number: _____ Formation date: _____ Termination date: _____

Members present: _____

_____

_____

Members absent: _____

General goals for the group: _____

_____

Goals for this session: _____

_____

Roles taken and by whom this session (Note the functional or dysfunctional nature of the role taken and whether functional or dysfunctional to the individual or the group; note the goal for future intervention): _____

_____

_____

Interaction in this session (Note the positive or negative tone for individuals and the overall tone for the group; note the goal for future intervention):

_____

_____

_____

Morale (Note the amount and the evidence of it; note the goal for future intervention): _____

_____

_____

Decision making in this session (Note the form used and the influential member or members; note the goal for future intervention): _____

_____

_____

Leadership in this session (Note the centers of influence, and whether task or social-emotional; note the goal for future intervention): _____

_____

_____

Sociogram of interpersonal relations in this session (Use the back of the page for this, noting the status and nature of interpersonal ties; indicate the goal for future interventions): _____

_____

Norms and values expressed in this session (Note which, and their effect on members; note the goal for future intervention): _____

_____

_____

Evidence of group movement seen in this session (Note the relation to group goals): _____

_____

_____

What needs specific attention in the next and future sessions? _____

_____

_____

What goals and what interventions (non-verbal activities, for example) seem indicated as the next steps? _____

_____

_____

Particular response from any individual or group of individuals that determines special attention, observation, or follow-up? Has this appeared before? (Note your specific plan for follow-up): _____

_____

_____

_____

_____

Worker _____

In the years since this format was first developed, it has been used in supervising paraprofessional and professional workers, in field instruction with graduate students in social work, in teaching recording to students in schools of social work, and in field instructor training for supervising students' field practice with people in groups. It has been judged by social work students to be excellent for comprehensiveness and usefulness, but only fair for time and ease. Completing the record after each session may be quite demanding in the beginning; however, it proves to be quite efficient with practice, once one has learned to look out for the items referred to on the recording form.

The format may be less useful in settings where the dimensions of a group entity are less evident (short-term hospital wards, for example) or where cohesive group formation may not be a goal.

Summary

The importance of recording cannot be overemphasized. The need exists for a format that helps the worker evaluate and plan, helps the worker be goal-oriented in her or his interventions, helps the worker focus on group and individual dynamics; and helps lay the groundwork for accumulating and communicating new knowledge in work with people in groups. The format proposed in this chapter may be a springboard to further experimentation and development.

The application of a four-dimensional approach to social work practice with people in groups for direct service is now concluded. The final chapter discusses the use of this practice approach with groups for other than direct service.

References

Bales, R. F. (1950). *Interaction process analysis.* Reading, MA: Addison-Wesley.

Broverman, I. K., & Broverman, G. (1970). Sex role stereotyping and clinical judgments of mental health. *Journal of Consulting and Clinical Psychology, 34,* 1–7.

Davis, L. (Ed.). (1984). Ethnicity in social group work practice [Special issue]. *Social Work with Groups, 7*(3).

DeMarche, D. F., & Iskander, G. M. (1950). On-lookers. *The Group, 12*(3), 7–12.

Emprey, L. J. (1977). Clinical group work with multi-handicapped adolescents. *Social Casework, 58*(10), 593–599.

Feldman, F. (Ed.) (1968). *Institutional racism and social work: Social work papers.* Los Angeles: University of Southern California, School of Social Work.

Fried, E. (1970). Individuation through group psychotherapy. *International Journal of Group Psychotherapy, 20*(4), 450–459.

Goodman, J. A. (Ed.). (1973). *Dynamics of racism in social work practice.* Washington, DC: National Association of Social Workers.

Haley, J. (1976). *Problem solving therapy.* San Francisco: Jossey-Bass.

Hollenbeck, H. (1954). The group dynamics concept of the "group." *The Group, 17*(1), 13–16.

Lewis, R. G., & Ho, M. K. (1975). Social work with native Americans. *Social Work, 20*(5), 379–382.

Lindsay, A. (1952). *Group work recording.* New York: Association Press.

Lum, D. (1986). *Social work practice and people of color.* Pacific Grove, CA: Brooks/Cole.

Mangold, M. M. (Ed.). (1971). La causa chicana [Special issue]. *Social Casework, 52*(5).

Mangold, M. M. (Ed.). (1976). Against the stormy seas [Special issue]. *Social Casework, 57*(3).

Martinez, C. (1977). Group process and the chicano: Clinical issues. *International Journal of Group Psychotherapy, 27*(2), 225–231.

Montalvo, B. (1973). Aspects of live supervision. *Family Process, 12*(4), 343–359.

NiCarthy, G., Merriam, K., & Coffman, S. (1984). *Talking it out: A guide to groups for abused women.* Seattle: Seal Press.

Papell, C. P., & Rothman, B. (Eds.). (1980). Co-leadership in social work with groups [Special issue]. *Social Work with Groups, 3*(4).

Rose, S. D. (1977). *Group therapy: A behavioral approach.* Englewood Cliffs, NJ: Prentice-Hall.

Ryan, R., & Gilbert, G. (1976). *Beyond ain't it awful.* Columbus: Ohio State University.

Symposium: Group therapy with minority group patients. (1975). *International Journal of Group Psychotherapy, 25*(4), 389–428.

Taft, J. J. (1949). Time as the medium of the helping process. *Jewish Social Service Quarterly, 16*(2), 189–198.

Vinter, R. (1967a). An approach to group work practice. In R. Vinter (Ed.), *Readings in group work practice.* Ann Arbor, MI: Campus Publishers.

Wilmer, H. A., & Lamb, H. R. (1969). Using therapeutic community principles. In H. R. Lamb, D. Heath, & J. J. Downing (Eds.), *Handbook of community mental health practice.* San Francisco: Jossey-Bass.

Wilson, G., & Ryland, G. (1949). *Social group work practice.* Boston: Houghton Mifflin.

Ziller, R. (1965). Toward a theory of open and closed groups. *Psychological Bulletin, 63,* 164–182.

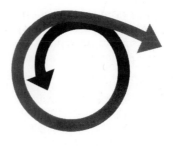

CHAPTER 10

GROUPS FOR PURPOSES OTHER THAN DIRECT SERVICE

The preceding chapters have been concerned with the use of groups for direct service purposes—enhancement of social functioning, restoration to former states of social functioning, achievement of yet unreached levels of social functioning, or correction of dysfunctional interpersonal or social relationships. The philosophical stance taken in this book is that life is lived in groups (family groups, work groups, social groups, voluntary associations, and so forth), and therefore groups are the appropriate form for offering service to people with personal needs that are socially oriented. There are other kinds of needs, however, for which groups are an appropriate form of service. These are needs outside a person's individual needs, ones that can be met in some formal organization: boards, committees, and task-action groups, for task accomplishment; agency in-service training, supervision, and staff development groups, for role performance; and consultation groups with decision and policy makers, with administrators, with direct service providers, or with interdisciplinary teams, for improving the functioning of an

248

organization. Groups of these three types are the focus of this chapter (see Toseland & Ephross, 1987).

This chapter applies the practice model to groups for other than direct service, but a therapeutic approach is not advocated for such groups. The chapter begins with a discussion of the group social forces described in Chapter 1, as they operate in groups for other than direct service. The practice approach set forth in Chapter 2 is then applied to such groups. Finally, the worker skills appropriate for these groups are discussed, and groups for purposes other than direct service are classified into three types, according to the unit of focus: individual contribution, group contribution, or both individual and group contribution to organizational functioning.

○

Group Social Forces

Group social forces, defined in Chapter 1, are summarized as they relate to groups for purposes other than direct service.

Membership selection and group composition, in other than direct service groups, may be self-generated, as in task groups for which people volunteer; or persons may be selected for their level of awareness in regard to a topic, as in task groups related to planning, or supervision, training, and staff development groups, or some boards and committees; or persons may be selected according to their role in an agency, as in some consultee groups, training groups, staff development groups, teams, and some boards and committees.

Direct service groups require a balance of homogeneity and heterogeneity in relation to the purpose for the group, with emphasis placed on problem homogeneity. By contrast, in groups for other than direct service purposes, homogeneity would be sought in awareness of a topic, and heterogeneity in the resources each person can contribute. The persons who compose these groups are assumed to be well functioning and capable of forming attachments to others and achieving enough cohesion to create a coalesced learning or action environment.

Whereas pregroup interviews are used in direct service groups to aid the selection of the group members, pregroup interviews are not used in groups for other than direct service purposes, except in the case of group hiring interviews or screening interviews. In group hiring interviews, a group of people interviews the prospective member; group-oriented contract negotiation is not part of the interview. Persons being considered for board or committee membership are sometimes asked to participate in some kind of screening interview (at least by telephone if not face-to-face).

Training and staff development groups, task groups, and consultee groups tend to have a stable membership and fixed time limits. The membership of boards and committees changes on a planned basis, coinciding with terms of service. The membership of some teams and supervision groups changes on an unplanned basis as a result of staff turnover.

Goals for groups for other than direct service are usually defined outside the group. They may be agency determined (as for training, staff development, supervision, or consultation), mandated by a charter of incorporation or legislative act (boards and committees), member determined (most task groups), or jointly determined by agency and members (teams and some task groups). The goals do not emerge over time as a synthesis of initial purpose, as they do in direct service groups. *External structural elements* tend to be more instrumental in groups for other than direct service than in direct service groups.

Time is not a medium of the process in groups for other than direct service. Some will have fixed time limits (training, staff development, task groups, and consultee groups); these resemble closed groups going through the stages of group development. Other groups have no time limits (boards, committees, and most teams); these resemble open groups recycling the stages of development.

Space is instrumental and subsidiary to the goals of groups of this type. Arrangement of the space is instrumental in training and staff development groups but is incidental in groups for other than direct service.

Size is a consideration in groups of this kind only insofar as it is a factor in insuring that there is a sufficient supply of persons for distributing the work (as in task groups, boards, committees, and teams). In groups for which distribution of work is not a factor, groups of any size may be utilized; however, too few persons may not provide enough resources to accomplish the group's goal, and too many persons tend to preclude interpersonal relationships.

Whereas the external structural elements are integral and facilitative in direct service groups, they are instrumental, incidental, or subsidiary for groups beyond direct service uses.

Internal structure is central to the capacity of the group to reach a mature level of functioning. Through role differentiation, leadership to followship patterns emerge among the members to aid the creation and sustainment of their group system. The worker role is apart from group member roles, since the worker is an actor in the system but not a member of it. Role differentiation is generally not developed by worker interventions with groups for other than direct service, except for teams, which attend to their own internal (social-emotional) processes as well as orienting themselves to their collective task.

Roles in both the internal and external systems will be activated in groups of any sort. As long as the role differentiation is not dysfunctional to the integrity of the group, the best thing for a worker to do is to let it be. With boards, committees, and task groups, worker attention would be directed to task (external system) roles more than to social-emotional (internal system) roles.

The worker/leader role is generally imposed on these groups from outside the group; this is the case with trainers, staff developers, agency-designated team leaders, and supervisors, and staff positions with boards, task groups, and committees. A worker role that is not imposed is that of the consultant who is invited to work on developing staff and organizational relationships as part of the task. Moreover, teams that attend to their own team building may not have an outside worker/leader.

In every case, where there is a professional person present to give service to the group, that person is not a member of the group. The professional person responsible for giving service to the group is sometimes referred to as the leader. However, a worker's leadership role is different from that of the formal, elected leader of a board or committee, and different from the role of the formal leader in some task groups.

Cohesion is less a focus of worker attention in groups for other than direct service. Some degree of cohesion may occur naturally, especially in boards and committees as they deliberate together, but it is not emphasized by the worker. In teams that engage in their own team-building, however, and in some self-help groups, the goals and the means for achieving goals tend to require some level of cohesion.

Communication and decision making are important for both types of groups. Communication—the verbal or nonverbal exchange of ideas, thoughts, and feelings—is central in task groups, boards, committees, consultee groups, and teams. Training, staff development, and supervision groups, which rely on an experiential mode for learning, do not require such exchange but rather the transmission and processing of information.

Decision making is a central element for boards, committees, some teams, and most task groups. It is less central in training, staff development, consultation, supervision, and some team groups. Decisions are made about using the consultation provided or the material acquired in training and supervision, or about correcting team functioning; but the worker/leader does not focus on aiding the group in its decision-making process.

Group influence and control are basic to the nature of groups for other than direct service. When the purpose of the group is individual contribution to organizational functioning, there is less emphasis on members' being under the influence and control of others; when the purpose of the group is both individual and group contribution to organizational functioning, there is a moderate emphasis on the influence and control of others; and when the focus is on group contribution to organizational functioning, the emphasis on influence and control of others is at a maximum (Festinger, 1953; Hartford, 1972; Sherif, 1947).

Norms help sustain the system, *group culture* helps define the system in relation to the rest of its environment, and *values* characterize the system. In groups for other than direct service, these social forces are generally not emphasized in worker interventions. However, for teams, which work at their own collective process, the normative structure, group culture, and values are part of the bond of cohesion among the team members; so they will emphasize these dynamics.

To summarize: group social forces are present in groups for purposes other than direct service. There is no social force that is absent from any group for other than direct service. Such groups differ from direct service groups in the degree of emphasis on and the use made of various forces.

Attention now turns to a consideration of the four dimensions of the practice approach presented in this book, as those dimensions apply to work with groups for purposes other than direct service.

○

Dimensions of the Practice Model

The discussion that follows represents the second of two flex points of this book's practice approach; the first flex point was presented in Chapter 9, when the use of this practice approach with open groups was described. These two flex points are places in the basic design of the model where exceptions, modifications, or revisions may be made so that the approach follows reality rather than requiring reality to bend to fit the design.

In this section, groups for other than direct service are considered from the viewpoint of the four dimensions—stage of group development, contract form in effect, role and location of the worker vis-à-vis the system, and program media.

Stages of Group Development

The stages of group development are similar to those of direct service groups: initial, convening, formation, conflict/disequilibrium, maintenance, and termination.

Training groups, staff development groups, task groups, and consultee groups tend to move through the stages in a regular way. These groups closely resemble direct service groups because they exist within fixed time limits and they have a stable, identified membership. There are differences, however. The people are present for the organization's purposes rather than for personal purposes. It is true that staff members, task group members, and consultee group members may benefit at a personal level through improving their skills, improving the situation they are in, or feeling a sense of accomplishment for doing work well; but those are not the reasons for their participation in these groups. They are present for task related reasons: to improve job performance, to prepare for advancement on the job, to acquire information essential to the agency's functioning, to accomplish a specific task, to solve a particular problem, or to work more productively or harmoniously.

The connectedness in these groups comes from the members' common work situation rather than from a common social situation; it is less individual and more organizational than in a direct service group. So, although groups for other than direct service go through the stages of development, the cohesion, role differentiation, and norms are more outward oriented than oriented inward toward personal growth and change.

Boards, committees, supervision groups, and some teams, on the other hand, more closely resemble open groups of the direct service variety. This is because they typically do not have fixed time limits and because they have memberships which change over time. The conflict/disequilibrium stage, for example, in an interdisciplinary team might be enacted in the following way.

●

Bernie had been employed at the center for children with developmental disabilities for four months, and things had been running smoothly. As a social worker, he had established himself on the team as a specialist in work with Hispanic families. He was pleased to notice that others on the team turned to him for expert advice when there was a case conference involving an Hispanic family.

Lately, he had been taking a certificate program in advanced family therapy at the local school of social work, and he started expanding his area of specialty in work with families. In team meetings, he began to propose the use of forms of family therapy other than the team's preferred form. He began speaking up to give advice to all the other team members on how they should be working with families according to the new therapies he was learning.

The other team members picked up on what they perceived as his "turf invasion," and began to try to be experts to each other in all areas. At several meetings the roles and relationships among the team members became completely blurred. The team leader than proposed that they spend a session retracing their tangential path and reorient themselves to the role-relationships they had established previously, which had worked so effectively for them.

●

Because the goal of a group of this subtype is a continuing one, when new members are added and old members leave the set of people regroups and reformulates itself in the open group variation of direct service groups. Groups of this subtype also form their member connection less on the basis of identification with each other than on the basis of their common identification with the mission of the organization of which they are a part. Roles do differentiate and norms do operate, but these are more often found in formal organizational form (offices, bylaws, and rules of parliamentary procedure, for example) than in an informal relationship-oriented form.

The following record shows a committee functioning in a way that reflects the members' abilities to perform their task even without the presence of the staff member.

●

The associate executive, who provided staff services to the family counseling agency's program committee, telephoned the branch where the program committee was meeting. He said he would not be able to get to the meeting because his son had been injured playing soccer and he had to be at the hospital. He suggested that the committee could go on without him.

When the meeting started, the chairperson announced that the group would go on without Walt. "I guess we'll be groping our own way, this time. But we've been meeting every month for seven months now, and the bylaws tell us what our task is, so I guess if we don't know our job by now, even having Walt with us couldn't help us much!" The others cordially agreed.

With the situation clearly before them, the committee got down to work and completed its task of reviewing proposed program objectives and budgets from all the agency's service units. The members found that they had among themselves the necessary resources for deliberating on the choices that needed to be made; that they could resolve their differences by arguing points on their own merits; and that they could come to decisions in an amicable consensus form.

●

The force that drives groups for other than direct service purposes through the stages of development is attachment to external, usually organization-oriented goals, rather than attachment to internal, personal growth goals as in the case of direct service groups. Further, groups for other than direct service differ from each other depending on whether they are open or closed with respect to membership and time limits.

Contract Forms

The contracts of training groups, staff development groups, and supervision groups most closely resemble those of direct service groups because they are oriented toward improving individual performance. Part of the contract is an agreement to attach oneself to the organization's purpose for making the group available. The interdependent contract form probably does not exist in these groups, because the purpose is not to create a cohesive group.

Task groups also resemble direct service groups in the evolution of contracts, because task groups are time-limited. Individual performance is not emphasized, but the group jointly appropriates the organization's purposes (or, in the case of a self-help group unrelated to an organization, creates its own organizational purpose). Some level of interdependent contract needs to exist, because the task group is collectively concerned with its relationship to organizational goals.

In groups for improving staff performance and in task groups, the individual contract is not taken heavily into account (other than in some hiring procedures or in briefly asking for people's learning needs), because the focus of these groups is individual contribution to organizational performance and not individual functioning per se.

For boards and committees, a reciprocal contract may be established through some kind of pregroup interview, as in the following example. The purpose of this would be to search for a match between the individual's aspirations and capacities and the organization's needs and purposes.

•

The advisory committee to the community social planning agency was formed by the staff using the nominational-reputational technique for identifying community leaders. Each prospective member of the committee was then interviewed by a staff member to determine the person's interest and willingness to serve on the advisory committee. At the end of each interview, each interviewee was asked to write a statement of commitment and agreement to serve. The wording was left to each person to frame within the overall purpose for which the committee was being formed. One prospective member wrote the following statement:

"I am willing to serve on the advisory committee and agree to attend all meetings of it unless I notify the agency in advance. I will have read the material furnished by the staff prior to each meeting, and I agree to add to committee discussions whatever knowledge and perspective I can. I will try to provide information about resources I am aware of whenever I am asked."

•

Board or committee members' individual contracts would be considered only tangentially, because the organization is probably not so concerned with what the person wants from life in general, but only with what the person hopes to contribute to the organization. No mutual contract exists among board or committee members, because their focus is less on their individual needs than on their collective aim. The interdependent contract is strongly emphasized, because there needs to be attention to the functioning of the group as a whole. This attention will probably manifest itself in some kind of formalized procedure for fixing tenure, assigning responsibilities, and determining the responsibilities of each board or committee member. A board or committee has no independent contracts; a board or committee member may agree with herself or himself about future requests to serve in such a capacity, but this would not represent an independent contract.

Teams have contracts that evolve like those of direct service groups—especially teams that involve all the members in the hiring procedures and then proceed to function as self-aware groups, attending to their own processes. Interdependent contracts are strongly emphasized for those engaging in team building and in team monitoring of the group processes. This contract form will probably be the most enduring, because the team's collective functioning is so crucial to its effectiveness. The following illustration shows this level of functioning and the contract which expresses that.

•

The interdisciplinary team had been working together for 18 months with no change of team membership. A level of trust and security had developed among them such that they were able to overlap their roles on occasion. Their agreement among themselves on this was that the members from any one discipline would rely on members from another discipline more often and more readily. Their task-effective, integrated, and coordinated team delivery of service to families of developmentally disabled children became the central group task (not an individual one). They agreed to use roles and functions according to each others' own unique strengths and skills; it was an agreement on true interdisciplinariness rather than multidisciplinariness.

•

The independent contract in a team will not be emphasized, because the focus is on group-as-a-whole rather than individual functioning. Consultee groups will emphasize interdependent contracts when the focus of the consultation is on strengthening the organization seeking consultant service. Because consultation typically focuses on group-as-a-whole functioning, little or no attention would be given to individual or independent contracts.

Role and Location of the Worker

The role and location of the worker vis-à-vis the group depends on the type of group.

Groups focused on individual contributions to organizational functioning—training groups, supervision groups, and staff development groups—have workers who occupy a central location and enact a primary role. Groups of this subtype are relatively less focused on autonomous functioning than are the other two subtypes. The group itself is deemphasized; the format is one of learning in the presence of others. Communication patterns (except for role plays and small work-groups) tend to be worker centered.

The goals have been determined by the agency, and the internal and external systems differentiate themselves relatively little. Cohesion is not encouraged beyond that typically seen in classroom-type settings. The agency-determined nature of such groups supports the aura of authority surrounding the role of the worker. Thus, both because the agency has determined that the group shall exist and because the group is structured to transmit information, the worker is in a primary role and a central location much of the time. For this reason these groups resemble direct service groups in the convening stage.

Groups focused on group-as-a-whole functioning and the contribution of that to the organization—boards, committees, and task groups— closely resemble direct service groups in the maintenance stage. The group is capable of autonomous functioning, and the members are able to create and sustain their own entity. They possess the skill of adopting and working toward their own goals, within the constraints of the group's societally mandated purposes as contained within charters of incorporation or legislation. Groups of this type have workers who occupy a peripheral location and enact a facilitative role, after a brief period of development in the areas of cohesion and role differentiation. The cohesion necessary to autonomous functioning is based on attraction to what the group does, rather than attraction to the experience or to other members. The differentiation of roles is necessary to create and sustain the group's internal and external systems (Cartwright & Zander, 1960). In these groups, the external (task-system) roles are typically formal, official roles—elected or appointed positions, for example; the internal (social-emotional system) roles are typically informal ones. No one has ever elected or appointed an encourager or a tension reliever, but these are crucial internal-system roles, nonetheless. Decision-making processes and norms are related in groups of this sub-type, because both are formally provided for in bylaws and guides to parliamentary procedure. The following example illustrates the worker's facilitative role.

•

This was the second meeting of the advisory board to the local affiliate program of the Council of International Programs for Youth Leaders and Social Workers. The members were community leaders and professionals, internationally minded people from the university and the community. The purpose of the meeting was to provide information to the members regarding the work of the advisory board.

Many of the tasks of implementing the program, which had been done the previous year by the staff worker, needed to be picked up by volunteer resources. The chairperson pro tem asked the staff worker to identify the range of tasks, which she did. Then the members were asked to categorize these tasks. The staff worker moved to the chalkboard and wrote the categories named by the board members. She then listed the specific tasks for each category.

From time to time the staff worker turned to the group to ask if they were agreeing with the way she was organizing their suggestions. Whenever there were disagreements, she asked the members who held differing points of view to exchange ideas with each other and thereby resolve the difference. Otherwise, she did not contribute to the discussion.

At the end of the meeting, all of the task forces and committees necessary to the operation of the program had been named, and a brief job description for each one had been created.

•

The persons who compose groups of this type are assumed to have experience in group decision making and the ability to contribute to the organization. From the worker they need aid in amalgamating the group, not aid in group functioning per se.

Groups that focus on both individual and group-as-a-whole contributions to organizational functioning—consultee groups and teams—have workers who occupy a pivotal location and enact a variable role. The group forces are to be maximized to a degree that makes coordinated functioning possible, but not to the same high degree as for boards, committees, and task groups. In teams and consultation groups, individual and group functioning are to be emphasized equally; in this respect, groups of this subtype resemble direct service groups in the formation stage, when norms begin to influence members' behavior and formally differentiated roles appear.

The composition of teams and consultee groups is such that the contribution of each individual is valued for the expertise she or he possesses. When any member leaves one of these groups, the valued expertise is sought, as much as possible, in the replacement member. The rationale for this is that the group has been composed as a balanced network of specific skills, and the group's effectiveness depends on maintaining that balance.

The example that follows shows a team dealing with the departure of a member and its decision about replacing him.

●

Rick, the first physician's assistant employed at the center, was leaving the city for advanced training. He had made an important contribution to the team's functioning, and his approaching departure was creating stress within the team.

As the team members talked about replacing him, they refused to consider hiring another physician's assistant. "We were lucky with Rick," they maintained. "I don't even want to think about taking the chance of looking for someone else who's a physician's assistant," said Miriam, the psychologist. Her resistance was shared by the others.

Finally, the team leader halted the discussion. "Look," she said, "Rick made a great contribution to our team. Other teams in the center envy us for our smooth functioning and for having had Rick with us. We'd do him a disservice if we made it appear that we couldn't go on without him; it would damage our sense of teamwork. Let's try to get ourselves together and look at what we want in another physician's assistant, rather than keeping our focus on Rick's irreplaceable qualities."

●

More emphasis is put on the differentiation of internal and external system in teams and consultee groups than in boards, committees, and task-action groups, because these groups have to hold themselves together while getting their work done. Members of a consultee group are selected for their expertise, and such a group is assumed to be capable of autonomous functioning only within the limits set by the organization's purpose for the group's existence.

The worker needs to coordinate the balanced system and to make space for the exercise of individual expertise. The pivotal location allows the worker to be central with respect to channeling communication and peripheral with respect to coordinating skill-specific roles. In a well-functioning interdisciplinary team, the members of each discipline are aware of the interface between their discipline and the other disciplines, and they keep their own system in balance; worker location at the periphery of that system does not affect the system's own balance. The variable role allows the worker to be primary with respect to keeping role definitions clear and to be facilitative with respect to helping the group define and act on its areas of commonality.

Rotating Team Leadership   In some settings, there is no formally designated team leader, or the leadership may rotate among the members of the group. A rotating team leader cannot be considered the worker; the definition used in this book is that a worker is a professional person assigned (by self or agency) to give service to a group. Groups that rotate the formal leadership position among peers include not only teams with a rotating team leadership role but also peer supervision groups, self-help groups such as Alcoholics Anonymous, and consultee groups focused on team building wherein formal roles are abolished. The convenor, chairperson, discussion leader, or facilitator of such a group is not a worker within the definition of this practice approach, even though she or he would enact the several worker roles and occupy the various worker locations vis-à-vis the group system.

The final dimension to be discussed for groups for other than direct service is program media.

Program Media

Groups for purposes other than direct service will require group-building, group-sustaining, and group-ending program media at successive points in their life span, although groups will differ in their respective purposes, emphasized entitativity, and openness on the membership and time dimensions.

Training and staff development groups are closed in terms of membership and time limits; their purpose is the transmission of information to improve the contribution of individuals to organizational functioning. Group-as-a-whole functioning is deemphasized; the focus is on individual performance in the organization. The need for such groups is typically determined by persons other than the group members; thus, except for a brief initial period when individuals attach to the stated objectives for training or staff development, groups of this subtype move very quickly through the group-building phase. Appropriate program media are get-acquainted exercises, goal-setting experiences, and discussion leading to a teaching-learning reciprocal contract.

The group-sustaining phase is extended in comparison to the other phases, for it is in this phase that the purpose of the group is worked on and fulfilled; however, no specific time frame is prescribed. Program media appropriate for the group-sustaining phase are didactic presentations, discussions, simulations, role plays, work groups, homework projects singly or in groups, and audio-visual presentations.

The following example shows a supervision group using planning for program media as a way of sustaining itself through a conflict situation.

●

The protective services unit of the department of social services had a confrontation with the supervisor over her plan to have case management information presented for three sessions; and the members of the unit modified the plan to fit their own identified needs. They began to function in a more coordinated fashion, taking more responsibility for deciding what content they wanted and how they wanted it presented. At the end of each meeting, they decided what they wanted for the next meeting; over the course of five sessions, they had case presentations, role playing, a film, a taped speech by Carl Rogers, and a speaker on Parents Anonymous.

●

The brief ending phase is focused on an evaluation of the experience by the group as a whole and by the members individually. Media appropriate for this phase include graphic arts done by the members, in which they depict what they have experienced and the value of the experience to them; written evaluation forms, which may then be discussed; and a discussion to wrap up unfinished business. The ending may be ritualized by giving certificates of completion at a closing ceremony, and concluded with refreshments.

Supervision groups, boards, and committees are alike in being open in membership and duration, and in the amount of entitativity sought. They are different, however, because both boards and committees focus on group contributions to organizational functioning, whereas supervision groups focus on individual contribution to organizational functioning. Because these three kinds of groups endure as continuing entities they need more cohesion than do groups of the previous type. More attention should be given to group-as-a-whole functioning because the purpose of boards and committees is group contribution to organizational functioning. Because the group is the vehicle through which individual contribution to organizational functioning is enhanced for supervision groups and because group contribution to organizational functioning is emphasized for boards and committees, all three of these kinds of groups will spend a relatively extended time in group building. Program media for group beginnings are get-acquainted experiences, goal-setting (or agenda-making) discussions, decision-making exercises, exercises that help people relate individual objectives to organizational goals, orientation-type presentations, and experiences that establish role differentiation patterns (formalized for boards and committees into elected or appointed officer positions).

Because these groups are open in membership and duration, their group-sustaining phase is also extended; it may be thought of as encompassing the lifespan of the organization. Since turnover does occur, there may be some recycling to earlier stages of development, as with direct service open groups; but most of the life of a board or committee is spent in the maintenance or work stage. Program media appropriate to this phase include discussion, deliberation, and decision making; review and monitoring activities; some retreat periods for reviewing goal setting or for enhancing interpersonal but task oriented relationships; action-research projects; and smaller task group or work group activities to strengthen task-oriented communication, which is then centrally integrated.

Endings for these groups are brief. Like the endings of direct service open groups, they mainly have to do with termination of individual members. The flavor of the ending program media is more concerned with ritualizing the departure of members than with evaluative activities. The program media utilized might be a meal or a reception; a recognition ceremony in which awards, certificates, or gifts are given; or statements of tribute given at the last session at which the departing member is present.

●

The family counseling agency had just completed a three-month membership drive that had, as its main purpose, developing a broader financial base for the agency. The board of the agency decided to hold a reception for the membership committee and to invite all board members, committee members, volunteers, and financial contributors. At the party, toasts were drunk to the membership committee workers who had performed such sterling service, and each of them was presented with a certificate of appreciation.

●

Consultee groups and teams focus on maximizing both individual and group-as-a-whole contributions to organizational functioning, and a high degree of entitativity is sought. The group is more than a vehicle for enhancing individual contributions to organizational functioning; the team or consultee group is equally important to the organization's functioning.

Consultation is usually a closed, time-limited relationship between worker and group; a team is usually an open, ongoing entity. In the beginning, some differences between these two types of groups will be evident. A consultant is usually brought into an already existing group, so the program media should focus on means for the worker and the group to become acquainted and to work out the details of the time they will spend together. A team will rather focus on the members getting acquainted with each other and the worker. The group-building phase, for both consultee groups and teams, will be extended in comparison to that of direct service groups, because the details of the worker-to-group relationship need time to be worked out in the group milieu rather than in pregroup interviews.

Other appropriate beginning program media include contract exercises, cohesion exercises, trust exercises, and experiences in balancing individual and group goals and objectives.

The following example shows the use of team-building media to aid a hospital department in its reorganization.

●

The social service department at the general hospital had just converted from a hierarchical form of organization to a team form and had added three new workers. It was therefore necessary to orient the new workers and to get all the team members on an equal basis. In the first few team meetings after the conversion, the content of the sessions was orientation to the hospital and the department, its philosophy of treatment, and the history of the changed organizational form. Details of the rotating team leadership pattern were worked out.

At the first meeting, the team leader for the month engaged all the members in team-building exercises so that new and old team members and the whole team could begin to work together. The team leader had everyone draw a figure of how they felt about working on a team, and to name three feelings that matched the figure. Then they were to draw a figure and name three feelings representing how they hoped the situation would be in six months. They then discussed their drawings in groups of three and reported to the whole group. In the whole group, the discussion focused on eliciting common aspirations and what they could do to realize those.

●

The middle phase for consultee groups and teams is extended, as was the beginning phase. Once they are established, their lifespan matches that of the organization (although the time with the worker is limited). The middle phase is the period of paramount work. Appropriate program media for the middle phase are role plays, simulations, decision-making exercises, goal-setting and goal-attaining exercises, cohesion-building exercises, role strengthening experiences (formalized roles, in both consultee groups and teams), and retreats or marathons.

The ending phase of consultee groups is different from that of teams. For teams, ending generally means the termination of a team member. The termination will be brief, concerned principally with a ritualized ending. The program media for boards and committees would be appropriate here—those which acknowledge a member's contribution both to the organization and to the group. The ending may be done once with the team and again with the organization as a whole.

For consultee groups, the group itself will go on, but the worker will terminate. Ending program media will focus on the evaluation aspects of termination rather than on recognition rituals. Some recognition of the worker's contribution either to the group or to the organization may be made, if the nature of the relationship has warranted that; but as this is a contractual arrangement, such recognition usually does not occur. The ending phase will be about the same as for direct service groups; it will be concerned with helping the group generalize and stabilize the changes that have occurred during the worker's time with them. Program media would include evaluative discussions, use of written evaluation forms, and exercises (a simulation, for example) that afford the opportunity for members to put into practice what they have gotten from the experience.

Task groups are similar to the prototype of direct service groups in that they are closed with respect to membership and duration. However, task groups have the purpose of maximizing group functioning for the sake of contributing to an organization's functioning, whereas direct service groups have the purpose of helping individuals. In task groups, therefore, the group-building program media need to help members connect with the task that is the group's reason for being. This entails some get-acquainted activity for members to know with whom they will work, goal-setting exercises, discussions about division of labor (role differentiation), practice of decision-making methods, and negotiations about time frames.

In the group-sustaining phase, where the main task is accomplished, the program media would involve deliberation and decision making, work done singly or in work groups and then centrally coordinated, homework projects, resource identification and information gathering, and review and monitoring activities. The group-ending phase of task groups is briefer than for direct service groups. The focus of the program media is evaluation of the functioning of the group as a whole. This could include writing a report, in parts and then collated; preparing a plan for action to follow; or setting a plan in motion. Depending on the kind of task undertaken, some recognition media would be appropriate, wherein the work of individuals or the task group as a whole could be honored for task accomplishments. The program media for the various types of groups for other than direct service are summarized in Table 10-1.

In general, with groups for purposes other than direct service, less attention is paid to the development of a cohesive unit than is the case with direct service groups. An emotional bond need not exist (and may, in fact, be inappropriate or dysfunctional) in groups for purposes other than direct service. Many groups for purposes other than direct service do have parties, luncheons, or receptions, and serve food and drink at their meetings, but such program media are used primarily to reinforce task performance by supporting a congenial atmosphere within which work may be performed.

Table 10-1

Program Media in Groups for Other Than Direct Service

	Training, Super-vision, and Staff Development Groups	Boards, Committees and Task-action Groups	Consultee Groups and Teams
Group-building media	Get-acquainted exercises Goal-setting experiences Discussion leading to teaching-learning contract	Get-acquainted exercises Discussion, deliberation, and decision-making exercises Relating individual objectives to the organization's Orientation Role training	Contract exercises Cohesion exercises Experiences balancing individual and organizational objectives
Group-sustaining media	Didactic presentations Simulations Role plays Work projects Discussions Homework projects Audiovisual presentations	Discussion Deliberation Retreats Action-research projects Work groups Review and monitoring	Role plays Simulations Trust and cohesion-building exercises Goal exercises Retreats Marathons Role-strengthening exercises
Group-ending media	Recapitulation and summary of learning Written evaluation Perhaps ritualized ending Wrap-up discussion Graphics	Formal, ritualized endings Evaluation sessions	Evaluative discussions Written evaluations Simulations

This concludes the discussion of the four dimensions of the practice model as they apply to groups for other than direct service. Differences between these groups and direct service groups are found in four major areas: the degree of entitativity necessary, the purpose for the existence of the group, whether the group is open or closed with regard to membership, and whether it is open or closed in duration. Within each of the four dimensions, subtypes of groups vary according to whether the group exists to affect individual contributions to organizational functioning, group contribution to organizational functioning, or both individual and group contributions to organizational functioning.

In the concluding section of this chapter, worker skills for groups for other than direct service are discussed.

○

Worker Skills

Groups oriented to the individual contribution to organizational functioning—training, supervision, and staff development groups—resemble the convening stage of group development, with the worker in a central location and enacting a primary role. Groups oriented to the group-as-a-whole contribution to organizational functioning—boards, committees, and task groups—resemble the maintenance stage of group development, with the worker in a peripheral location and enacting a facilitative role. Groups that exist for both individual and group-as-a-whole contributions to organizational functioning—consultee groups and teams—resemble the formation stage of group development, with the worker in a pivotal location and taking a variable role. Each of these subtypes is taken up in turn in this section of the chapter.

Groups Focused on Individual Contributions

In its early state, a group for other than direct service has the dynamics of beginning affiliation. People stand apart as separate individuals; as they are in the presence of others, there is simultaneous, but not unified, activity. Such is the case with training and staff development groups; the collection of people is assembled for a specific task and for a fixed period of time. In the case of supervision groups, the group is ongoing, somewhat resembling an open group of the direct service type; because of its specific learning task, however, it is classified with the other learning-oriented groups.

Another dynamic seen in these groups echoes the approach-avoidance dilemma of direct service groups. The persons are willing to enter into first-order decision making about tasks and relationships and to undertake joint activity; yet they are not fully integrated into a cohesive whole. The full commitment to joining—which implies giving up some part of one's separateness in favor of a greater good—is neither sought nor made. There is merely enough accord and unity to permit participation in common activities. The ambivalence is resolved by balancing individual learning aims with organizational needs.

The worker skills for these groups are similar to those for direct service groups in the convening stage: assessing the learning needs, planning, facilitating connection, modeling new skills, and observing and assessing member behavior.

The first worker skill with training, supervision, and staff development groups is assessment in relation to the learning needs of the members of the group. The purpose of the group is to improve the contribution of individuals to the functioning of the organization. The individuals' learning needs may be assessed in a variety of ways. The worker (trainer, supervisor, or staff developer) may meet with an agency or organization manager to determine what the management has in mind as necessary content, and then meet with members of the staff (a planning group, standing or ad hoc; staff members at random; or all staff members) to refine the content and shape it to the specific persons' experiences.

The worker needs to ascertain the job requirements for those who are to be members of the group. This may be done by reading agency documents or by asking the planning group members directly. The worker will form an educational assessment, a process something like a force-field analysis (Lewin, 1947). The gap between the members' present information and the information needed in the future constitutes the field of learning within which the worker will plan (see Figure 10-1).

Figure 10-1
Educational Assessment

Worker-defined
- Previous experience
- Previous training
- Previous education
- Length of time in position or until taking new position
- Anticipated use of content

Agency-defined
Job requirements
- Educational
- Experience
- Previous training
Job specifications
- Tasks
- Accountability point
- Linkages to rest of system
Content focus

Defined area of need for training,
supervision, or staff development

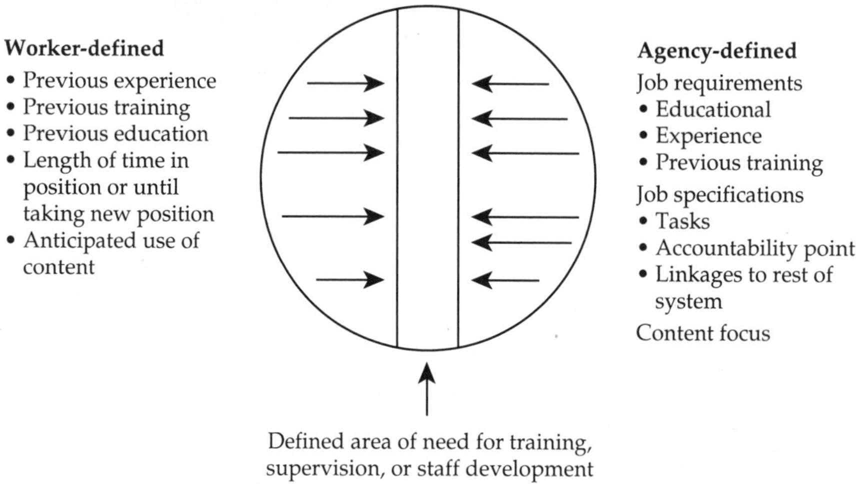

The worker occupies a primary role and central location in defining what she or he needs to learn from the organization and the group members, the form into which that information is put, and the way to transmit the information to the group and manage the group processes as well.

Once this assessment has been completed, the worker plans the training, supervision, or staff development program. Using the educational assessment, the worker designs the content, determines the sequencing for the content, designs learning opportunities (media), and chooses an evaluation mechanism. The worker will share this plan with the group members, ask for additional input, and revise the original plan accordingly. This exchange and the working agreement that emerges from it are equivalent to a reciprocal contract in a direct service group.

In facilitating connection, the worker gives attention to the communication and interactional nets that exist. For groups of this subtype, the facilitation of connection is not highly emphasized; the participants join in cooperative activities such as role plays, small group activities, discussion, simulations, and exercises, but a fully cohesive entity is not required. Communication flows mainly from the worker to the group as a whole or from the worker to each individual, rather than between individuals. Interpersonal forces are not mobilized, except in very specific program media.

The worker is central and primary in bringing information and learning materials to the group or in answering questions, referring to resources, or leading the group in problem solving.

The worker facilitates connection in engaging the members in the learning opportunities (program media) and encouraging them to participate in such simulations, role plays, and exercises as the worker proposes.

In the modeling skill, the worker uses herself or himself as a resource in a particular way, as well. The worker's methods may represent a model of the techniques being taught. In addition, the worker might take a role in a role play, to demonstrate what is being taught, or might suggest specific phrases or demonstrate a specific technique.

To keep faith with the assessing and observing skills, the worker should engage in periodic monitoring with the group. This skill is similar to contract review and renegotiation, although only contracts resembling the reciprocal and mutual forms are utilized in groups of this subtype. The worker should seek feedback from the members and from organizational officials as to whether the course of action taken so far is congruent with the original stated needs. Midcourse corrections may be made, if necessary, on the basis of this feedback; or the plan may continue to be implemented.

This kind of evaluation is a shared activity between the worker and the group, both because the participants are capable of autonomous functioning and because the focus is on individual contributions to organizational functioning, achieved through a learning environment. The members should know and be able to express the value of the group experience as measured against the stated objectives. The worker's role will be to provide the mechanism—a form to be filled in and/or a discussion—for evaluating and to engage the group in it, individually and collectively.

Some of the feelings and behaviors of termination may be manifested during the ending of groups of this subtype, and workers should be prepared to handle these. The doorknob phenomenon sometimes occurs, with members wanting to introduce new topics at the last moment. Sometimes members decide that the experience has not been what they wanted or expected, and they may criticize the worker for that. Periodic monitoring is not always a sufficient preventive measure. If such behaviors surface, the worker should handle them as a worker with a direct service group would do, except that a worker with a group of this subtype would not encourage deeply personal expressions of need or loss. That would be contrary to the purpose of groups of this kind; such expressions, if they do arise, are best dealt with by suggesting that the person meet the worker at the end of the final session.

A useful technique for unanswered questions of any sort is to provide space at the bottom of an evaluation form where persons can write in requests for specific information. The trainer or consultant will agree to answer such questions directly; she or he might also agree to treat questions of this sort as confidential.

Groups Focused on Group-as-a-whole Contributions

Boards, committees, and task groups exist because an organization has determined that such a group is necessary to the functioning of the organization; this determination may be stated in a charter of incorporation, bylaws, or legislation. Some task groups constitute their own organization, but the same skills apply: the focus remains on group-as-a-whole contributions to organizational functioning. With groups of this subtype, the worker has a facilitative role and a peripheral location. The members are capable of autonomous functioning, and this type of group is the most mature group form. The appropriate worker skills parallel those of direct service groups in the maintenance stage: guiding and supporting; however, the worker does not actively encourage expressions of difference. The worker is present to facilitate the group's functioning, to furnish information, and then to execute the results of its actions.

The first skill, guiding, focuses on the ability of the group to sustain its functioning in order to accomplish its task. This would be done by observing group sessions and analyzing the group's functioning in its internal and external systems, communication and decision-making methods, and operation of norms. The results of this observation and analysis are then shared with the formal leader (president, convenor, or chairperson), and the worker and the leader together may develop a plan for improving, correcting, or giving orientation information about any of these aspects of the group's functioning. Depending on the plan that is developed, the worker may be primary in these activities, the formal leader may be primary, an outside resource person may do them, or some combination of persons may be used. If either correction or orientation is chosen, it would proceed after the fashion of training groups, described in the preceding subsection. If improvement is chosen, it would follow the practice with teams and consultee groups, described in the next subsection.

The agenda for group sessions is developed collaboratively by the worker and the formal group leader. In some organizations, the agenda is developed by the worker alone, by the formal leader alone, or by the group as a whole at the outset of each session; however, since the worker and the formal leader are the two persons most responsible for the functioning of the group and the implementation of actions issuing from the group, they ought to be the ones who define the work to be done by the group and the sequence in which it is done. They receive input, of course, from the other units, subunits, and groups, and they would be responsive to requests to consider particular items of business.

Besides giving attention to group functioning and relaying her or his observations to the formal leader, the worker observes the group's progress toward its organizationally determined goals. The worker will collaborate with the formal leader to schedule points for checking progress. This could result in a midcourse correction, a decision to redouble efforts, or a decision to continue as planned.

Usually, organizations have some regular process, and a fixed time frame, for evaluating their work. The worker contributes documents and supporting materials that will be addressed by the group as a whole in a discussion led by the formal leader. The worker collaborates with the formal leader in identifying what these materials and documents should be and adds information that might otherwise be overlooked.

The worker's facilitative role and peripheral location are manifested in two basic forms: the worker contributes information and other resources to the whole group, and she or he supports role performance and decision-making by being a resource to the formal leader. A worker with a group of this subtype may supply missing information (asked or unasked), point out consequences of proposed decisions, refer to formal or informal rules of procedure to clarify issues, raise questions, and propose ideas or alternative courses of action; but the worker never supplants the role of the formal leader. The worker does not make motions or vote on issues. Once a decision is taken, however much the worker may have preferred a different outcome, the worker's role is to execute the decision (Wilson & Ryland, 1949). In doing this, the worker supports the group's own autonomous functioning and acknowledges the maturity of its development.

Although the worker has no active part to play in encouraging members of these types of groups to express differences, the worker may enact a facilitative role in that respect. The worker may pay attention to the order in which people indicate an interest in being recognized, or pay attention to the nonverbal signals from members, and may relay that information to the formal leader. The worker with groups of this subtype is in a secondary or backup position to the formal leader and enacts her or his facilitative role from that peripheral location.

Sometimes the worker may be assigned the task of recording group sessions. There is said to be value in having the official record of group sessions kept by the professional person with the group. On the other hand, this may so preoccupy the worker that other skills cannot be executed. It is therefore recommended that the recording be done by someone else, so that the worker can give full attention to utilizing her or his professional skills.

Throughout the life of the group, the worker attends to the location and spatial arrangement of the place where group sessions are held.

Groups Focused on Individual and Group Contributions

Consultee groups and teams focus on both individual and group contributions to organizational functioning. The need for such groups is determined by the organization or by the group itself (Stringer, 1961), on the basis of a decision favoring an effective structure for service delivery. Because the focus is on both individual and group-as-a-whole contributions to organizational functioning, the worker needs to move between the central location and primary role and the peripheral location and facilitative role, as progress and performance warrant.

Once the worker is identified and engaged, she or he meets with the group to observe its functioning and to gain insight into its stated and unstated needs. As with boards, committees, and task groups, the worker should use a scheme of group functioning to determine the areas of group work that need attention. The worker is a backup to the group as a whole rather than to a formal leader, as is the case with boards, committees, and task groups. There are formal leaders in consultee groups, but the channel for working with groups of this subtype is to the whole group and not to the formal leader.

This subtype of groups resembles direct service groups in their formation stage. Norms are emerging by which member behavior is regulated on behalf of the group; roles are differentiated according to formal positions in the organization; and decision-making processes operate the group. The worker skills are parallel to those for direct service groups in their formation stage: helping the synthesizing process, encouraging participation, and reinforcing interactional patterns.

In helping the synthesizing process, the worker coordinates efforts and should also pay particular attention to the balance between individual uniqueness and collective unity. Groups of this subtype should be viewed as a mosaic in which each part is recognized as distinct even while belonging to a larger pattern.

The worker skill of encouraging participation reflects one of the ways in which the variable role is enacted. The worker joins the plan envisioned by the group or organization; she or he aligns with it and acts on that alliance. At the same time, the worker openly states that she or he may contribute information that would cause the plan to be redesigned. This understanding, negotiated between the worker and the group, resembles the mutual contract in a direct service group. The worker would give such input on the basis of her or his initial observations and her or his sense of how such a group ought to function and what means may be used to move the group to that state of functioning.

In involving members of the consultee group or team in identifying needs, in formulating the goal and the plan for the worker's engagement with the group, and in uniting the members in action toward reaching the goal, the worker supports and encourages participation.

The worker will design a scheme for helping move the group to where it wants to go. The program media to be used will address the group's stated needs, the worker-assessed needs, and the agreed plan, and the media will establish patterns of behavior that lead the group to its desired state of functioning.

In employing the skill of reinforcing interactional patterns, the worker strengthens role performance through relatively direct action, using the primary aspect of the variable role. The worker may stop the group's action to point out what she or he is observing, or to redirect role performance by members. At the end of a session, the worker may feed back to the group what has been observed and may propose alternate ways of acting.

Periodically, the worker should stop the action of the group and ask for direct feedback and review of progress. On the basis of this, mid-course corrections could be made, the effort could be redirected, or the work could proceed just as it is going. The monitoring is collaborative and relies equally on observations by the group and by the worker. The monitoring should take into account both the group functioning and individual contribution to that functioning.

Evaluation is a joint activity between worker and group, because of the members' capacities for autonomous functioning. Consultations are usually done within fixed time limits, whereas teams tend to be ongoing; in both cases, the evaluation needs to be a specific event occurring at a recognized time. Evaluation may be a regular part of the group's operation as well as marking the end of the relationship between the worker and the consultee group.

Summary

This chapter has discussed the differences and similarities between direct service groups and groups for purposes other than direct service. The first section of the chapter described group social forces, where the differences existed primarily in the degree of emphasis on, attention given to, and use made of selected social forces.

The second section considered the four dimensions of social work practice with respect to groups for other than direct service. These groups differ from direct service groups because of the degree of entitativity necessary, the purpose for the existence of the group, and whether the group is open or closed with regard to membership and time limits.

The final section described the worker skills employed in the three subtypes of groups for purposes other than direct service: those focused on individual contributions to organizational functioning (training, supervision, and staff development groups), those focused on group-as-a-whole contributions to organizational functioning (boards, committees, and task groups), and those focused on both individual and group-as-a-whole contributions to organizational functioning (consultee groups and teams). Worker skills with these three subtypes parallel those in, respectively, in the convening stage, the maintenance stage, and the formation stage of direct service groups.

References

Cartwright, D., & Zander, A. (Eds.). (1960). *Group dynamics research and theory* (2nd ed.). Evanston, IL: Row, Peterson.

Festinger, L. (1953). An analysis of compliant behavior. In M. Sherif (Ed.). *Group relations at the crossroad*. New York: Harper and Bros.

Hartford, M. E. (1972). *Groups in social work*. New York: Columbia University Press.

Lewin, K. (1947). Frontiers in group dynamics. *Human Relations, 1,* 5–41.

Sherif, M. (1947). *The psychology of ego involvements*. New York: John Wiley.

Stringer, L. A. (1961). Consultation: Some expectations, principles, and skills. *Social Work, 6*(3), 85–90.

Toseland, R. W., & Ephross, P. (1987). Working effectively with administrative groups [Special issue]. *Social Work with Groups, 10*(2).

Wilson, G., & Ryland, G. (1949). *Social group work practice*. Boston: Houghton Mifflin.

REFERENCES

Abrahamson, L. (1979). Termination as a stage of group development. Class assignment, University of Denver, Graduate School of Social Work.

Affective Education Office, Philadelphia. (1975). *The together book*. Board of Education, Philadelphia. Mimeographed.

Alissi, A., & Casper, M. (1985/86). Time as a factor in groupwork [Special issue]. *Social Work with Groups, 8*(3/4).

Anderson, J. R. (1977). Clinical diagnosis as a factor relating to optimal group composition. Class assignment, University of Denver, Graduate School of Social Work.

Asch, S. (1955). Opinions and social pressure. *Scientific American, 193*(5), 31–35.

Asch, S. (1956). Studies of independence and conformity: Vol. 1. A minority of one against a unanimous majority. *Psychological Monographs, 70*(9), 1–70.

Asch, S. (1960). Effects of group pressures upon modification and distortion of judgements. In D. Cartwright & A. Zander (Eds.), *Group dynamics research and theory* (2nd ed.). Evanston, IL: Row, Peterson.

Bales, R. F. (1950). *Interaction process analysis*. Reading, MA: Addison-Wesley.

Bales, R. F., & Borgatta, E. (1955). Size of group as a factor in the interaction profile. In A. P. Hare, E. Borgatta, & R. F. Bales (Eds.), *Small groups: Studies in social interaction* (pp. 396–413). New York: Alfred A. Knopf.

Bales, R. F., Strodtbeck, F. L., Mills, T. M., & Roseborough, M. E. (1951). Channels of communication in small groups. *American Sociological Review, 16*(4), 461–468.

Bavelas, A. (1960). Communication patterns in task oriented groups. In D. Cartwright & A. Zander (Eds.), *Group dynamics research and theory* (2nd ed.). Evanston, IL: Row, Peterson.

Beall, L. (1972). The corrupt contract: Problems in conjoint therapy with parents and children. *American Journal of Orthopsychiatry, 42*(1), 77–81.

Benne, K., & Sheats, P. (1948). Functional roles of group members. *Journal of Social Issues, 4*(2), 41–47.

Bennis, W., & Shepard, H. (1970). A theory of group development. In T. Mills & S. Rosenberg (Eds.), *Readings on the sociology of small groups*. Englewood Cliffs, NJ: Prentice-Hall.

Berlson, B., & Steiner, G. A. (1964). *Human behavior*. New York: Harcourt, Brace, & Jovanovich.

Bernstein, S. (1965). Group work and conflict. In S. Bernstein (Ed.), *Explorations in group work*. Boston: Boston University School of Social Work.

Biddle, B. J., & Thomas, E. J. (1966). *Role theory: Concepts and research.* New York: John A. Wiley.

Bossman, L. J. (1968). An analysis of interagent residual-influence effects upon members of small, decision-making groups. *Behavioral Science, 13,* 220–233.

Brager, G. (1969). Commitment and conflict in a normative organization. *American Sociological Review, 34*(4), 482–491.

Broverman, I. K., & Broverman, G. (1970). Sex role stereotyping and clinical judgments of mental health. *Journal of Consulting and Clinical Psychology, 34,* 1–7.

Burgess, R. (1968). Communication networks: An experimental reevaluation. *Journal of Experimental Social Psychology, 4*(3), 324–337.

Cartwright, D., & Zander, A. (Eds.). (1960). *Group dynamics research and theory* (2nd ed.). Evanston, IL: Row, Peterson.

Cassano, D. R. (Ed.). (1989). Social work with multi-family groups [Special issue]. *Social Work with Groups, 12*(1).

Churchill, S. (1959). Pre-structuring group content. *Social Work, 4*(3), 52–59.

Churchill, S, (1970). *Worker behavior and rationale in troublesome management incidents in groups.* Unpublished doctoral dissertation, University of Chicago.

Council on Social Work Education. (1964). *A conceptual framework for the teaching of the social group work method in the classroom.* New York.

Coyle, G. L. (1930). *Social process in organized groups.* New York: Richard R. Smith.

Coyle, G. L., & Hartford, M. E. (1958). *Social process in the community and the group.* New York: Council on Social Work Education.

Crawford, J. (1957). *Impact of activities on participant behavior of children.* Unpublished master's thesis, University of Michigan, Ann Arbor.

Croxton, T. (1974). The therapeutic contract in social treatment. In P. Glasser, R. Sarri, & R. Vinter (Eds.), *Individual change through small groups.* New York: Free Press.

Cunningham, R. (1951). *Understanding group behavior of boys and girls.* New York: Columbia University Press.

Davis, L. (Ed.). (1984). Ethnicity in social group work practice [Special issue]. *Social Work with Groups, 7*(3).

DeMarche, D. F., & Iskander, G. M. (1950). On-lookers. *The Group, 12*(3), 7–12.

Dunphy, D. (1968). Phases, roles and myths in self-analytic groups. *Journal of Applied Behavioral Science, 4*(2), 195–225.

Emprey, L. J. (1977). Clinical group work with multi-handicapped adolescents. *Social Casework, 58*(10), 593–599.

Erikson, E. (1968). *Identity: Youth and crisis.* New York: W. W. Norton.

Estes, R. J., & Henry, S. (1976). The therapeutic contract in work with groups: A formal analysis. *Social Service Review, 50*(4), 611–622.

Feldman, F. (Ed.). (1968). *Institutional racism and social work: Social work papers.* Los Angeles: University of Southern California, School of Social Work.

Feldman, R. (1968). Interrelationship among three bases of group integration, *Sociometry, 31*(1), 30–46.

Festinger, L. (1953). An analysis of compliant behavior. In M. Sherif (Ed.), *Group relations at the crossroad.* New York: Harper & Bros.

Fried, E. (1970). Individuation through group psychotherapy. *International Journal of Group Psychotherapy, 20*(4), 450–459.

Garland, J., Jones, H., & Kolodny, R. (1965). A model for stages of development in social work groups. In S. Bernstein (Ed.), *Explorations in group work.* Boston: Boston University School of Social Work.

Garvin, C. (1969). Complementarity in role expectations in groups: The member-worker contract. In *Social Work Practice, 1969*. New York: Columbia University Press.

Glick, O., & Jackson, J. (1970). The effects of normative similarity on group formation of college freshman. *Pacific Sociological Review, 13*(4), 263–269.

Goodman, J. A. (Ed.) (1973). *Dynamics of racism in social work practice*. Washington, DC: National Association of Social Workers.

Goroff, N. (1972). Unique properties of groups: Resources to help people. *Child Welfare, 51*(8), 494–504.

Gump, P. (1955). The 'it' role in children's games. *The Group, 17*, 3–8.

Gump, P., & Sutton-Smith, B. (1955). Activity-setting and social interaction: A field study. *American Journal of Orthopsychiatry, 25*, 755–760.

Hackman, R., & Vidmar, N. (1970). Effects of size and task type on group performance and member reactions. *Sociometry, 33*(1), 37–54.

Haley, J. (1976). *Problem solving therapy*. San Francisco: Jossey-Bass.

Hall, J., & Williams, M. S. (1970). Group dynamics training and improved decision making. *Journal of Applied Behavioral Science, 6*(1), 39–68.

Hare, A. P. (1962). *Handbook of small group research*. New York: Free Press.

Hare, A. P., Borgatta, E., & Bales, R. F. (Eds.). (1955). *Small groups: Studies in social interaction*. New York: Alfred A. Knopf.

Hartford, M. E. (1962). The social group worker and group formation. Unpublished doctoral dissertation, University of Chicago.

Hartford, M. E. (Ed.). (1964). *Working papers toward a frame of reference for social group work*. New York: National Association of Social Workers.

Hartford, M. E. (1966). Changing approaches in practice theory and techniques. In *Trends in Social Work Practice and Knowledge: NASW Tenth Anniversary Symposium*. New York: National Association of Social Workers.

Hartford, M. E. (1972). *Groups in social work*. New York: Columbia University Press.

Hartley, E., & Hartley, R. (1952). *Fundamentals of social psychology*. New York: Alfred A. Knopf.

Henry, S. (1964). *An exploration of the association between group interactional behaviors and four program activities*. Unpublished master's thesis, Western Reserve University, Cleveland, OH.

Henry, S. (1972). *Contracted group goals and group goal achievement*. Unpublished doctoral dissertation, University of Denver.

Henry, S. (1974, October). Use of contracts in social work with groups. Paper presented at the School of Applied Social Sciences Alumni Association Symposium, Cleveland, OH.

Hocking, W. (1941). The nature of morale. *American Journal of Sociology, 47*(3), 302–320.

Hollenbeck, H. (1954). The group dynamics concept of the "group." *The Group, 17*(1), 13–16.

Homans, G. C. (1950). *The human group*. New York: Harcourt, Brace.

Jennings, H. H. (1952). Leadership and sociometric choice. In L. Swanson (Ed.), *Readings in social psychology* (rev. ed.). New York: Henry Holt.

Jennings, H. H. (1953). Sociometric structure in personality and group formation. In M. Sherif (Ed.), *Group relations at the crossroads*. New York: Harper & Bros.

Johnson, D. W., & Johnson, F. P. (1975). *Joining together group theory and group skills*. Englewood Cliffs, NJ: Prentice-Hall.

Klein, A. (1970). *Social work through group process*. Albany: State University of New York, School of Social Welfare.

Kolaja, J. (1968). Two processes: A new framework for the theory of participation in decision making. *Behavioral Science, 13*, 66–70.

Kolodny, R., & Garland, J. (Eds.). (1984). Groupwork with children and adolescents [Special issue]. *Social Work with Groups, 7*(4).

Kubler-Ross, E. (1974). *Questions and answers on death and dying.* New York: Macmillan.

Lang, N. (1972). A broad range model of practice in the social work group. *Social Service Review, 46*(1), 76–89.

Lee, J. A. G. (Ed.). (1988). Group work with the poor and oppressed [Special issue]. *Social Work with Groups, 11*(4).

Lewin, K. (1947). Frontiers in group dynamics. *Human Relations, 1*, 5–41.

Lewis, R. G., & Ho, M. K. (1975). Social work with native Americans. *Social Work, 20*(5), 379–382.

Lindsay, A. (1952). *Group work recording.* New York: Association Press.

Linton, R. (1936). *The study of man.* New York: Appleton Century.

Lippitt, R., Watson, J., & Westley, B. (1958). *The dynamics of planned changed.* New York: Harcourt, Brace & World.

Lott, A., & Lott, B. (1965). Group cohesiveness as interpersonal attractions: A review of relationships with antecedent and consequent variables. *Psychological Bulletin, 64*(10), 259–309.

Lum, D. (1986). *Social work practice and people of color.* Pacific Grove, CA: Brooks/Cole.

MacLennen, B. W., & Felsenfeld, N. (1968). *Group counselling and group psychotherapy with adolescents.* New York: Columbia University Press.

Maloney, S., & Mudgett, M. (1959). Group work and group casework: Are they the same? *Social Work, 4*(2), 29–36.

Maluccio, A., & Marlow, W. (1974). The case for the contract. *Social Work, 19*(1), 28–36.

Mangold, M. M. (Ed.). (1971). La causa chicana [Special issue]. *Social Casework, 52*(5).

Mangold, M. M. (Ed.). (1976). Against the stormy seas [Special issue]. *Social Casework, 57*(3).

Martinez, C. (1977). Group process and the chicano: Clinical issues. *International Journal of Group Psychotherapy, 27*(2), 225–231.

McGrath, J., & Altman, I. (1966). *Small group research: A synthesis and critique of the field.* New York: Holt, Rinehart & Winston.

Middleman, R. (1968). *The non-verbal method in working with groups.* New York: Association Press.

Middleman, R. (Ed.). (1983). Activities and action in groupwork [Special issue]. *Social Work with Groups, 6*(1).

Miller, G. A. (1956). The magical number seven, plus or minus two: Some limits on our capacity for processing information. *Psychological Review, 63*, 92–95.

Mills, T. M. (1967). *The sociology of small groups.* Englewood Cliffs, NJ: Prentice-Hall.

Mills, T. (1970). Toward a conception of the life cycle of groups. In T. Mills & S. Rosenberg (Eds.), *Readings on the sociology of small groups.* Englewood Cliffs, NJ: Prentice-Hall.

Montalvo, B. (1973). Aspects of live supervision. *Family Process, 12*(4), 343–359.

Moreno, J. L. (1960). Organization of the social atom. In J. L. Moreno (Ed.), *The sociometry reader.* Glencoe, IL: Free Press.

Morris, S. (Ed.). (1984). Use of group services in permanency planning for children [Special issue]. *Social Work with Groups, 5*(4).

National Association of Social Workers. (1979). *The Code of Ethics.* New York.

Newcomb, T. (1960). Varieties of interpersonal attraction. In D. Cartwright & A. Zander (Eds.), *Group dynamics research and theory* (2nd ed.). Evanston, IL: Row, Peterson.

Newstetter, W. I. (1935). *What is social group work?* Proceedings of the National Conference of Social Work (pp. 291–299). Chicago: University of Chicago Press.

NiCarthy, G., Merriam, K., & Coffman, S. (1984). *Talking it out: A guide to groups for abused women.* Seattle: Seal Press.

Osmond, H. (1959). The relationship between architect and psychiatrist. In C. Goshen (Ed.), *Psychiatric architecture.* Washington, DC: American Psychiatric Association.

Papell, C., & Rothman, B. (1966). Social group work models: Possession and heritage. *Journal of Education for Social Work, 2,* 66–77.

Papell, C. P., & Rothman, B. (Eds.). (1980). Co-leadership in social work with groups [Special issue]. *Social Work with Groups, 3(4).*

Phillips, H. U. (1954). What is group work skill? *The Group, 16(5),* 3–10.

Phillips, H. U. (1957). *Essentials of social group work skill.* New York: Association Press.

Pincus, A., & Minahan, A. (1973). *Social work practice: Model and method.* Itasca, IL: F. E. Peacock.

Postman, N., & Weingartner, C. (1969). *Teaching as a subversive activity.* New York: Dell.

Prisoners sign contract for correction. (1971, December 13). *The Denver Post.*

Raven, B. H., & Rietsema, J. (1960). The effects of varied clarity of group goals and group path upon the individual and his relation to his group. In D. Cartwright & A. Zander (Eds.), *Group dynamics research and theory* (2nd ed.). Evanston, IL: Row, Peterson.

Redl, F. (1951). The art of group composition. In S. Schulze (Ed.), *Creative group living in a children's institution* (pp. 76–96). New York: Association Press.

Reed, B. G., & Garvin, C. (Eds.). (1983). Groupwork with women/groupwork with men: An overview of gender issues in social groupwork practice [Special issue]. *Social Work with Groups, 6(3/4).*

Reid, C. (1969). *Groups alive—church alive.* New York: Harper & Row.

Reid, W., & Epstein, L. (1972). *Task-centered casework.* New York: Columbia University Press.

Richards, C., & Polansky, N. (1959). Reaching working class youth leaders. *Social Work, 4(4),* 31–39.

Rose, S. D. (1977). *Group therapy: A behavioral approach.* Englewood Cliffs, NJ: Prentice-Hall.

Rose, S. D., & Feldman, R. A. (Eds.). (1986). Research in social group work [Special issue]. *Social Work with Groups, 9(3).*

Ryan, R., & Gilbert, G. (1976). *Beyond ain't it awful.* Columbus: Ohio State University.

Ryland, G. (1967). *Exploring human space.* New York: Young Women's Christian Association of the U.S.A.

Sarri, R., & Galinsky, M. (1967). A conceptual framework for group development. In R. D. Vinter (Ed.), *Readings in group work practice.* Ann Arbor, MI: Campus Publishers.

Saul, S. (Ed.). (1982). Groupwork and the frail elderly [Special issue]. *Social Work with Groups, 5(2).*

Schmidt, J. T. (1969). The use of purpose in casework practice. *Social Work, 14(1),* 77–84.

Schmitt, A. (1972, November). The pattern of Rankian growth process. Paper presented at the annual meeting of the Otto Rank Association, Doylestown, PA.

Schopler, J., & Galinsky, M. (1974). Goals in social group work practice: Formulation, implementation, evaluation. In P. Glasser, R. Sarri, & R. Vinter (Eds.), *Individual change through small groups* (pp. 201–230). New York: Free Press.

Schutz, W. (1958). *FIRO: A three-dimensional theory of interpersonal orientation*. New York: Holt, Rinehart & Winston.

Schutz, W. (1966). *Interpersonal underworld*. Palo Alto, CA: Science and Behavior Books.

Schwartz, W. (1961). The social worker in the group. In *The Social Welfare Forum* (pp. 146–177). New York: Columbia University Press.

Schwartz, W. (1962). Toward a strategy of group work practice. *Social Service Review, 36*(3), 268–279.

Schwartz, W. (1964). Analysis of papers. In M. E. Hartford (Ed.), *Working papers toward a frame of reference for social group work* (pp. 53–61). New York: National Association of Social Workers.

Schwartz, W. (1966). Neighborhood centers. In H. S. Maas (Ed.), *Five fields of social service: Reviews of research*. New York: National Association of Social Workers.

Schwartz, W. (1971). On the use of groups in social work practice. In W. Schwartz & S. R. Zalba (Eds.), *The practice of group work* (pp. 16–31). New York: Columbia University Press.

Seabury, B. (1976). The contract: Uses, abuses, and limitations. *Social Work, 21*(1), 16–21.

Shalinsky, W. (1969). Group composition as an element of social group work practice. *Social Service Review, 43*(1), 42–49.

Shapiro, S. B. (1968). Some aspects of a theory of interpersonal contracts. *Psychological Reports, 12*, 171.

Shaw, M. E. (1971). *Group dynamics: The psychology of small group behavior*. New York: McGraw-Hill.

Sherif, M. (1947). *The psychology of ego involvements*. New York: John Wiley.

Shulman, L. (1967). Scapegoats, group workers, and the pre-emptive intervention. *Social Work, 12*(2), 37–43.

Shulman, L. (1971). "Program" in group work: Another look. In W. Schwartz & S. R. Zalba (Eds.), *The practice of group work*. New York: Columbia University Press.

Siegel, A. E., & Siegel, S. (1960). Reference groups, membership groups, and attitude change. In D. Cartwright & A. Zander (Eds.), *Group dynamics research and theory* (2nd ed.). Evanston, IL: Row, Peterson.

Slater, P. E. (1955). Role differentiation in small groups. *American Sociological Review, 20*, 300–310.

Slavson, S. R. (1964). *A textbook in analytic group psychotherapy*. New York: International Universities Press.

Smalley, R. (1971). Social casework: The functional approach. In J. B. Turner (Ed.), *Encyclopedia of social work* (p. 1287). New York: National Association of Social Workers.

Snyder, N. (1975). An experimental study on optimum group size (Doctoral dissertation, University of Pittsburgh). *Abstracts for Social Workers, 12*(3).

Stein, J. (1971). *The Random House dictionary of the English language* (unabridged ed.). New York: Random House.

Stinson, J. E., & Hellebrandt, E. T. (1972). Group cohesiveness, productivity, and strength of formal leadership. *Journal of Social Psychology, 87*, 99–105.

Stringer, L. A. (1961). Consultation: Some expectations, principles, and skills. *Social Work, 6*(3), 85–90.

Symposium: Group therapy with minority group patients. (1975). *International Journal of Group Psychotherapy, 25*(4), 389–428.

Taft, J. J. (1949). Time as the medium of the helping process. *Jewish Social Service Quarterly, 16*(2), 189–198.

Taylor, M. (1970). The problem of salience in the theory of collective decision-making. *Behavioral Science, 15,* 415–430.

Thibaut, J. W., & Kelley, H. H. (Eds.). (1959). *The social psychology of groups.* New York: John Wiley.

Thomas, E. J. (1967). The socio-behavioral approach: Illustrations and analysis. In E. J. Thomas (Ed.), *The socio-behavioral approach and applications to social work.* New York: Council on Social Work Education.

Thomas, E., & Fink, C. (1963). Effects of group size. *Psychological Bulletin, 60*(4), 371–384.

Toseland, R. W., & Ephross, P. (1987). Working effectively with administrative groups [Special issue]. *Social Work with Groups, 10*(2).

Tuckman, B. W. (1965). Developmental sequence in small groups. *Psychological Bulletin, 63,* 384–399.

Veiga, J. F. (1974). *Life goals inventory.* Mimeographed.

Vidmar, N. (1970). Group composition and the risky shift. *Journal of Experimental Social Psychology, 6*(2), 153–166.

Vinter, R. (1967a). An approach to group work practice. In R. Vinter (Ed.), *Readings in group work practice.* Ann Arbor, MI: Campus Publishers.

Vinter, R. (1967b). The essential components of social group work practice. In R. Vinter (Ed.), *Readings in group work practice.* Ann Arbor, MI: Campus Publishers.

Vinter, R. (1967c). Program activities: An analysis of their effects on participant behavior. In R. Vinter (Ed.), *Readings in group work practice.* Ann Arbor, MI: Campus Publishers.

Ward, C. D. (1968). Seating arrangements and leadership emergence in small discussion groups. *Journal of Social Psychology, 74*(1), 83–90.

Weathers, L., & Liberman, R. P. (1976). The family contracting exercise. *Journal of Behavioral Therapy and Experimental Psychiatry, 6,* 208–214.

Weitzel, K. (1961). *Endings as related to beginnings.* Western Reserve University, Cleveland, OH. Mimeographed.

Whittaker, J. (1970). Models of group development: Implications for social group work practice. *Social Service Review, 44*(3), 308–322.

Wilmer, H. A., & Lamb, H. R. (1969). Using therapeutic community principles. In H. R. Lamb, D. Heath, & J. J. Downing (Eds.), *Handbook of community mental health practice.* San Francisco: Jossey-Bass.

Wilson, G. (1976). From practice to theory: A personalized history. In R. W. Roberts & H. Northen (Eds.), *Theories of social work with groups.* New York: Columbia University Press.

Wilson, G., & Ryland, G. (1949). *Social group work practice.* Boston: Houghton Mifflin.

YWCA of Metropolitan Denver. (1969). *YWCA Denver Dares.* New York: Research and Action.

Zajonc, R. B., Wolosin, R., Loh, M. A., & Loh, W. B. (1970). Social facilitation and imitation in group risk taking. *Journal of Experimental Social Psychology, 6*(1), 26–46.

Zander, A. (1971). *Motives and goals in groups.* New York: Academic Press.

Ziller, R. (1965). Toward a theory of open and closed groups. *Psychological Bulletin, 63,* 164–182.

NAME INDEX

SUBJECT INDEX

Page numbers in italics refer to figures.

TO THE OWNER OF THIS BOOK:

I hope that you have found *Group Skills in Social Work*, 2nd Edition, useful. So that this book can be improved in a future edition, would you take the time to complete this sheet and return it? Thank you.

School and address: _____

Department: _____

Instructor's name: _____

_____

1. What I like most about this book is: _____

_____

2. What I like least about this book is: _____

_____

3. My general reaction to this book is: _____

_____

4. The name of the course in which I used this book is: _____

_____

5. Were all of the chapters of the book assigned for you to read? _____

   If not, which ones weren't? _____

_____

6. In the space below, or on a separate sheet of paper, please write specific suggestions for improving this book and anything else you'd care to share about your experience in using the book.

_____

_____

_____

_____

_____

_____

_____

Optional:

Your name: _____ Date: _____

May Brooks/Cole quote you, either in promotion for *Group Skills in Social Work*, 2nd edition
or in future publishing ventures?

Yes: _____ No: _____

Sincerely,
Sue Henry